# The Heart That Would Not Hold

*A Biography of* Washington Irving

# The Heart That Would Not Hold

## A Biography of

## WASHINGTON IRVING

by Johanna Johnston

*Published by M. Evans and Company, Inc., New York*
AND DISTRIBUTED IN ASSOCIATION WITH
*J. B. Lippincott Company, Philadelphia and New York*

For even thus the man that roams
    On heedless hearts his feeling spends;
Strange tenant of a thousand homes,
    And friendless, with ten thousand friends.

Washington Irving—1822

# Contents

vii

### Part Three · By the Alhambran Fountain

### Part Four · An American Theme

# Part One

## "A Being Borne In Air . . ."

# I

# Jonathan Oldstyle

HE WAS, as he might have phrased it himself, your least likely candidate. Aside from the hope that he might be considered a gentleman, he had no ambitions when he was young.

Whim was the word. To follow one's whims wherever they led was the way to be truly alive. Washington was supposed to be studying law, preparing himself for a legal career, but he had found the law dreadful stuff, "a pile of dull rubbish." And so he put in the required, or almost the required, hours at Judge Hoffman's law offices on Wall Street each day, and through those hours he yawned and sighed, waiting for the time of release when he could come alive again. Then he could stroll with his friends along the Battery with its elms "like brooms on end." He could idle away an hour or so in a coffee house or at the bookseller's or junket out to the country with congenial souls to imbibe iced punches at a crossroads inn. (New York was a manageable little city in 1802; one walked into the country within a mile of the Battery.) Then, in the evening, he could go to the theater or a dance. He wanted no more, really, except the opportunity to talk it all over now and then in a certain familiar parlor.

That he suddenly did something more was only another whim, brought on by circumstance.

One of his older brothers—Peter, whom he liked to call the Doctor, because he had studied medicine once and actually practiced briefly—was able to gratify a long-standing ambition in the fall of 1802. He finally found backing to publish a daily newspaper in which he could espouse his favorite political theories. His theories were chiefly those of Aaron Burr, a magnetic man who had quite hypnotized Peter during the years when Burr was making his headquarters in New York, but no one took this amiss. Every one of New York's eleven newspapers existed to promote the policies of one or another of the nation's leaders. Peter called his paper the *Morning Chronicle*, and it was an elegant little sheet in the judgment of the family, beautifully printed on fine paper. But dull, thought Washington.

On a whim, he pushed aside the law books on the deal table in the back room of the offices where he worked, sharpened his quill, and prepared to write a letter to the editor.

He was just nineteen, a good-looking youth with curly chestnut hair, widely spaced blue-gray eyes under winging brows, and a mouth that seemed to conceal a secret smile, lurking in one corner. Being so young, he was amused to fancy himself an old and crusty bachelor, sharp-eyed, patient, but not to be put upon. (How else win the confidence of those solemn readers of the *Chronicle*, so concerned about Jefferson's mad ideas for the nation and Bonaparte's insane ambitions in Europe?)

An old bachelor lamenting—something not at all important for a change—lamenting, for instance, the sad deterioration in manners since the days of his youth. Nothing could be easier. The past had always exerted a curious fascination on young Washington Irving. Born in 1783, just after the Revolution had ended, just as peace treaties were being signed and the new nation of the United States was coming into being, he was forever imagining, as he roamed New York, the way things had been *before*. Walking past Federal Hall, he imagined the men in powdered wigs and flared coats who had walked the same street in the days of the British governors. Or strolling past one of the old stepped-roof Dutch houses that still stood, surrounded by gardens, he conjured up visions of old Dutch burghers in their voluminous breeches who had once smoked their pipes before such houses. But he laughed even as he indulged his fancies. Life surely had been as ridiculous in the past as it was now.

The old bachelor's letter spun along, no trouble to write. How courteous people had been when attending balls in the past. "Then, ah then, how delightful to contemplate a ballroom. Nothing more common than to see half a dozen gentlemen knocking their heads together as they bent to pick up a lady's fan or snuff box."

He signed the letter Jonathan Oldstyle. The pseudonym was not especially original. Joseph Dennie, the Philadelphia editor, had been signing himself Oliver Oldschool in his magazine, the *Port-Folio*, for several years now. But what did that matter? Old-Fellows-something-or-other had been in style ever since the days of the *Spectator* papers. He handed the scrawled sheets to Peter diffidently. It was just some nonsense, he told Peter. Peter did not have to use it. But the paper *was* a bit on the heavy side, wasn't it?

Peter read the letter and smiled. He was a man of whim and humor himself, in spite of his serious political convictions. He printed it.

Readers of the *Chronicle* felt a mild surprise when they came across the letter in all its mock solemnity, not set off in any way from the other communications in dead earnest. But they smiled as Peter had. And the next week they had opportunity to smile again when another letter from Jonathan Oldstyle appeared, this one recalling nostalgically the courtship and marriage customs of yesteryear. "Then, Mr. Editor—then were the happy times; such oceans of arrack—such mountains of plum-cake—such feasting and congratulating—such fiddling and dancing;—ah me! who can think of those days and not sigh when he sees the degeneracy of the present: no eating of cake nor throwing of stockings . . . ."

Peter continued amused. Certainly write another letter, he said when he stopped in, as he frequently did, at Judge Hoffman's offices for a chat with his youngest brother. So Washington picked up his quill and flicked its feathered shaft as he wondered what more he could say about the manners of yesterday. He had covered most of what he could imagine about them. Perhaps Jonathan Oldstyle should take up another subject altogether. His thoughts drifted, as his thoughts had a way of doing, and somehow he was thinking about the evening before at the theater.

He had arrived early into the glow of the lamps flaring outside the theater, lighting the playbills and the gathering playgoers, and felt his usual lift of anticipation. He had smiled, making his way through the hubbub of the lobby which was lined on either side with tables laden with gingerbread, pies, and apples for sale and crowded with rough gallery patrons making purchases of such refreshment. There was an equal hubbub in the auditorium where men were shoving about in the pit to find places on the backless benches there, while above the men and boys who could afford only balcony seats also shoved, shouted, sang snatches of song, and munched on the provender they had acquired in the lobby. Only the ladies in the boxes between the two scenes of confusion preserved a quiet gentility, smiling archly at one another from box to box, displaying their bare shoulders as they turned and nodded and bowed. And then, at last, the curtain had gone up and the play had begun.

And what a gathering disappointment the production had been. Sitting at the deal table in Judge Hoffman's offices,

Washington's eyes closed in remembered pain as he recalled the babbling speeches of the principals, the ridiculous caperings of the supporting actors, the alternating paralysis and confusion of the supernumeraries masquerading as villagers.

Suddenly Washington stopped his idle recollections, felt the stab of inspiration, picked up his quill and began to write.

"Sir, There is no place of public amusement of which I am so fond as the Theatre. To enjoy this with the greater relish I go but seldom; and I find there is no play, however poor or ridiculous, from which I cannot derive some entertainment . . . ."

He had hit it, just the subject that would allow him to run on and on. Far from going to the theater "but seldom," he was a constant attendant and had been ever since someone had taken him, at the age of ten or eleven, to a performance at the old John Street Theater, just around the block from the family house on William Street. He had been so charmed by the experience, so determined to re-enter that magic world again and again, that sometimes he had crept out of his second-story bedroom window onto the neighboring roof and made his way from that roof to the next to drop to the street at the far corner and so get to his goal without his family's knowledge. He had remained as loyal when the John Street Theater was replaced a few years later by the new Park Theater. He had become acquainted with the clever, talented, one-eyed manager of that theater, William Dunlap. He had come to know personally the actors and actresses most frequently seen on the Park's stage—Thomas Abthorpe Cooper, George Frederick Cooke, John Hodgkinson, and New York's favorite leading lady, Mrs. Whitelock, sister of England's Mrs. Siddons. And of course he had become familiar with most of the plays that made up the Park's repertory, able to fancy himself a connoisseur of performances in Shakespearean dramas or plays by Sheridan or Congreve.

But only someone so fond of the theater could be so aware of its lapses into excess and folly, wincing when tragedians lurched about in drunken confusion, when plot and sense were subordinated to spectacular stage effects, or when everything was lost in a hysteria of patriotism or national pride. Only someone so fond of it could laugh at it with understanding.

"I was very much taken with a play bill of last week," Washington's quill scratched on, "announcing, in large capitals, 'The Battle of Hexham, or, Days of Old,'—Here, said I to myself, will be something grand—Days of Old—my fancy fired at the words. I pictured to myself all the gallantry of chivalry . . . ."

He then launched into Oldstyle's report on what had happened to him when he attended the advertised play and the mystifications and disappointments that had befallen him.

Readers who had been mildly amused before were delighted by this epistle from Jonathan Oldstyle. They too had attended plays and been baffled by scenes that seemed to have nothing to do with the plot, or by the sudden eruption of a "gallery song," some comic air inserted simply to please the rougher elements in the audience.

> The Welshman lik'd to have been chok'd by a mouse,
> But he pull'd him out by the tail . . . .

They too had been let down by plays that advertised a battle and then ran their course without offering one until at last the play was ended "by the falling of the curtain." Especially they were familiar with scenes in native American dramas such as one that Oldstyle described as part of the after-piece, a short play entitled *The Tripolitan Prize.*

"Then came the cream of the joke. The captain wanted to put out to sea, and the young fellow, who had fallen desperately in love, to stay ashore. Here was a contest between love and honour—such piping of eyes, such blowing of noses,

such slapping of pocket-holes! But *Old Junk* was inflexible—
What! An American tar desert his duty (three cheers from
the gallery) impossible! American tars forever!! True blue
will never stain &c. &c. (a continual thundering among the
gods)."

"I say," one New Yorker said to another that day in November, 1802, when the letter was published, "there's an
amusing sort of thing in the *Chronicle*. Did you see it? Written by some fellow who calls himself Oldstuff or some-
such."

Peter suggested that his younger brother write another
letter on the theater, and Washington, nothing loath, com-
plied. The whim was still on him and he could think of
many more things to say. So he wrote about the behavior of
the audience and the "waggery and humor of the gallery,"
and of how, on a recent visit, "the anger of the gods seemed
to be aroused all of a sudden, and they commenced a discharge of apples, nuts, and gingerbread, on the heads of the
honest folk in the pit." Oldstyle had been hit on the head by
an apple core and rose to shake his cane at the offenders. But
"I was prevented by a decent-looking man behind me," he
wrote, "who informed me that it was useless to threaten or
expostulate. They are only *amusing themselves* a little at our
expense, said he; sit down quietly and bend your back to it."

The drama critics were mentioned, and the way they often
sat with their backs to the stage, sucking their canes and re-
garding the audience. And the musicians also, who came out
of their "cavern under the stage," and bravely tuned up in
opposition to cries from the gallery for some popular air like
*Molly in the Wad* or *Tally Ho, the Grinders*.

New Yorkers were buying the *Chronicle* especially to look
for Oldstyle letters by this time. And by midwinter of 1803,
Peter learned that various out-of-town editors, who received
the *Chronicle* on an exchange basis, were clipping the letters
and reprinting them in their own newspapers. Readers in

Boston, Philadelphia, Baltimore, and Richmond were laughing at Oldstyle's sallies and asking one another, just as New Yorkers were, "Who do you suppose he is, really?"

But that no one should know had been Washington's insistence from the beginning. Peter remonstrated with him as Oldstyle's popularity increased. The letters were having a vogue. Didn't he want the credit? No, no, Washington was firm. To have their authorship a mystery was really the best part of the whim. Peter must not tell.

Washington had been attracted to anything that smacked of mystery since childhood. Out on the same roofs that he later traversed to get to the theater secretly, he had, at the age of six or seven, dropped stones down neighboring chimneys of an evening, simply to cause mystification below. Gravely, he had stood by the chimneys under the dark sky, and imagined the agitated questions that the neighbors must be asking. Where could that stone have come from? Could evil spirits be abroad? Now he was just as grave when anyone speculated in his presence as to who Jonathan Oldstyle might be. The smile that pulled his mouth up at one corner just deepened a little.

Some people found out, of course. It was impossible to keep the secret from his family—his mother and father, his other older brothers, William, Ebenezer, and John, his sister Sarah. One of them could not resist sending copies of the *Chronicle* containing Oldstyle letters to sisters Ann and Catherine, who were both married and living in the frontier village of Johnstown, in upstate New York. Judge Hoffman could not remain ignorant forever that his apprentice's unusual industry had nothing to do with a sudden interest in the law, and if the Judge knew, how could Washington keep it a secret from the Judge's young wife? He confessed also to William Dunlap, telling him that he hoped Dunlap would not take the criticisms personally. Washington knew how valiantly Dunlap struggled to raise the artistic standards at the Park. But Dunlap was pleased rather than otherwise to have public attention drawn to the theatrical follies he himself deplored, and urged the young writer on. However, it was probably Peter who gave Aaron Burr a clue as to Oldstyle's real identity. Burr was in Washington, D.C., these days, serving as Vice President to his old antagonist, Thomas Jefferson—and clipping the Oldstyle letters as they appeared to forward them to his daughter, Theodosia. "Not bad for someone so young," he commented.

Still, Washington found the mystery he had created the most entertaining part of the project. In Philadelphia, chief city of the Union, people were speculating as to who Jonathan Oldstyle might be, and so were people in Boston, in Baltimore, and in Richmond. His pleasure in this kept his whim alive through a sixth letter on the theater and then a seventh.

The architecture of the Park Theater, much admired by city-proud New Yorkers, came up for comment. "Observe," Jonathan Oldstyle asked a fellow theatergoer, "the fine effect the dark colouring of the wall has upon the white faces of the audience, which glare like stars in a dark night!" But Oldstyle's companion could not forbear commenting on the way the great chandelier in the ceiling spilled dollops of candle wax on his shoulders from time to time, and at last spoke with something less than enthusiasm about the house itself. "Wasn't there rather a—sort of a—a kind of *heavyishness* about the house? Didn't it have a sort of *undergroundish* appearance?"

Then, suddenly, Washington's inspiration flagged. He tried half-heartedly, as spring advanced on the ctiy, two letters on other topics. In one letter he had Jonathan Oldstyle expound on dueling, that prevalent method of settling points of honor between gentlemen. Oldstyle reported on a young friend's suggestion that "no persons should be allowed to fight without taking out regular licenses from what might be called the Blood and Thunder Office . . ." and that the public should be "admitted to the show." Since men fought, nine times out of ten, for fear of being branded a coward, was it not fitting that the world should judge the issue? With this last recommendation (not so foolish, perhaps, with the Burr-Hamilton duel two years in the future), Washington's whim had run its course. The Jonathan Oldstyle correspondence was finished.

He sighed with relief more than anything. And he was astonished when Charles Brockden Brown came to New York from Philadelphia in the late spring and made a special point of looking him up and talking to him. Brown, it turned out, was starting a new magazine in Philadelphia and wanted young Irving to contribute to it. Washington could not help being flattered. Brown was one of the few accredited literary men in the United States. He had written novels that were published not only in America but in England, works that had actually won some attention there. Almost as surprisingly, Brown had recently announced his plan to make writing his means of livelihood, something that no one in the United States had ever attempted. Almost everyone with pretensions to culture wrote. Lawyers, politicians, farmers, gentlemen of leisure—all of them wrote reams and reams of essays, political polemics, poems, translations—but for their own amusement and their friends, never as a means of making a living.

Washington Irving could only shake his head politely when Mr. Brown urged him to think about writing for his magazine. He could only look politely unbelieving when Brown said that his Oldstyle letters had shown a real comic talent and a nice use of language.

But they had been written only on a whim, Washington said. They were just a joke and the joke was over.

All his life Washington would maintain that attitude toward his Oldstyle letters, considering them the overflow of youthful good spirits, rough, unpolished, and spontaneous. He never had any consciousness of having struck a new note in American writing—on a whim at the age of nineteen. Satire there had been before and gibes at the various awkward postures which citizens of a new nation assumed in their efforts to be both worldly and unique, but the satire had been literary in tone and full of classical allusions. What the Oldstyle letters offered was everyday humor, easy and conversational in style, a kind of mockery that allowed Americans to laugh at themselves good-naturedly, without the sense of being flayed as fools. Washington Irving was unaware of having given his countrymen this gift. Conscious only of how remote his letters were from accepted, foreign models, he never was able to see that they had a small, new, domestic sparkle of their own, and he was outraged, some years later, when a London publisher collected them and put them out in a little book.

He had no pride in the letters later, nor did he take them seriously when he was talking to Charles Brockden Brown. Besides, he had no ambition to begin polishing his skills and start writing on some regular basis, if that was what Brown was suggesting. The idea was ridiculous.

To the nineteen-year-old Washington Irving, life itself was fairly ridiculous. It seemed to him that almost everybody took it too seriously, worrying about making a living, about making a name for oneself, about convincing others that one's own political or religious theories were the only correct ones.

He had no such ambitions, no desire to do or be anything except a generally cheerful young New Yorker, strolling in the Battery, going to the theater, flirting with pretty girls, and talking it all over, now and then, in a certain familiar parlor.

# 2

# Good-to-Everybody

It was a pleasant room, solidly weighted with a few chests and settles in the old colonial style but lightened with some new chairs and tables from Duncan Phyfe's workshop on William Street. A Turkish rug, French draperies at the tall windows, and polished brass gave it color and warmth. Maria Fenno Hoffman, sitting at the tea table of an afternoon, felt a quiet pride in the way she had refurbished the room with the new pieces and new fabrics after coming to the house as a bride.

A native of Philadelphia, where her late father, John Fenno, had been editor of Alexander Hamilton's Federalist paper, the *Gazette of the United States*, Maria had felt very much a stranger in New York when she first arrived in the late summer of 1802, and a little abashed by the extent of the new roles she was essaying. Not only was she marrying one of New York's most prominent attorneys, she was also becoming the stepmother of his five children by his first wife who had died several years before. Within a few weeks of her settling in at the Judge's house on the Broad Way, however, her sympathetic manner had won twelve-year-old Ann and ten-year-old Matilda to regard her as a loving older sister and the three younger children to cling to her with affection. Friends and acquaintances of Judge Hoffman had called and welcomed her with invitations to teas, to dinners, to balls, and Maria, raised in Philadelphia's sophisticated political and social circles, had met the demands of such engagements with a poise that soon established her in her husband's set.

Her friendship with her husband's young clerk, Washington Irving, had grown even more quickly. The Judge had brought him home to dinner one evening, as it seemed he had been in the habit of doing ever since the young man had gone to work for him, and Maria had been amused and pleased by Washington's good looks and shy humor. She had invited him to stop in for tea one day soon and he had accepted the invitation. Before long he was stopping in every day or so, hoping that he was not interrupting but with some new bit of gossip or story to tell her that he was sure she would enjoy. He never did interrupt for he was quick to adapt himself to any situation. He had obligingly moved furniture when she was redoing the parlor and studied swatches of toile with her when she was choosing the material for the new draperies. He was helpful with the children when their demands were importunate, and was an agreeable, amusing addition to the group when other guests called.

Maria was soon aware of his admiration, aware of the way his eyes followed her as she moved about the room, aware of his eagerness to amuse her. But perfectly sure of herself, and of him as well, she saw no harm in his devotion. He was like a younger brother, five or six years younger than herself, and somehow very much in need of the approval of a woman a little older than himself. Now and then she pondered about why this should be, and considered him in relation to his family. She had met his mother, a friendly, generous woman, whose face still had an English handsomeness about it, though she was in her sixties. Washington's laugh was like hers, quick, throaty, impatient. Maria had also met his father, Deacon William Irving, and saw him when her shopping took her over to William Street where his business was located. He was a tall, gray-bearded man who seldom smiled but merely nodded his greeting as she went by. She knew he was a pillar in New York's Scottish Presbyterian Church, and that he imposed a daily ritual of morning and evening prayers on his family. Washington had mentioned it as an aside, his eyebrows lifted, and never referred to it again. Maria sensed his lack of sympathy with his father and wondered how much that contributed to his general irreverence and to his periodic moods of depression as well.

But it was not a time when people worried overmuch with such analyses. In general, they found it sufficient to say that somebody's parents were "good people," and Washington's certainly were that, honest, upright, respected, and, if not rich, not poor either. His older brothers, William, Peter, Ebenezer, and John, whom Maria also knew, were all that and more—diligent, clever men, making their way in the intellectual and social life of the city as well as in business or a profession. So Maria's conjecturing as to why Washington was as he was usually came to rest on the fact that he was the youngest of his family. Babied by his older brothers and sisters too, he had never felt the need to take anything seriously. Content with that, she laughed at his jokes, was sympathetic with his moods, cherished him as her "favorite," and knew that her husband was wholly undisturbed.

As for Washington, he did not allow the thought that he might be in *love* with Mrs. Hoffman to cross his mind. She was *Mrs.* Hoffman, the wife of his employer—a beautiful, modish, witty young woman who was gracious enough to welcome him whenever he appeared—another "older sister" of a sort, he told himself. He brought his friends to meet her, the young men with whom he laughed in the coffee house or strolled with along the Battery. He brought lanky James Kirke Paulding, who was an in-law to Washington, since Washington's oldest brother, William, was married to James' older sister, Julia. Paulding's grave, hawknosed countenance gave no clue to the dry humor of his conversation which delighted his friends. Washington brought Gouverneur Kemble, John Furman, and half a dozen others. In turn, he met Maria Hoffman's friends, the people she was meeting in New York and old friends who came visiting from Philadelphia. He spent more time, in fact, at the Hoffman house than he spent at his own family dwelling on William Street.

But of course he was not in love with Mrs. Hoffman. He was simply devoted to her, her knight in the medieval sense, wearing her colors on his arm, dreaming of ways in which he could please her or be of service to her.

The possibility of an unusual opportunity to serve her began to loom in the early summer of 1803, just as he had finished his dalliance with the Oldstyle letters. Judge Hoffman was projecting a trip to northern New York and Canada. Like many other farsighted men, the Judge had been investing in wilderness land, anticipating the steady push of pioneers outward from the settled regions along the coast. In company with an associate, Ludlow Ogden, the Judge had bought some tracts along the St. Lawrence River, a region particularly fraught with possibilities because of the busy, if illegal, fur-trading across the border with Canada. Sometime in June, the Judge decided that he and Mr. Ogden should make a trip of inspection to the area, confer with their land agents there and start platting the land into townships and farm sites. With little thought, seemingly, of how rigorous a trip to the St. Lawrence might be, Judge Hoffman asked his wife and his oldest daughter, Ann, to accompany him. Ludlow Ogden invited his wife and daughter, Eliza. Then the Judge suggested that Washington go along also, partly for the services he might render as a law clerk, but chiefly as a general aide to help with the luggage and the comfort and amusement of the ladies.

Washington was delighted to accept. He liked any sort of traveling. Twice in the years previous he had made the journey up the Hudson River to Albany to visit his sisters Nancy and Kitty in Johnstown. The rich, fantastic scenery of the highlands and the Catskill Mountains bordering the river had laid a spell upon him. Now, imagining the joy of voyaging past those great, mysterious hills with Mrs. Hoffman and sharing with her some of the curious legends he had heard about the region, he hurried to prepare for the trip. And though writing of any sort was still only a whim, he did buy a small leather notebook in which to keep a journal of the adventure.

On July 31, 1803, the party repaired with its luggage to a wharf on the Hudson River, where it was joined by three young men who planned to accompany the group as far as Saratoga Springs. Washington made an entry in his journal that evening.

"I sailed from New York for Albany in company with Mr. & Mrs. Hoffman, Mr. and Mrs. Ludlow Ogden, Miss Eliza Ogden, Miss Ann Hoffman, Mr. Brandram & Mr. Ready & Stephen Van Rennselaer. We set off about 3 o'clock in the afternoon and came to anchor in the evening at the entrance of the highlands."

Such terse notes reflected none of the good nature and excitement of the occasion. As the sloop moved slowly up the river, the young men of the group fired guns to wake the echoes, sang songs and rattled on with jokes and puns until the ladies and girls were breathless with laughter. When the boat came to anchor in the evening, Washington was filled again with the awe he had experienced on earlier voyages, but this time his feelings were intensified as he thought that Mrs. Hoffman, in the ladies' cabin, was sharing with him the dark and solemn stillness, broken now and then by an owl's cry or the splash of a sturgeon in the water.

The next day, the sloop came in to shore briefly so that Washington, Mr. Ogden, and Brandram could get some milk from a farmhouse near the riverbank. "We found a mean house with a lazy-looking fellow seated at the fireplace," Washington wrote later in his journal. "While the woman of the house was milking the cows, we were entertained by some enquiries & speculation of Brandram, who was lately from England. He declared that the man lived in 'luxury and disapation' having nothing to do except to work a little on his farm. That he had good milk to drink and rye bread to eat—at the same time Brandram wished he had a *bottle of wine* from onboard the sloop that he might cool it in a neighboring spring . . . ."

"Luxury and disapation . . ." The phrase pleased Washington. Soon he was using it as a descriptive tag for everything that went wrong—or right—on the expedition. But mostly, except for comic discomforts, everything went right. After a thirty-nine-hour boat trip from New York, the group landed at Albany. There a carriage was hired to take the company to Ballston Springs. Washington had visited this primitive resort, established in an old trading post, two years before with Kitty's husband, Daniel Paris. Little had changed since then. The springs still bubbled out of a broken barrel sunk into the ground. The inn was still much like a trading post, unpainted and ramshackle. However, the Hoffman-Ogden party managed to find amusement in the efforts of the innkeeper to create the illusion of a stylish hotel and in the fashionable pretensions of a guest named Mrs. Smith. A big, bare room on the second floor, with an old harpsichord in the corner, was designated the ballroom and a ball was held one night of their stay.

"Mrs. Smith's dress for the Ball was of Muslim with large gold sprigs," Washington noted later, obviously fascinated by her toilette for the gala. "A gold ribbon round her waist her hair turned up over a cushion powdered pomatumed and covered with lace and trinkets. She was surrounded with an atmosphere of perfume. She carried an enormous Bouquet of Artificial flowers, in addition to which I presented her with a stylish assortment of poppies, Hollihocks and asparagus."

Mrs. Smith giggled and blushed her pleasure at this attention. Washington danced with all the ladies and played his flute for Mrs. Hoffman to sing. Outside the open windows crickets chirped, a woodland breeze blew in to make the candles flicker, but with everyone entering into the spirit of the occasion the ball was as merry as any more formal gathering in New York.

Another sightseeing stop was made at Saratoga Springs, a short journey from Ballston. Here the facilities for a health resort were somewhat more advanced than at Ballston Springs. The hotel and the waters nearby already were attracting a certain number of southerners who welcomed the cool northern climate in the summertime. But the long table where meals were served and the hit-or-miss cuisine still maintained a primitive note. Washington and the others of the party laughed at the "high airs" of the southern rice or cotton heiresses as they were forced to mingle, higgledy-piggledy, with less-mannered guests. Then, after saying good-bye to the young men, Brandram, Ready, and Van Rennsselaer, the party was making its way inland to Utica, where the real journey into the wilderness would begin.

In Utica, Judge Hoffman hired wagons, horses, and oxen. One wagon, pulled by the oxen, was filled with the party's luggage. The Hoffmans, Ogdens, and Washington took their places in the horse-drawn wagons, and the little caravan started off down the road to the north.

Washington now burned with the desire to make everything pleasant for Mrs. Hoffman, and he hoped vaguely that the wilderness might offer him some opportunity to distinguish himself. But nothing dramatic happened for some time. The road out of Utica quickly became a rutted trail through the forest, and on every side there was the litter that marked the advance of American civilization—felled trunks of trees lying at grotesque angles, rotted stumps, the remains of fires. The passengers in the wagons, jolted and jarred by their progress, could only turn from the contemplation of such scenery to amusing themselves through the long hours of travel. Ann Hoffman had brought a copy of *Romeo and Juliet* with her, and from time to time she read aloud from that. Sometimes Washington played on his flute and Mrs. Hoffman sang—an eerie, floating music in the forest.

At night, they did as all travelers did on such a journey, stopped at some hunter's shack or isolated farmhouse. The owners of such shelters were glad to make a few pennies by allowing wayfarers to take cover under their roofs and to prepare what food they had with them on their hearths. During such halts, Washington found various ways to be helpful to Mrs. Hoffman and the other women. He could fetch and lay down the pallets on which they slept. He could hang blankets across a room to screen off a private sleeping area for them. He could make them smile as they ate their breakfast of hard crackers and gingerbread which were soon all that remained of their provisions. "Luxury and dissipation," he reminded them.

On the third day of their traveling through the forest, heavy rain began to fall. The road became a sucking mire into which the horses sank deeper with every step. Then Washington joined Judge Hoffman and Mr. Ogden in helping the women and girls from the wagons and made jokes to cheer them as they walked through the brush and mud beside the trail while the drivers struggled to get the horses moving.

The next day the party was able to escape the difficulties of wagon travel for a while and ride a scow for a distance down the north-flowing Black River. The travelers disposed themselves about the rough barge to enjoy the quiet movement along the river. Parasols were raised against the sun. Fishing lines were put out to lure a better dinner than had been available for some time.

Then came Washington's first real chance to distinguish himself. As the scow rounded a turn in the river, the passengers on board saw ahead two hunters in a canoe and a deer swimming frantically toward the shore. Everyone was interested at once. The pilot steered the scow toward the bank and all the men prepared to do what they could to aid in the capture of the deer. One of the hunters in the canoe leaped into the river to swim after the deer. Impetuously, Washington also leaped into the river, planning to seize some part of the deer's anatomy.

Unfortunately, instead of landing near the deer, Washington dived directly onto the swimming hunter, sinking both the hunter and himself. In a great welter of water and with much gasping and struggling, Washington and the hunter finally surfaced. By that time the deer had gained the land and Mr. Hoffman, Mr. Ogden, and the other hunter were in pursuit. Through their combined efforts the animal was captured while Washington retired into the forest to change into dry clothes. Still, he later managed to laugh with the others at his contribution to the hunt and enjoyed the venison steaks that evening which were the group's share of the trophy.

The party returned to land travel the next day and at once ran into more bad weather. This time the storm was so violent and the mud so deep that the horses lay down in the mire and refused to go on. Again everyone had to quit the wagons.

"We helped the ladies to a little shed of bark laid on crotches," Washington wrote in his journal, "about large enough to hold three, where they sat down. It had been a night's shelter to some hunter, but in this case it afforded no protection. One-half of it fell down as we were creeping under it . . . The wind blew a perfect hurricane. The trees around shook and bent in a most alarming manner . . . The ladies were in the highest state of alarm and entreated that we should walk to a house which we were told was about half a mile distant . . ."

They achieved that goal at last only to discover that two drovers, taking wagons to Canada, were already settled in at the house and well gone in drink. The drovers greeted the entrance of the Hoffman and Ogden women with loud and ribald cries. The firelight flickered, the candles guttered, the rain poured down without ceasing, and then the door opened and in staggered one of the Hoffman-Ogden drivers streaming blood. At this point, and to Washington's horror, Maria Hoffman fainted.

She soon revived after sal volatile was held to her nose. It was learned that the driver, who had cut himself with his ax while chopping down a sapling in the course of tethering the horses, was not seriously injured. But in a passion of concern for Mrs. Hoffman, Washington not only hung the usual blankets to provide the ladies with a private sleeping place but stayed awake most of the night guarding them. As the rain still poured and leaked in erratic streams through various holes in the roof, he sat holding an open umbrella and moving it about over Mrs. Hoffman and the other women, trying to shield them from the falling water.

But they were not far from their destination by now. A day or so later they emerged from the forest to see the glittering water of the Oswegatchie River flowing toward the St. Lawrence. They made their way along it until, at the wide river mouth, they arrived at an old French fort, currently occupied by an American who was a friend of Judge Hoffman's.

Baths, clean clothes, a decent meal, and real beds soon restored the party. Judge Hoffman and Mr. Ogden met with their land agent and rode about looking over their holdings, while Washington walked with Mrs. Hoffman, Ann, Mrs. Ogden, and Eliza along the shores of the St. Lawrence River and marveled at the grand, wild scenery. Or he took the girls out in a canoe on the river's waters. Or he went off by himself with his gun and his flute, losing himself in romantic fantasies as he went deeper and deeper into the primeval forest. Once he found the remains of an old sawmill where he sat down and leaned against the ruins to rest and then fell asleep. The forest was darkened in twilight when he awoke, and the walk back to the fort had an eerie feel to it; so he was glad to be scolded and petted in turn by his friends who had been waiting anxiously for his return.

Washington was of brief service as a law clerk one day when he rode with Judge Hoffman around some of his land and wrote up several deeds for him. Another day, the Judge sent him, along with his agent, to speak with an Indian who might rent the party a bateau in which to journey down the St. Lawrence to Montreal before returning home. Washington and the agent made their way to the Indian's wigwam, which was on a small island in the river. The Indian was not there when they arrived so they settled themselves on a bench near the opening of the wigwam to wait his coming.

The brave appeared before long, accompanied by his wife, and from their swaying progress it was evident that both had been drinking. The Indian woman especially seemed freed from inhibition. Catching sight of Washington and charmed by his youthful good looks, she sat down beside him and began smiling, chattering, and patting his hands flirtatiously. Embarrassed, Washington forced a smile.

Suddenly he was knocked from the bench to the ground by a blow from the enraged Indian. Struggling to his feet, he saw the Indian threatening him with a knife. Fortunately, the agent was acquainted with the brave and rushed to the rescue. Washington was ordered to the boat at the shore while the agent pacified the Indian and made the necessary arrangements for the bateau.

The Judge was delighted when he heard the story later and at once began to tease Washington about his fatal charm. What had Washington done to encourage the woman? the Judge asked. Or was it unnecessary for him to do anything but cast a melting glance? Washington, smiling ruefully at first, began to cringe at the very mention of the subject. It was not by becoming the butt of such a joke that he had meant to distinguish himself before Maria Hoffman. And there was no one to wonder if the Judge, twenty years Washington's senior, had at last become a little jealous of the young man's gallantry toward his wife and finally found a way to express it. Once started on a teasing course, the Judge seemed unable to stop.

In due course, the party did take off for Montreal in a bateau. One evening, they stopped for the night on the shore near an Indian village. The Indians were friendly and welcomed the visitors cordially. The chief was so obliging, in fact, that before the evening was over, he had been convinced by the Judge that he should honor Washington by giving him an Indian name.

Before Washington knew what was happening he was led to the center of the rough hall where everyone had gathered. The chief stamped around him, chanting incomprehensible words, while the watching Indians contributed responsive grunts. The chief then stopped in front of Washington, made a long speech and finally conferred upon the young man the Indian name Vomonte, which, being translated, meant Good-to-Everybody.

Washington usually laughed promptly at jokes on himself and he liked nicknames almost as much as small mysteries. He had nicknames for all of his brothers and sisters and most of his friends. One can even imagine a certain dissatisfaction with his own name underlying this passion (was there not a certain "heavyishness" about it that did not match his character very well?) and an unspoken wish that someone would nickname him in return. His pleasure in a pseudonym, like Jonathan Oldstyle, was also something that would continue in years to come as he invented one pen name after another for himself.

But *Vomonte*—Good-to-Everybody! To Washington there was something insulting about it, some implication that he was so spineless and pliant that he might have the same feelings toward a drunken Indian woman as he had toward Maria Hoffman. He felt a hint in it that he was too shallow to have real emotions at all.

He had seen Mrs. Hoffman and Ann, Mrs. Ogden and Eliza, standing in the doorway, trying to repress their laughter while the ceremony was being played out. His own smile was tight and his cheeks were flushed as he thanked the chief for the honor but told him that it had been misplaced. The really distinguished person in the party was Judge Hoffman himself, who had been Attorney General of the great state of New York for several years. Somehow, in the intensity of his reaction against the name Vomonte, Washington was able to persuade the chief that the Judge must indeed be honored. He made his way to join Mrs. Hoffman and the others in the doorway to watch while the chief drew the Judge into the center of the room, danced around him and finally named him Citrovani, or Shining Man.

Washington's smile was again his usual one, and his whole

bearing was more relaxed as he greeted the Judge after the ceremony by his new name. The small maneuver was not exactly the way he had planned to distinguish himself in the wilderness, but at least he had shown the Judge that he was not altogether an amiable child to be laughed at with impunity.

# 3

# The Lads of Kilkenny

In the old walled French city of Montreal there was a wild, rich mingling of commerce, adventure, and an almost feudal hospitality. The center for some years now of the North-West Fur Company, Montreal's narrow streets were busy with the comings and goings of traders and trappers, merchants and captains, and a mingling of Indians as well. The various officers of the great fur enterprise, living in old, narrow but lavish stone houses, kept a kind of open house at all times, the long tables in their big halls laden with food and drink. Judge Hoffman and Mr. Ogden were acquainted with some of these men and Washington went with them as they called, entranced by everything. He could not hear enough of the talk by the traders who had just returned from interior posts. Some of them had passed years away from civilization among distant Indian tribes. They had encountered every sort of adventure, it seemed—trial by water, by forest, by wild beast and hostile aborigine. The puny adventures that had befallen the Hoffman-Ogden party began to look like picnic discomforts to Washington. When one trader to whom he talked at length invited him to accompany him on his autumn trip up the lakes and rivers to a remote post, Washington wanted very much to accept the invitation. There, in the real wilderness, facing true hazard at every turn, he would shed his frivolity, find challenges that really tested him and emerge—how? Taller, stronger, more taciturn, more compelling?

But it could not be. Duty as well as emotion held him to the Hoffman-Ogden party. Judge Hoffman was expecting him back in his law offices on their return to New York. Mrs. Hoffman was expecting him to return with the party. He could not run away to adventure as he had dreamed when he was a boy. Or so, at least, it seemed to him.

The frustrated desire made him envious of a young New Yorker his own age whom he met while in Montreal. Henry Brevoort, a good-looking fellow with a large, candid face, was working as an agent for John Jacob Astor and had already enjoyed some of the adventures that tantalized Washington. He had traveled to trading posts on the banks of lakes with romantic names. He had dickered with Indians, learned a little of their various languages, observed as well some of the difficulties that were engulfing the Indians as the onrushing and grasping civilization of the whites turned their ancient ways and values topsy-turvy. Soon, however, Washington's jealousy disappeared in friendly laughter. Brevoort, he discovered, talked his own language, mocking pretension and self-satisfied pride. No unique qualities of daring had led him to what adventures he had known, Brevoort confessed. He was a cousin of Astor's wife. Looking for some sort of gainful employment, he had gone to Astor who had, by now, a monopoly on the importation of furs to the New York market. Astor had sent him off into the wilds. So he had had adventures, gotten acquainted with Indians, known hardships. That was all there was to it. Washington and Brevoort agreed to meet again after both had returned to New York.

Brevoort would not return for some weeks, but Washington and his party were soon on their way.

Washington had stopped making entries in his journal just before the episode of the amorous Indian woman. He made no notes on the trip back along the St. Lawrence, up the Oswegatchie and through the forests of New York to civilization. But the difficulties were, after all, very like those that had been experienced on the outgoing trip and had lost their ability to shock. One "Temple of Dirt," as Washington named the worst of their overnight accommodations, was very like another and no further opportunities to distinguish himself, even comically, seemed to appear.

Back in New York, and at his law books, Washington was soon recalling the whole journey in waves of nostalgia. Day after day, through the strange and sometimes sublime surroundings of the forest, he had been at Maria Hoffman's side. At night he had been privileged to hold an umbrella over her. Now he was just the tea-time visitor again, helping with the hot water and amusing the children.

In the early fall, Henry Brevoort returned to the city. Washington and he discovered that the kinship they had sensed in Montreal had not been based simply on meeting someone from home in strange surroundings, but was a real pleasure in each other's company. Soon Brevoort was accompanying Washington on his visits to Maria Hoffman. Washington became a familiar visitor at the Brevoort farm out in the country at Broad Way and Fourth Street (where the Broad Way took a jog because the elder Brevoort refused to let the city authorities run a road across his property). Washington was meeting Brevoort's friends and Brevoort was meeting Washington's. Somehow, before long, the two of them had become the focal figures of a group that included some of Henry's friends, some of Washington's, and his brothers too; but all now repolarized into what James Paulding called the "Irving-Brevoort set."

"The Ancient and Honorable Order," "The Ancient Club," "The Nine Worthies"—in the months and years to come the members of this loose and wholly unorganized group, which rarely included just nine, would refer to themselves by all those lofty designations. From the beginning, however, Washington most liked to call this cluster of friends, gallants, and drinking companions "The Lads of Kilkenny." And it was Washington, so obsessive about nicknames, who invented aliases for all the Lads. Brevoort was sometimes Anthony Quoz, after a character Washington had invented in the Oldstyle Letters, and sometimes "Nuncle." Paulding was "Billy Taylor," William and Peter Irving were "The Membrane" and "The Doctor." Ebenezer was "The Captain," or "Captain Greatheart," and there were equally cabalistic names for Gouverneur Kemble, Henry Ogden, James Furman, and the others who moved in and out of the group. Further emphasizing their solidarity and exclusivity, most of the Lads developed a distinctive manner of talking, a way of making shocking or outrageous remarks in a bored, throwaway tone of voice, and a distinctive way of laughing—a sort of buried chuckle that seemed a special tribute to the person who had wrenched forth the laughter. Irving, Brevoort, and the Lads became a recognizable entity at the city's balls and assemblies that winter. They separated to dance and to flirt with all the prettiest girls and regrouped to comment on their partners and give them nicknames—"The Divine Hen," "Little Rule Britannia"—and to amuse themselves by their killingly sophisticated observations on the assemblage.

Still, as the fall gave way to the winter of 1804, it became clear to his family that something was wrong with Washington. A cough, from which he suffered periodically, returned, and he complained of not sleeping well. Since his infancy, when his oldest sister, Ann, had called him "a little rack of bones," his family had considered him less than robust. When a yellow fever epidemic had swept New York City in 1798 he was sturdier but still the one member of the family who was sent to the country—to friends who had a farm in the Sleepy Hollow area of Westchester County—to escape the plague. Both of his trips up the river to visit Ann and Catherine in Johnstown had been instigated chiefly for reasons of health. He had been coughing and had "pains in his chest."

Now, though he pursued his whims and distractions as restlessly as ever, he seemed less well than he had during those years. He went off on sleigh rides with the Lads and various young ladies, into the country and across the "Kissing Bridge," and came home so chilled that his mother filled stone bottles with hot water for his feet and wrapped him in blankets before letting him go to bed. More and more often he came home early from the theater, flushed and coughing. As for his law studies, his progress in them as he huddled in Hoffman's cold offices, barely warmed by open fires, had fallen to a new low.

In the early spring, Maria Hoffman told him that she was expecting a child. He was, above all, a young man who hid feelings of shock, dismay, or deep hurt. He was, as he had always known, nothing but her knight, her humble vassal. Washington rallied to a show of sympathetic joy. How happy she and the Judge must be! How splendid it would be for the five young Hoffmans to have a little brother or sister! He redoubled his efforts at gallantry, fetching and carrying, minding the youngest children, amusing Matilda with drawing lessons.

But his cough and his general health grew so much worse that his family became seriously alarmed. Consumption was the fatal ailment, the fear of it so omnipresent that everyone hesitated to speak the word aloud. No one spoke the word in the Irving household as glances darted toward Washington when he coughed. By the end of March, however, his mother and his brothers were taking quiet counsel with one another, convinced that something had to be done about Washington's health and soon.

# 4

# Deacon Irving's Youngest

THAT HIS mother and brothers should have left his father out of their consultations at first was quite logical. Deacon William Irving, a man in his seventies, had suffered a partial stroke several months earlier. He had recovered sufficiently to go now and then to his shop, just down the block on William Street, but his family thought of him as an ailing man to be spared any unnecessary worry.

His poor health made it easier for them to ignore, as they much preferred to do, a certain strangeness between Deacon Irving and his youngest son, a distance between them that was never openly expressed but which was evident to all and bypassed whenever possible.

The distance was nothing new but had been there since Washington's childhood. He had been a sensitive, high-strung boy, reacting quickly to all the sights and events of his small world. Years later, he would recall "an impossible flow of spirits that sometimes went beyond my strength. Everything was fairy land to me." His older brothers and sisters had found this entertaining and, in the way of families, had sometimes abused his sensibilities. Taking advantage of his quick emotional responses, they told him fantastic stories to see how swiftly they could swing him from laughter to tears and then back to laughter again. Naturally, this had only increased his excitability.

To his father, there was something offensive about this emotionality in a boy. Unaware of his own emotionalism, the tears that rolled down his face when he led the family in morning and evening prayers and hymns, the fierce joy that he felt as he contemplated the salvation that awaited God's chosen few, he had shown only distaste for his youngest son's quick laughter and tears. Whether he rebuked the boy openly or only turned away, was never recorded.

In later years, Washington would write lovingly about every member of his family—except his father. In none of the many stories that he ultimately wrote was there any figure who reflected, even remotely, the man that Deacon Irving might have been. Going further, Washington rarely, either as a youth or a man, spoke of his father in conversation. Fascinated by the past, he found no romance in any stories of his father's youth in the Orkney Islands, where he had been born. Charmed by legends, Washington was unimpressed by a legend that traced his father's family back to an early Irving who had helped Robert Bruce in an escape and been rewarded by a seal bearing the device of a holly branch. In love with the sea and the ships that sailed it since his childhood, when he had spent hours watching the great-sailed schooners beat out to sea from the East River wharves, Washington seemed wholly uninterested in the fact that his father had loved the sea when he was young and had, for some years before his marriage, been a petty officer in His Majesty's merchant service, making regular packet runs between Liverpool and New York.

His father's life, by every token of his son's interests, should have been filled with drama for Washington. His marriage to Sarah Sanders, granddaughter of a Church of

England clergyman, in Plymouth in 1761, his decision to give up the sea and emigrate to the New York colony, his original success as a merchant in the thriving little city at the tip of Manhattan Island and his reverses as first the Stamp Act and then the ensuing difficulties with the mother country marked the inexorable progress toward revolution—all this was part of the past that Washington was so fond of imagining. Then there had been the war, the occupation of New York by the British, the commandeering of the Irving house, the family's flight to New Jersey, and its subsequent return to a city ruined by fires and harassed by British troops. Washington turned a blind eye to it all. What his father had lived had nothing to do with him, it seemed. It was outside the past so nostalgically remembered by Jonathan Oldstyle.

Once, in his middle age, Washington said elliptically to a nephew, "When I was young, I was led to think that somehow or other everything that was pleasant was wicked." He did not say that his father was the one who had led him to such a belief. Neither did he mention his father when he wrote that as a child "religion was forced upon me before I could understand or appreciate it. I was made to swallow it whether I would or not, and that too in its most ungracious forms. I was tasked with it; thwarted with it; wearied with it in a thousand harsh and disagreeable ways; until I was disgusted with all its forms and observances . . ."

New York City was not and never had been a community organized around religion as New England towns and cities were. Its Scottish Presbyterian Congregation, of which William Irving was a member, was not one of its more important or influential churches. Dutch and Anglican churches were more numerous and popular. But the elder Irving, who had embraced Presbyterianism as a youth, bore his church title of deacon with a gravity and sense of importance that were commensurate with his belief in the lonely election of his own group to God's mercy. Daily prayers and hymns were not the only ritual of religion that he imposed on his household. On Sundays, the young Washington was required, with the rest of the family, to attend the three long church services held during the course of the day. His Thursday half-holidays from school were by custom devoted to a study of the catechism on which the Deacon would quiz his son in the evening. Beyond this, the Deacon had the Calvinist habit of examining any small wrongdoing in the light of God's awful wrath and eternal punishment. Life was short, the Deacon warned his son, and all that was mortal withered away like grass. He must take heed of his soul in the brief moment allowed him.

Life was short—everything passed. Somehow, of all the religious precepts with which Deacon Irving "taxed, thwarted and wearied" his son, this was the only one that caught the boy. Everything passed. He could see proof of that everywhere. Where were the old Dutch burghers who had sat before their gabled houses? Where were the men in their buckram-stiffened coats who had once walked Wall Street? Gone, gone. Everything passed. If a flick of terror stirred at the thought, he was unable to exorcise it by some vision of a remote heaven where all was as it had been, now and forever. He thought of how everything passed and a melancholy of acceptance came over him, a melancholy which he could escape only by some rapid move to a distracting scene or by seizing on some sight or action or snatch of conversation that made him shout with laughter.

His older brothers, William, Ebenezer, Peter, and John, had all managed somehow to slip away from their father's teachings without this sort of self-willed detachment from life, this conclusion that nothing mattered very much anyway. Deacon Irving had struggled with each in turn, hoping to move at least one son's ambitions toward the ministry. But William, seventeen years Washington's senior, had first gone to up-state New York to try his luck as a fur trader, and then returned to the city to marry Julia Paulding and to set himself up in a merchandising business similar to his father's. His free time he devoted to literary clubs, political conversations, the theater, and other worldly pursuits. With Peter, who had studied medicine and with Ebenezer, who joined William in his mercantile operations, it had been the same. John, a serious lad, just five years older than Washington, had raised his father's hopes briefly by contemplating a minister's career, but in the end he had not been able to resist the freedom his brothers had found or their mocking advice, "Mind, Jack, you must preach dashing sermons." Finally John had turned to the law. Still, all four of the older brothers had remained considerate and respectful of the gray-bearded patriarch their father had become and spoke of him as "that good old man."

Only Washington was forever unable to say anything like that, or to say anything at all about his father. Once, at the age of twelve or thirteen, he dreamed of running off to sea. For a week he had tried to live on salt pork and had slept on the floor of his room, attempting to harden himself for a sailor's life. But the flare of rebellion had died away. His hardships at home were not really that great. Besides, there was the thought of how hurt his mother would be if he were to run away from home.

From the beginning, Washington had found his mother a protection from the alarm his father could generate in him. The rigors of the war years that had hardened her husband's character had not been able to banish Sarah Sanders Irving's quick smile or change her cheerfully impatient ways. She had been profoundly relieved when the war came to an end, profoundly grateful to the national hero who was most responsible for the American victory. When her eleventh child, the eighth to survive, was born on April 3, 1783, just as peace treaties were being signed, she had murmured,

"Washington's work is over. Let us name the child after him."

Of course, as it turned out, George Washington's work was not over. Six years later, the city was filled with parading, cannonading, and fanfare as the general returned to be inaugurated the first President of the United States on the balcony of Federal Hall, just a few blocks from the Irving home. That same summer, the youngest Irving, walking down the Broad Way with the family servant girl, was suddenly whisked into a shop inside which the girl had spied the tall figure of the President. The girl was telling the President that here was a child who had been named after him and the great man was laying his hand on the boy's head and uttering appropriate blessings.

Sarah Sanders Irving was undoubtedly the first to laugh when her misjudged prophecy about Washington's work being over was pointed out to her. All the Irving sons and daughters, with the possible exception of John, had the gift of laughter and a talent for seeing the comic side of things. They had not received that gift or talent from their father nor been encouraged in them by him. The gift and talent must have come from Sarah Sanders Irving.

A laughing woman, a loving woman, she did what she could to mitigate the sense of gloom and doom with which her husband filled the household at times. When Washington had wandered away from home, as he often did in his early childhood, staying gone so long that sometimes the town crier had to be alerted: "Deacon Irving's youngest missing. Anyone seeing him requested to send him home," she welcomed him back with a sorrowful look and disappointed words. "Oh, Washington, if you were only good." But then she hugged him and ruffled her hand through his chestnut curls. She found it impossible really to scold him.

She always had a firm belief that her youngest child was uniquely talented. Through his school years, as he idled and dreamed away the hours under the discipline of first one master and then another, she had repeated the little refrain, "Oh, Washington, if only . . ." But however she regretted his lack of application, his occasional truancy, or his secret visits to the theater, which did not escape her attention, she never ceased believing that some day this child would show his abilities and surprise everyone.

"Everything pleasant somehow wicked." His father might have hammered that teaching into one corner of his son's soul to leave an alarm that would go off whenever anything became *too* pleasant. But all the while his mother denied that concept with her loving looks and actions. All the while his brothers and sisters entertained him with their lively lives and introduced him to many pleasant things. Ann Sarah, the oldest girl, who had sung Scottish lullabies to him when he was a baby, had married Richard Dodge and gone upstate to live when Washington was only five. But Catherine, nine years older than he, was still at home until he was fifteen. One of Kitty's beaux was John Anderson, the brother of a well-known painter and an amateur artist himself. When Anderson was whiling away an hour or so waiting for Kitty, he amused himself by giving her little brother sketching lessons or showing him large books of engravings. "Everything pleasant somehow wicked"? Wherever he turned, away from his father, he could see that it was not so.

William, Peter, and Ebenezer had saved him also from the need to stage any open rebellion against his father. When Washington finally refused to spend all day Sunday at church, when he began to go openly to the theater, his father might give him a long look and then turn away, but there were no words. If Washington needed someone to lead the way into the worlds of politics, literature, and art, there were William, Peter, and Ebenezer. They had opinions which they could express with wit and clarity, and they were as ready to laugh at their own opinions as to mock the excesses of others. Life in New York City in 1804 was busy and full of incident for William, Peter, and Ebenezer.

Happily enough for Washington, life was also prosperous for William and Ebenezer that year. Their importing business was doing very well and so they were able to think rather grandly when they took counsel with their mother and Peter about Washington's health.

The talk circled about, at first. The brothers recalled that Washington's health always seemed to improve when he traveled away from New York. They spoke of the trips he had made up the Hudson to visit Nancy and Kitty, and how well he was when he came back from the Canadian expedition. They mentioned the fact that Washington would be twenty-one years old on April 3, 1804. Attaining one's majority was a milestone of sorts, never mind if Washington did seem as far from any settled approach to maturity as ever. It was remembered that Washington had not gone to college as Peter and John had, never mind that he had not qualified for Columbia College as they had done.

Finally, the sum of these facts and recollections was a proposal from William and Ebenezer that they send their youngest brother on a European tour to extend over the course of a year or two.

Mrs. Irving and Peter may have gasped at the first suggestion of the idea. The Irvings did not move in the circles of New York society where grand tours in the English tradition were accepted, at least to a degree, as part of a young man's education. But William and Ebenezer repeated their satisfaction with the profits they were making from the business and glowed with the pleasure that only the contemplation of an unselfish gesture can bestow. They spoke of how educational a trip abroad might prove for Washington. Exposed to the culture and glory of past civilizations, he might begin to see his direction in life and come back not only restored in health but matured emotionally and intellectually. If no one referred to the fact that it might also be helpful for him to be separated for a long time from the object of his youthful and hopeless affection, Maria Hoffman, that did not necessarily mean that no one thought of it.

Finally, when the idea of the European trip had been accepted by all of them, they spoke to Deacon Irving about it. The Deacon said little. But his own importing business, which dealt in the same sort of hardware, wine, sugar, and "segars" as William's and Ebenezer's, had long since recovered from the reverses of the war and was also prospering. After the project had been outlined, the Deacon said he would contribute from time to time to the funds necessary for Washington's European tour.

Washington was incredulous when he heard what his brothers planned for him. After incredulity came a passion of gratitude, and then the intoxicating pleasure of hurrying out to tell everyone of his good fortune. Henry Brevoort must be told and Jim Paulding and all the Lads. He wished every one of them was going with him, but he promised long letters in which he would describe everything, particularly the girls of every country and how they varied from nation to nation. He was less ebullient when he told Maria Hoffman. He realized as he sat looking at her that it would be a long time before he saw her again. Her child would be born before his return. Then he tried to banish those thoughts and asked her what she wanted him to send her from abroad. Ann and Matilda came in and he promised to send them sheet music, laces, gloves, books—and to Matilda especially, because of the drawing lessons they had shared, engravings from Italy.

After that, there were new clothes to be chosen, ordered, and fitted. Passports had to be acquired and letters of introduction to various people abroad. Soon it appeared that half of Washington's friends in New York knew someone in

Europe, or else knew someone who did know someone. Before he was through, Washington had a thick packet of letters to present here and there throughout France and Italy with more promised to be sent after him later.

William and Ebenezer had taken passage for him on a vessel bound for Bordeaux, due to sail May 19th. As the day approached, Washington began to feel a certain nervousness mingling with his anticipation. But this he could almost forget in the last-minute gatherings with Brevoort, Paulding, Kemble, and the other Lads at Dyde's Coffee House.

The young men grew boisterous as they lifted glass after glass, toasting Washington, his good fortune, the countries of Europe that he would visit, and the belles whom he would meet. Then Washington, flushed and excited, had to respond, toasting them in return and the belles of New York whom he was leaving behind. Finally he had to toast Maria Hoffman. He lifted his glass to her.

"My Mistress! he called her, in all love and innocence.

Suddenly it was the day to say good-bye to her and her family. Then it was time to kiss his mother good-bye and bid farewell to his father. Time to get his trunks into the hack that had been hired and make his way with his brothers to the wharf. Time to step into the rowboat in which his brothers were going to row him out to the ship that rested at anchor in the river. Time to mount the rope ladder over the ship's side, to say good-bye to his brothers and promise again that he would keep a journal faithfully and write them long letters. He would not disappoint them, he promised. He would learn, he would study. They would be amazed.

But the sails were shuddering up the masts. His brothers were disappearing over the side and into the rowboat. Orders were echoing back and forth across the deck. Sailors were scrambling about. The sails were filling. He was on his way.

# 5

# Traveling Incog

His brothers were right about one thing. Travel was beneficial for his health. He had been pale, coughing, and disconsolate when he boarded the ship, already feeling pangs of homesickness, nor had he been cheered to discover that all the passengers aboard the vessel were French and spoke almost no English. But by the time the ship was two days out, Washington had his sea legs and was roaming the deck. Soon he was feeling so energetic that he was climbing the rigging in imitation of the sailors and finding his new "round jacket" and pantaloons very convenient for the activity. He discovered a perch for himself on the main topsail yard and sat there for hours, gazing out over the water toward the horizon, dreaming the long, wordless dreams to which he had been addicted since childhood, dreams which he once said were sometimes a "substitute for thought" with him.

The weather held fair day after day. They were having a "lady's voyage," the sailors said. But in the year 1804, a voyage across the Atlantic took six weeks in the best of weather. Toward the end of June Washington had a glimpse of the coast of Spain and felt the usual pilgrim's awe at the first sight of a foreign land. The Moorish conquest of Spain, and the story of the last Moorish king, Boabdil, had been part of his favorite reading as a boy, and he thrilled as he gazed at the coastline. There, on that very land, the proud and unfortunate Boabdil had walked. But the ship was not putting in at Spain. A few days later, she was riding at anchor in the Gironde, off Bordeaux, while the passengers waited out their time of quarantine. At last, on June 30th, Washington was setting foot on French soil, bursting with health and anticipation.

Where his brothers had been optimistic, if not visionary, was in imagining Washington might be transformed by the European environment into a serious, studious being, imbibing draughts of history, comparing political theories, and pondering philosophical problems. It was not that Washington did not try. At first he really made an effort. Scribbling a postscript to a letter home which he had been writing throughout the voyage and which he wanted to send back by a westbound ship, he did not forget to mention the scraps of political news he had picked up. Napoleon was about to declare himself "emperor of the Gauls," Murat was in prison. Then he sought out lodgings for himself with a Bordeaux family because he planned to spend several weeks in the city perfecting his French.

An eager tourist, he wandered through the streets of Bordeaux, pleased by every evidence of antiquity. Old churches, old buildings of every sort held his eye. "Ancient piles," he called them, using a phrase from Congreve's writings that had caught his fancy. The lively marketplace with country people in their picturesque native dress seemed a positive carnival to him, and of course he went to the theater, to compare Bordeaux's Grand Theater with his own Park in New York. He made copious notes on everything in his journal and read diligently in the travel and guidebooks he had brought with him.

That other form of research which he promised his friends in New York, a study of the girls and women of every country, was not neglected. Everywhere he went he watched girls shyly but constantly and soon was able to write at length about his observations to friend Quoz. "A sunbeam falling on one of the Bordeaux bells, renders her perfectly transparent, and a slight zephyr betrays the contour of every limb, and the working of every muscle . . . .The ladies of France . . . generously display to the very garter . . ."

Such remarks had a fine worldly sound, but they could not blot out some thoughts of home. "My mistress, you say is *growing in grace*," he wrote Brevoort. "Heaven grant her an accouchement as pleasant as the Virgin Marys, (who if I recollect right sat out on a journey a day or two afterwards). Often do I trace in my fancy her sweet & gentle features, and at this very moment 'the light of her countenance' is beaming upon me with one of her usual smiles that a seraph or a crying cherubim might envy . . ."

When his weeks in Bordeaux were over his itinerary lay across southern France to Marseilles and Nice. Soon after starting on this cross-country journey his tour began to take on the elements of a romp.

"To be pleased with everything and if not pleased, amused," was the creed that Washington had chosen for himself even before leaving home. His brothers might well have wondered then about their hopes for his serious self-improvement. Being pleased or amused by everything might prevent him from emulating the disagreeable Smellfungus character in Laurence Sterne's *Sentimental Journey*, who carped at everything foreign. It was not so likely to lead to the study and reflection his brothers were hoping for.

He was pleased and amused, just a day out of Bordeaux, to meet a short, cheerful man named Dr. Henry, who was sitting beside him in the cabriolet at the front of the diligence.

Dr. Henry, Washington soon learned, was an American, a native of Lancaster, Pennsylvania, but after practicing medicine there for several years he had been enabled by a stroke of fortune to leave his practice and start traveling. Since then, according to Dr. Henry's account, he had been almost everyplace and met almost everybody. Certainly he had a fine command of French and various other languages as well. Washington was even more entertained when Dr. Henry began to show a brilliant talent for improvisation and masquerade.

The journey across southern France was scenic and rich with history, details of which Washington noted in his journal so as to rework them later into letters for William and Ebenezer. But now it was further enlivened at every stop by Dr. Henry's "continually passing himself off on the Peasants for a variety of characters—Sometimes a Swede, sometimes a Turk now a German & now a Dutchman . . ." Soon the doctor began embroiling young Washington Irving in his impersonations as well.

At one inn where the diligence had deposited its passengers to spend the night, Dr. Henry introduced Irving to the landlady as a "young mameluke of distinction, *traveling incog.*" He presented himself as the mameluke's interpreter and begged for a large chair so that his master might sit crosslegged in the manner of his country and also for a pipe so that he might smoke perfumes.

Another day, at a noon halt when the passengers of the diligence were wandering along the streets of a small town, the doctor and Washington stopped at an open door to look at some French maidens busy at a quilting frame just inside. Here the doctor was inspired to introduce his companion as a young English prisoner. Nothing could have been more believable. In France as in England, even the smallest towns were feeling the tension building from Napoleon's slow but steady moves toward an English invasion. The French were ready to expect English spies anywhere. Washington looked very much like an Englishman. A short distance down the street the French girls could see a French army officer who was also a passenger on the diligence and might well be the young man's captor. "Yes," said the doctor gravely, nodding at Washington, "he is on his way to being sentenced."

"*Ah, le pauvre garçon!*" the French maidens cried. "What will they do to him?"

"Oh, nothing serious," answered the doctor. "Perhaps shoot him or cut off his head."

The sympathetic girls caught no note of foolery and hurried to fill Washington's pockets with fruit and to bring him a bottle of wine.

That particular masquerade, which seemed both sweet and amusing at the time, soon had troubling consequences. Perhaps some other passenger on the diligence overheard enough of the charade to begin wondering about the young traveler. Whatever the reason, a small cloud of suspicion began to form over Washington's head and travel with him from town to town. He left Dr. Henry to make a detour to Avignon so that he could visit the tomb of Petrarch's beloved 'Laura' and became convinced that he was being followed the whole time. Later, stopping at an inn, he was visited by an official who demanded to know his country of origin and departed quite unsatisfied that he was really from North America as he claimed.

The suspicion seemed to have died down when he arrived in Marseilles. There he was pleased to meet Dr. Henry again. They went to the theater together and Washington was shocked, or so he wrote to his brothers, by its "lascivious exhibitions"; but he was not too prudish to be amused by the young bootblacks on the street who sought his patronage with scraps of English, "Monsieur, God damn, God damn son de bish son de bish."

All continued serene until he and Dr. Henry arrived at Nice, from which port Washington was going to sail to Genoa. In Nice, the casual masquerade of a few weeks before tripped up Washington completely. He was told that his passport was of the kind given to suspected persons. He could not travel any farther until he had obtained something more satisfactory. In vain Dr. Henry poured out his facile French, vouching for the young man with his person, his property, his all. Washington was halted in Nice until he could offer some more valid proof of his identity and citizenship. He and Dr. Henry hurried to write letters to acquaintances scattered across Europe. Washington wrote a special plea to an old acquaintance from New York, Hall Storm, who was currently vice-consul in Genoa. To speed matters, Dr. Henry boarded a ship for Genoa to deliver this letter in person.

"To be pleased with everything and if not pleased, amused" was not quite as easy as it had been when week succeeded week and Washington had nothing to do but haunt the anterooms of officials or walk aimlessly along the Nice waterfront. At last, after six weeks, enough papers had arrived to reassure the authorities. Washington was soon aboard a felucca bound for Genoa and in such a frenzy of high spirits at his release that the other passengers stared in amazement at the crazy American.

Genoa, under Hall Storm's sponsorship, brought him the gaiety that Nice had failed to provide. Dr. Henry had already departed to continue his wanderings when Washington arrived, but Storm, delighted to have a guest from home, arranged dinners and outings and introduced Washington everywhere. One of the happiest introductions was to the wife of the English consul in Genoa, a Mrs. Bird, who lived with her husband and daughters in a beautiful villa surrounded by gardens high on the hills in the Sestri Ponente. A youthful and vivacious mother, pretty and merry daughters—the grouping was irresistible to Washington, echoing all his memories of Maria Hoffman and Ann and Matilda. He put on his best frilled shirt and black silk breeches to visit the Birds, day after day. He walked with them in the gardens overlooking the Mediterranean, or danced with the girls in the cool parlors as Mrs. Bird played the harpsichord, or just sat and chatted with them about anything and everything. Particularly, Washington like to hear whatever romantic stories the Birds could tell him of the banditti who roamed the Italian hills. Banditti—the very word fascinated him, and when an especially notorious brigand was captured and sentenced to be hanged in the city square, he foreswore a visit to the Birds to witness the grisly execution. Later, he made an entry in his journal describing the scene and admiring the dignity of the outlaw as he went to his death.

Day after day, week after week, he lingered in Genoa. He had other pleasant friends as well as the Birds and his usual research was not neglected. "I have found far more handsome women in proportion in Genoa than in any other city that I have visited in Europe," he wrote to Brevoort. "They have charming figures, beautiful features and fine black eyes. . . . They are said to be as *kind* too as they are *fair*. . . ." He was cryptic as to how he had tested this kindness, writing only of "some transient attachments that are necessary to give *flavor* to existence. . . ." but he had a great deal to say about the differences between the French and the Italian women: "a French woman is much given to gallantry, but an Italian woman to love." He compared the great restraints laid on the behavior of young unmarried ladies in Italy to customs at home. "The innocent familiarities that prevail between young people of both sexes in America & England are unknown in this country and to press the *ruby lips* of a fair damsel would be a howling abomination. Such favors are bestowed by the *married* ladies—*in private*. . . ." He wrote of the proverbial jealousy of Italian husbands and declared that he was convinced they had cause for it. "In fact, friend Quoz—though to a single man the Italian women are a mighty agreeable accomodating set of beings, yet, were I what is called a *marrying man* I would as soon put my neck into a hempen noose as into the hymenial one, with any of them."

But for all the pages he wrote in this vein and whatever time he spent in pursuit of the material for it, the affectionate Birds, up on the hills, were the friends who held him in Genoa, his touchstone of home.

At last, however, William and Ebenezer, who had also received quite a few letters from Genoa, though of a more scholarly nature, wrote to ask what was so remarkable about the city to cause Washington to linger so long. They asked when he was going to proceed to Sicily, an island which they had set their hearts on his visiting.

Washington found it difficult to leave. The coronation of Napoleon was finally taking place and distant as Genoa was from the scene, the city was buzzing with social affairs triggered by that event. There were balls and concerts to which he had been invited. Above all, he grieved to leave Mrs. Bird and her daughters. But he could not ignore the message from his brothers. On December 21, 1804, he boarded the ship *Matilda*, bound for Messina.

The voyage down the coast of Italy took a week or more. Washington had already spent a dull and homesick Christmas Day aboard the little vessel when the pirate ship was seen bearing down on her.

"Pirates?" Washington said to the captain incredulously.

Just then two cannon shots whistled over the bow of the *Matilda*. Washington still could not quite believe it. Two years before he had mocked the play, *The Tripolitan Prize*, for showing him no real pirates. Was he about to see some in the actual flesh?

He was. The pirate ship hove alongside—no bigger, Washington noted with one part of his mind, than a North River ferryboat. A gang of dirty and fierce-looking characters with daggers in their belts leaped aboard. The pirate captain put up a pretense of legality by demanding health certificates. But the captain of the *Matilda*, pale and frightened, shook his head. He knew no Italian. Washington, who had picked up a few Italian phrases by now, put in a few words. He was seized promptly as an interpreter and he and the *Matilda's* captain were hurried onto the pirate ship. There they were pushed into chairs and a couple of ruffians were left to guard them and ask desultory questions while the rest of the pirates ransacked the ship. The ordeal did not last long. After an hour or so Washington and the captain of the *Matilda* were allowed back on their own vessel. Washington arrived in time to see one pirate throw down the packet of introductory letters which had been in his trunk and through which the the pirate had been riffling in search of currency.

"*C'est un home qui court tout le monde,*" said the pirate in disgust, kicking away the packet. Disgust was the general mood of the raiders. They had found a few pipes of brandy, some writing paper, and two boxes of quicksilver in the ship's hold. Lugging this loot they began to make their way back onto their own ship.

"What? No throat cutting?" cried one of the sailors on the *Matilda*, stung by the tameness of the encounter.

"I have no wish to take your life," one of the pirates replied, climbing over the rail onto his own ship.

"What a piracy!" cried the outraged sailor.

What a piracy indeed, thought Washington, as the *Matilda* got underway again. That night in his berth he tried to reimagine the episode and started up by fancying pirates with stilettos pressed against his bosom. But it was no use. He lay back again. There were truly bloodthirsty pirates in these waters. The United States had been warring against them for several years and good men had been killed by them. But it was simply not his luck to meet the genuine article.

In the harbor at Messina, riding out the quarantine there, he became acquainted with some of the officers aboard an American naval vessel, the *Nautilus*, in the area to deal with just such genuine pirates as Washington had failed to meet. Rowing over to the *Nautilus* in one of the *Matilda's* small boats, Washington shouted greetings and exchanged pleasantries with the young Americans on deck. By the time the twenty-one-day quarantine was over, he had arranged to continue his journey on to Syracuse aboard the *Nautilus* and moved his trunks to that ship.

Chatting with his new friends in the wardroom, he heard some of the political and war news. Spain's alliance with the Emperor of France had recently been announced. Plainly, Napoleon was planning to have the French, Spanish, and Dutch fleets foregather somewhere off the French coast in preparation for the invasion of England. The young men on the *Nautilus* knew, however, that England's Admiral Nelson was already in the Mediterranean with his fleet, hoping to bottle up in that sea any allied ships that might be on their way to the rendezvous. The young men said that even now Nelson was reported to be somewhere near Messina.

One fine morning in late January came proof that the *Nautilus* men had not been misinformed. Panic swept the town of Messina as the townspeople first caught sight of the English fleet sailing in through the Strait. Soon, however, it became clear that the fleet was simply sailing past, with which realization everyone relaxed to enjoy the spectacle. Later, Washington described the event dramatically for his brothers. "We wished to have a good view of the fleet. . . . It consisted of eleven sail of the line three frigates & two brigs all in prime order and most noble Vessels. . . . The fleet continued in sight all day. It was very pleasing to observe with what promptness and dexterity the signals were made, answered and obeyed. The fleet seemed as a body of men under perfect discipline. Every ship appeared to know its station immediately and to change position agreeably to command with the utmost precision. Nelson has brought them to a perfect discipline. . . . He takes great pride in them and says there is not a vessel among them that he would wish out of the fleet. . . ."

A few days later, the *Nautilus* weighed anchor for Syracuse. There was an unexpected passage through the famed channel between Scylla and Charybdis, which Washington found less alarming than the East River's Hell Gate at home. Soon, in Syracuse, he was involved in all manner of expeditions ashore with various members of the ship's company. A masquerade ball entertained the young men one evening. Dangerous climbing experiments in the natural wonder known as Dionysus' Ear amused them for several days. Washington, courting risk, dangled at the end of a rope over a crevice while someone inside the cave fired a pistol to test the echoes.

Later, Washington set off on a land excursion accompanied by two of the young officers, a servant and various mules and muleteers, to travel along the Sicilian coast and then inland over the mountains, past various antiquities, to Termini. The young men were pleased to learn that their route took them through wild country known to be the haunt of bandits and outlaws and happily made sure they were well-armed with pistols and dirks.

The area was even wilder and more desolate than they expected, and they were not quite as carefree as they pretended when they were forced to take refuge, one stormy night, in a rude and abandoned chapel high in the hills. At midnight or later they were awakened by a stealthy rattling of the door and other small but unmistakable signs of someone trying to enter. They sprang to their feet, hands on pistols. The servant crept silently toward the door to fling it open and surprise the intruder. He put his hand on the latch and swung the door wide. There stood a thin and eager dog, drawn by the scent of the bones that had been left from the group's dinner.

Collapsing in relief and laughter, Washington may well have wondered if his case was hopeless. Would promised adventure and danger always end in comic anticlimax for him?

Laughing, meeting colorful and hospitable notables in the towns at which they now arrived, becoming involved again in masquerade balls, flirtations, and other merriments, Washington must have remembered now and then his brothers' ambitions for him, their hopes that this tour would steady him and fill him with serious goals and his own promises that they would be amazed. If he did, he did not let the memories worry him. His tour still had another year to go. Ahead lay Naples, Rome, Paris, England. Who knew what serious and profound event might occur in that year and along that route which might change everything? And if it didn't? He could still be pleased with everything and if not pleased, amused.

# 6

# To Turn Painter?

BACK HOME, the flow and activity of life went on. Ebenezer
Irving, twenty-eight years old, was courting a young lady
named Elizabeth Kip. Sister Sally was being courted by a
young man, Henry Van Wart, lately connected with the
Irving purchasing activities in England. Little word of all that
reached Washington as he roamed Sicily. Aaron Burr had
challenged Alexander Hamilton to a duel. They had met on
the heights of New Jersey just above the Hudson River, and
Hamilton had been fatally wounded. Washington did hear
about that and was dismayed, both by the death of Hamilton
and the fall this would mean for Burr, so long Peter's hero.
Maria Hoffman's child, a girl, was born; and in the fall the
Republican Thomas Jefferson was returned to office as President with a sweeping majority. Deacon Irving, long alarmed
by the talk of Jefferson's Godlessness, shook his head and
feared the worst, but William, Peter, and Ebenezer, still generally Federalist in their views, merely sighed and hoped that
business would continue as healthy as it had been during the
last four years of Jefferson's administration. New buildings
were being erected in the city, business was still doing well,
and so they saw no reason to be unduly alarmed.

Meantime, the Irvings, the Hoffmans, Henry Brevoort, James Paulding, and the other friends with whom Washington was corresponding followed—with a lag of the six or seven weeks it took letters to cross the ocean—the path of Washington's travels in Europe and wondered what was really happening with him.

William, not altogether bemused by the long paragraphs on history, monuments, and cathedrals with which Washington studded his letters, had begun to have his suspicions when his young brother had lingered so long in Genoa. Washington might well be reacting happily to strange and curious sights and to the evidences of antiquity, but what truly interested him was the people he met. If they were pleasant, there was no telling how long Washington might linger in one spot. If they were dull, or if he found no one with whom he was sympathetic, he was likely to move on at once, ignoring all the historical claims of the place to his attention.

The time came when William felt he must enter a brotherly, even a quasi-fatherly protest.

"You have determined to *gallop through Italy.* Has it been reserved for you, my dear brother, to make, in *these latter days*, the discovery that all that is worth a stranger's curiosity in Naples and in Rome, may be completely viewed in the short space of time comprised between the 7th March, the time you arrived in Naples, and the 4th April, the date of your last letter, when you inform me that you are detained a week longer in Rome *only* on account of its being Holy week! And as you propose to be at Paris to attend the lectures which are to commence in May, all Italy, I presume, is to be scoured through, (leaving Florence on your left and Venice on your right,) in the short period of eight or nine weeks! Good company, I find, is the grand desideratum with you; good company made you stay eleven weeks at Genoa, where you needed not to have stayed more than two, and good company drives you through Italy in less time than was necessary for your stay at Genoa . . ."

"Good company . . . the grand desideratum. . . ." William was not wrong. In Naples, Washington had met a young American from Virginia, Joseph C. Cabell, as interested as he in observing and making the acquaintance of pretty girls. Cabell also had a methodical approach to the business of studying history, art, and architecture, which for him, as for Irving, was the serious purpose of his European tour. With Cabell leading the way, Washington swept through Naples, seeing the proper buildings, bridges, and monuments. After two weeks, the two were ready to travel on to Rome.

In Rome, thanks to Cabell's letters of introduction, Irving found more good company. One new acquaintance, in particular, was soon impressing him to a degree that might really have staggered William, had Washington been confiding everything in his letters.

Washington Irving began to know Washington Allston (both of them smiling at the coincidence of having the same given name) at a gathering of young British and American artists and writers who were making Rome their headquarters as they studied, experimented, and labored over the creations with which they hoped to amaze or delight the world. Samuel Coleridge and George Gordon, Lord Byron—often part of the group—were not in the city at that time, but Irving had no sense of missing anything. Neither Coleridge nor Byron had won fame as yet. Washington Allston, a native of South Carolina, and in Europe to study painting, seemed the focal figure of the group to Irving from the beginning. Black-haired, blue-eyed, and with a "pale, expressive countenance," he was the perfect image of "artist," and his conversation held Irving enthralled as he talked compellingly about various theories of painting, the comparative virtues of the great masters, the glory of Michelangelo, and the treasures of beauty to be found in Rome. At the end of the evening,

Irving asked Allston if he would accompany him to a gallery some day to help him to a better understanding of what he was seeing. Allston agreed willingly and a date was set.

For Washington Irving, it was the beginning of his first real case of hero worship. Allston, four years older than he, was dedicated to his art as no one Irving had ever known had been committed to anything. All Irving's impulses toward mockery vanished as he stood with his mentor before Michelangelo's *Moses*, or walked slowly beside him through Saint Peter's Basilica, or listened as Allston explained what to look for in a work of sculpture or painting. One or two paintings were all one should dream of trying to look at in the course of a morning, Allston told him—that is, if one really wanted to discover their scope and meaning.

It was a time, in the appreciation of art, when great storytelling canvasses, full of sumptuous techniques and rich contrasts of light and shadow, were admired. Under Allston's guidance, Irving began to respond more completely than before to such paintings and to realize his own affinity for such works. The revelatory moment, accented by the lines of composition, the mystery of a shadow, the gleam of an eye—these were what caught him in nature. Now his comments, gradually growing less diffident, brought pleased responses from Allston. "You have an artist's eye," he told Irving.

Half-forgotten pleasures of his childhood came back to Irving's memory as he and Allston met daily for further tours of Rome's galleries and churches. He remembered the hours that he had spent sketching under the tutelage of Kitty's beau, John Anderson. He remembered a few more formal lessons in drawing from the famous engraver and painter, Archibald Robertson, who had presided over his Columbian Academy of Art just down the block on William Street from the Irving home. He spoke of those early introductions to art to Allston, and then, with Allston's encouragement, began to do a bit of sketching as they walked through the city or out into the countryside. "But that's very good," Allston would say. "That's really good."

The praise stirred curious emotions. Irving thought of the law, his destined career, and the boredom he felt as he studied it. He contrasted his reluctance to return to that study with Allston's eagerness for each day's work. He looked about him, at a city suddenly grown magically rich in beauty and inspiration, and thought of how endlessly stimulating such surroundings must be. Something like an ambition began to crystallize.

Ambling along Rome's streets, stopping now and then for coffee, the young men soon were talking about themselves as well as about art and aesthetics. Irving heard about Allston's childhood on a South Carolina plantation, a life that seemed a world away from the life Irving had known in New York. Allston told one story that was almost incredibly romantic. His mother, he said, had once been in love with a young man who was presumably lost at sea. After his death seemed certain, she had married the man who became Allston's father. And then, several years later, in the midst of a dreadful storm, she had beheld the French windows of the Allston home burst open and the figure of her long-lost love appear before her. He had not been drowned years before after all. Saved, returned to land, and discovering that his fiancée had given him up and married another, he had gone to sea again only to be involved in another shipwreck that had cast him up on the very shore where his lost love now lived. Irving had no story to compare with that one, but he did have his quota of legends that had their birth in the mysterious Hudson Highlands or the old Dutch settlements around Sleepy Hollow. Entertaining each other with strange and marvelous tales, they heightened the interest of each story for themselves by conjuring up the painted scene that would most dramatically evoke the essence of the tale.

Irving was twenty-two on April 3, 1805. He spent the day

with Allston, making an excursion into the hills beyond Rome to a villa where some especially fine paintings could be viewed on invitation. Walking back to the city in the pale, transparent rose of an Italian sunset, the poplars dark smudges on the hills, Irving suddenly voiced the wish that had been forming.

"Oh, if I could only remain here—and turn painter."

"But why not?" said Allston, turning to him. "Nothing could be more feasible."

Irving looked at his friend. "You think that?" he asked.

Allston's eyes were shining with his interest and belief. "You have talent. An artist's eye. I could teach you. Perhaps we might take an apartment together. I could instruct you and help you in every way that was in my power, and you would succeed, I am sure."

Irving was in a daze as they re-entered the city. Wonderingly, he told himself that the miracle had happened. His tour abroad was not to be just entertainment and laughter. He had found a direction in which to go. Allston talked eagerly of the course Irving should follow, the schedules of study he must set for himself, the sketching from models, the progression to oils, and each detail made Irving see his future as an aspiring artist more solid and believable.

Still, he did not mention a word of his new plan to William when he wrote to him the next day. Curiously, he wrote only that he would be detained in Rome through Holy Week. Perhaps, in addressing himself to his oldest brother he realized for the first time the enormity of what he was contemplating.

Two days, three days, almost all of Holy Week went by and the city's streets were filled with the religious pageantry for which Rome was famous. Gradually, as the colorful and glittering parades and processions passed before Irving's eyes, the bright dream began to fade. A creature of whims he might be, but he did have some picture of himself as he was.

He saw that he had none of the dedication to art that Allston felt. He liked to sketch, to look at the scenes about him
and feel emotional responses. But he did not burn to translate
those responses into paintings.

Haltingly, he told Allston that he had reconsidered. He did
not think he had it in him to "turn painter" after all. Allston
was understanding. One had to do what one sensed was right.
He still felt that Irving showed talent in his sketches and in
his intuitive recognition of pictorial composition. Perhaps
some day he would find himself more able to make use of
those talents. Meantime, they would always be friends.

Subdued, feeling a sense of loss, Irving moved through
various social engagements. He was entertained by Baron
von Humboldt, brother of the Alexander von Humboldt who
had recently stirred scientific circles with his explorations in
South America and Mexico. Baron von Humboldt introduced
him to Madame de Staël, the French novelist and political
*femme fatale*, who talked constantly and bombarded the
young American with questions. Irving wrote some long, dull
letters reporting on this and on various antiquities of the city
to William and Ebenezer.

Then, on April 14th, he was fleeing Rome entirely, to
"gallop through Italy," just as William had surmised, traveling to Paris in the good company of Joseph Cabell.

Irving and Cabell laughed and teased their way through the
long, jolting journey over the Alps, across Switzerland and
into France, flirting with innkeepers' daughters and any other
young females who crossed their paths. They had long, silly
discussions with other passengers in the diligence about where
exactly America was on the globe, about the curious political
parties in America, and about the reports heard in Europe of
the matchless fidelity of American women. "*Mon dieu*," said
a gentleman from Lyons, "*c'est un pays malheureaux pour les
garçons*."

"*Certainement*," replied Cabell airly, "*il faut se marier là*."

Then at last they were clattering into Paris, getting out of the diligence in the Faubourg Saint-Antoine and taking lodgings at the Hôtel de Richelieu.

The dream of "turning painter," of becoming serious and dedicated, was further banished as Irving staged a "levee of tailors, shirt-makers, boot-makers et al," so that he might rig himself out "à la mode de Paris." After that he went walking in the gardens of the Palais Royale where he was soon saluted by a *fille de joie*. According to his journal, he strolled and chatted with her for most of the afternoon. The latest news of the emperor, the changes that he was making in the city—new avenues, new buildings, new monuments—provided a helpful structure for conversation between two strangers. Then Irving parted from the young woman, with no inclination, it seemed, to pursue the acquaintance further. "What singular beings these French women are!" he commented in his journal. "Very lively and witty and remarkable for turning a disappointment in a pretty manner."

Another evening he went to a play, attending what he was pleased to discover later was "the most disreputable theater in the city." After the play he wandered again in the royal gardens and was again accosted by one of the "frail, fair nymphs" who lingered there. This one wanted him to buy a bouquet of flowers, which he did, paying double for it because he sensed that she was working in partnership with an old flowerseller. Gratefully, the girl kissed him and begged him to go home with her.

He did not say in his journal how he responded to the invitation, nor is it likely that he would have. William and Ebenezer would be wanting to read the journals on his return, so might his father, to whom "everything pleasant was somehow wicked." So he recorded no dalliances, but in the following weeks he did enter a surprising number of sexually oriented anecdotes—a story of a minister and a *fille de joie*, a story about a home for women of loose virtue, various stories about mistresses who were beautiful, mercenary, abandoned, or otherwise.

There were, as well, one or two notes in his notebook to indicate he had not altogether forgotten the family plan, of which William had recently reminded him, that he should attend some lecture course at the university while in Paris. Botany was the subject that had been suggested, that being a science of great current interest in the United States, where so much vegetation was new and strange to Old World knowledge. Washington noted registering for such a course and buying a botanical dictionary. And there was an entry that recorded his attendance at one lecture.

But in Paris there were a thousand things to distract him from any regular course of study. He found it a pleasure just to walk through the streets of the city, and soon there were a number of new acquaintances, thanks to his letters of introduction and Cabell's, with whom to attend the theater, the opera, or go sightseeing.

Among these new friends was still another young American artist, John Vanderlyn. After the impact that Allston had made on him, and his own brief dream of an artist's career, Washington met every artist eagerly. Vanderlyn, he learned, had once been a protégé of Aaron Burr's and was in Paris because he had been commissioned by New York's recently established Academy of Arts to buy paintings and sculptures for it abroad. Unfortunately, no funds from the Academy had reached Vanderlyn for some time and he was having difficulty scraping up money to live on. Washington wrote at once to William and Ebenezer, entreating them to intercede with the Academy for his new friend. Meantime, he did what he could for Vanderlyn personally by ordering a portrait of himself. Sittings for that brought him again into the studio atmosphere he had enjoyed in Rome, and he met still more artists. The portrait, when Vanderlyn finished, turned out to be a profile likeness which hid Washington's quirking smile but showed a very young man with regular features, his firm chin half-buried in a high collar and stock, his curly hair falling over a smooth high forehead.

The days and weeks went by and Washington was finding that it was easier to be amused in Paris than anywhere else he had been. In a letter to Peter he tried to explain why. He wrote of the climate, the theaters, and the opera, the public walks and the friendliness of the people. The greatest charm of Paris he left for the last—"the perfect liberty of private conduct."

The perfect liberty had to end. In October of 1805, after seventeen weeks in Paris, he set forth with two acquaintances to tour Holland briefly and then embark for England. The flat and tidy land of dikes and windmills seemed a letdown after the beauties and gaieties of Paris, however, and Washington suddenly decided that he knew enough about the Dutch already. He had grown up with descendants of the early Dutch settlers of New York. He knew the snug, quiet houses of the Dutch farmers along the Hudson. Why should he study them further? Besides, there were rumors that Prussia was about to join Napoleon and his allies in the assault on England, which continued as a brooding threat to the future. If Prussia did ally herself with France, there was no telling how packet service to England would be disrupted. Washington hurried to board the channel packet and get to England while he could.

London, foggy and gray in November, enveloped him in a sense of familiarity and homecoming. "Here I am in the land of our forefathers," he wrote to William and Ebenezer, ignoring the fact that Deacon Irving was from the Orkney Islands and Scotland, not England. What gave him a sense of already knowing London was all the reading he had done in his boyhood and youth. Novels, plays and poems alike had mapped out the city for him. There had been also the *Gentleman's Magazine*, to which his brothers had subscribed, with its dark engravings of the Tower, Westminster Abbey, and London Bridge. He even knew how the city should look and it did not disappoint him.

It was as well that the place made him feel at home. He knew no one in the city and his letters of introduction for England, which were to have been awaiting for him there, had miscarried somehow. But there was always the theater to entertain him, and he did have one letter with him from Mrs. Johnson of the Park Theater to Marie Therese De Camp, a young actress. So he went to the theater and saw John Kemble, "Glorious John," the imposing chief of the famous English stage family, and decided that he was not especially impressed by Kembel's talents. He went again and saw the renowned Sarah Kemble Siddons, sister of New York's prize actress, Mrs. Whitelock, and he gave up his native prejudice to write home that Mrs. Siddons was "incomparable," despite her age. Before too long, he presented his one letter to Miss De Camp and was invited to dinner at her lodgings, where he met, among others, Charles Kemble, also of the famous clan, whom the young actress was soon to marry. During the days, he visited the Tower and the Abbey and other historic spots, and he did not have a dull time.

Washington happened to be again at the theater one evening when the performance was suddenly interrupted by the manager stepping forward to make an announcement. News had just been received that Nelson's fleet had scored a magnificent victory over the French and allied fleets at Trafalgar. A long shout began to rise, but the manager lifted his hand to stop it. There was further news. Admiral Nelson had been fatally injured in the battle. He was dead. Washington, remembering the sight of Nelson's brilliant, orderly fleet moving past Messina the year before, felt a sympathetic response to the mingled grief and rejoicing that now filled the theater and was beginning to sweep the city and the nation. The long, long threat of invasion had been averted, but at a price.

After the New Year, Washington set off on a short tour of Oxford, Bath, and Bristol with yet another new acquaintance. But he was growing weary of traveling, weary of new acquaintances, however pleasing or interesting. Good company might indeed be a desideratum to him, but more and more he was longing for the good company that he knew in New York, his family, his friends, Maria Hoffman. He gave up a plan to tour Scotland which would have taken him to his father's native territory and on January 17, 1806, boarded a post chaise from London to Gravesend. The next day he was aboard the ship *Remittance* bound for New York.

The homeward journey was no "lady's voyage" as the trip out had been. Week after week, the ship tossed and plunged through the winter storms of the North Atlantic. The passengers, when not lying miserably in their narrow berths, came crowding in on one another in the cramped confines of the general cabin. Half-ill, generally unwashed, sometimes wrapped in soiled dressing gowns, they tried to while away the time by reading aloud and by making jokes and puns. But the jokes soon grew as familiar and irksome as the sight of one another's persons. The voyage seemed to have lasted an eternity when the *Remittance* came into New York harbor at last, March 24, 1806, fifty-two days out of Gravesend.

Washington Irving was almost breathless in his eagerness to be ashore in his own city again, to see his family and his friends and to walk the well-known streets. He was even looking forward to being back in Judge Hoffman's law offices, vowing to himself that from now on he would really apply himself and be a model of industry. His two years abroad *had* changed him, he told himself, and even his brief ambition to turn painter had left its mark. He was more serious. Then he burst out laughing in the sheer joy of being home again.

# 7

# A Traveled Man

In Philadelphia, Rebecca Gratz read the letter from her friend, Maria Hoffman, and smiled. Washington Irving was back from Europe. How pleased Ann and Matilda would be and how delighted by their stepmother's suggestion that they take a brief holiday from school for a visit to New York. Rebecca was quite pleased herself at the idea of accompanying them, and seeing her dearest friend, Maria. She was also curious to see Washington again. Rebecca remembered him as she had known him two years before when she visited Maria. A charming young man with a gift for seeing the comic side of things, and still, at the same time a young man in whom Rebecca had sensed a curious undertone of sadness. Or, sensitive as she was to sadness about which one could not speak, had she only imagined that?

She rose to put on her cloak and bonnet. It was almost the hour when the girls at Mrs. Greland's boarding school went out for their afternoon walk. If she hurried she might be able to meet them as they were starting off. Tying the scoop bonnet under her chin, she wondered how the two years abroad had affected Washington. Would he have changed—grown less merry and less melancholy?

It was, of course, the question that was in the minds of all his family and friends as they greeted him on his return. He was healthier, certainly. He looked well and somehow firmer, more pulled together physically, less a boy and more of a man. And he was in wonderful spirits, more eager at first to find out what had changed at home than to begin relating his own adventures. But that was to be expected. They would have to wait to find out if anything more basic than physical improvement had occurred.

The clamor of welcoming went on and Washington rejoiced to find his brothers, his sister Sally, and his mother looking well. He admitted privately to his brothers that their father had aged considerably. Washington congratulated Ebenezer on his marriage to Elizabeth Kip, met his new brother-in-law, Henry Van Wart, and was suitably impressed by the way William's children had grown. He marveled at the changes in the city—so many new buildings—a new hotel near the Park Theater—streetlamps on Broadway now that were lighted at night, just as in London. He was told that there were rumors of John Jacob Astor buying the Park Theater with a view to remodeling it, that the Vauxhall had been rebuilt, and that he would have to see for himself how far northward the city now extended.

Very soon after his arrival he hurried to call on Maria Hoffman. He saw her and she seemed as dear to him as always, as warm and affectionate. Nothing had changed. And yet, something had changed a little. She brought in her year-old daughter to show him, but the child was not the whole reason for the change. Somehow the experiences of the last two years had caused an emotional shift in him. Had Maria Hoffman, the ideal whom he called "my mistress" two years before, become at last what he had so often tried to tell himself that she was—"an older sister"?

Rebecca Gratz arrived from Philadelphia with the two

Hoffman daughters and there were more welcomings. Washington saw that Ann, now sixteen, had become quite a beauty, and Matilda, slight and shy, was no longer a child but budding into maidenhood. As for Rebecca Gratz, Washington stared at her a moment. He had forgotten how lovely she was. Small, slender, her dark hair curling in tendrils over her wide brow, she seemed in a way more exotic than any of the women he had observed so carefully abroad. Perhaps her eyes were the clue to the mystery. Large, dark, lustrous, with a vaguely Oriental slant, they seemed to have a haunting quality, secret and sympathetic at the same time.

With Ann and Matilda, Washington laughed and teased in the old vein. With Rebecca he was quieter. Somehow with her he found himself talking about some of his European experiences that had really touched him—his friendship with Allston, his brief dream of turning painter, the way he had felt at home in London with none of the hostility that so many Americans seemed to feel obligatory toward everything British. And yet, with Rebecca he could also laugh and be as mocking as he chose, confident that she would respond to his humor as she did to his more serious conversation. He began to wonder about this darkly beautiful friend of Maria Hoffman's, sensing some sadness beneath her surface grace even as she had sensed his own inner melancholy.

Meantime, of course, he had to greet the Lads, Brevoort, Paulding, Kemble, and the others. With them he was very much the "travelled man," reporting in person on the "frail, fair ones" of Paris, and the belles of every land, elaborating extravagantly on the ways in which necessary triflings had "lent flavor to existence."

Soon enough, however, Rebecca and the girls had returned to Philadelphia, Rebecca exacting a promise from him that when he next visited that city he would stay at the Gratz house on Chestnut Street. Soon enough the excitements of the first reunions were over. It was time to return to Judge Hoffman's law offices and test his resolution that he would really apply himself and study seriously to become a lawyer.

Alas, for all his resolve, he had not been back in the offices a week before he realized that nothing had changed. The law was as boring to him as ever. The vows that he had made during his last weeks in England and on shipboard had crumbled with the first casebook he opened.

Still, he no longer suffered quite the same frantic boredom that he used to know in the office. Lounging in his chair, puffing a segar, he could dream of laughter and champagne in Paris, and the "sunshine in some fair Hunka-munka's eyes." When Peter stopped by in the old fashion he could ramble on about what he had done and seen in a glow of recollection, making everything even more amusing, impressive, or instructive with each telling. For a while, Peter could not hear enough of Rome, Paris, pirates, Dr. Henry, Washington Allston, Madame de Staël, the banditti of Sicily, and the rest. Then suddenly, it was too much for Peter. He was twelve years older than Washington and he had never known any of the scenes and adventures that Washington had experienced. Within a few weeks of Washington's return, Peter was making arrangements to dispose of the *Morning Chronicle*. He was booking passage on a ship and was off on his own tour of Europe. Washington was hardly surprised. Nothing could quite compare with the sense of being "a travelled man."

Ann and Matilda Hoffman, their school out, returned from Philadelphia and with Ann's return, another young girl entered Washington's consciousness—Mary Fairlie. Washington had not known her before, but during the years that he was away, she had become Ann's closest friend. She was at the Hoffman house now as often as he was (and the frequency of his visits there was something else that had not changed). Mary was the daughter of Major John Fairlie who had served under General Washington in the Revolution, and had won special distinction as a man who had managed to make the austere general laugh aloud on various occasions. Mary seemed to have inherited her father's wit, and was pretty and charming as well. She and Washington soon established an almost competitive relationship, testing who could be the most amusing. On the picnics, sailboat rides, garden parties, and junkets into the country with which the young men and women of the town entertained themselves during the summer, Washington and Mary Fairlie set the pace for extravagant badinage.

The summer was already going well so far as distractions went when Gouverneur Kemble crowned it with glory for the Lads of Kilkenny. An uncle of his had died and left him a country house on the banks of the Passaic River, a mile or so out of Newark, complete with outbuildings, summerhouse, orchard, and an elderly black couple who took care of the place. In an expansive gesture, Kemble declared the house to be totally at the disposal of all the members of the "Ancient and Honorable Order."

Kemble was at once christened "The Patroon" by Washington, and the house instantly became the favorite resort of the Lads. Every Friday or Saturday through the summer they made their way, by twos or by threes, laden with bottles and other provisions, to the North River Ferry, and then, once across the river, traveled by rented carriages or horses to their own delectable country playground.

Cockloft Hall was Washington's name for the house and it suited the place—a curious old mansion which had once pretended to Georgian elegance but was now a generally decaying structure with a variety of additions, ells and ornamentations, bespeaking the eclectic taste of Kemble's late uncle. Inside, equal fantasy and dilapadation marked the rooms that opened into one another, all decorated in the antique style—the Green Moreen Room, the Red Silk Room, the Pink Chintz Room. The young men were delighted with the décor, with the shabbiness, with everything about the place. Before long, following Washington's lead, they were peopling the dusty rooms and corridors with legendary figures from the Hall's romantic past, all members of the Cockloft family who, the Lads were sure, looked with ghostly benevolence on the current revels in their old home.

The word "whim" took on new dimensions here. The Lads ate when and how they would, drank rather constantly, and sometimes fell asleep in heaps, but soon rose again to play leapfrog on the lawn, climb trees, pelt each other with cherries, or indulge in equal foolishness indoors. Good humor and quick wit were all that mattered. Pretension was the only enemy. They pounced on it whenever they saw it. Excesses of patriotism dismayed them. "God," said Brevoort, leaning against the porch railing on the Fourth of July and listening to the cannonading echoing from across the river in the city, "What a great nation we are!" They were equally sarcastic about the city's politics, the latest fashions, and anything they saw or read that seemed pompous or affected.

One afternoon at Cockloft Hall Washington and James Paulding were convulsed by a new magazine called *The Town* that had recently appeared in New York. Laughing at its solemn, self-satisfied tone, they amused themselves by talking about how easy it would be to parody the pretentious little publication. Jim had written several light pieces for the *Chronicle* while Washington was away. He was even fonder of scribbling in his spare time than Washington was. They were sure that together they could quite laugh *The Town* out of town.

But that was only a whim. Nothing had changed for Washington. William and Ebenezer, who had been so hopeful about what two years abroad might do in maturing their youngest brother, were quite undeceived by now. They saw that he had no more serious ambitions than he had ever had. Still, they did not regret the investment they had made. They loved the good-looking, amusing young man and told each other that perhaps he needed only time to steady him.

He was supposed to be studying for his bar examination which had been scheduled for November. Instead, he could not resist a sudden trip to Philadelphia, so much easier to reach than it had been, only a day's traveling by the "Swift-Sure Stage." Once arrived, he stayed, as he had promised, at the spacious and welcoming Gratz house. He enjoyed becoming acquainted with Rebecca's father, mother, brothers, and sisters, but most of all he was happy to see Rebecca again.

He had learned, in the weeks since he had last seen her, the explanation for that hint of sadness he thought he saw in her eyes. Maria Hoffman had told him the story. Rebecca had been courted for several years by a handsome and intelligent young Philadelphian, Samuel Ewing. For a long time, Maria had been sure they would marry. To her it had seemed no problem that Rebecca was Jewish and Samuel was Christian. Christian prejudice against Jews was almost nonexistent in those days. Most of the Jews in Ameria had come as refugees from Spain or Portugal and had often been wealthy, sometimes titled people in their own countries. In general, they had made their way easily in the business and social circles of the cities where they settled. As it happened, Rebecca's family had come from Germany, but her father, Michael Gratz, and his brother, Barnard, had established themselves with the same lack of difficulty in Philadelphia, going into business as importers and merchants. Wealthy men by the time of the Revolution, the Gratzes had contributed heavily to the American cause, outfitting private men-of-war at their own expense and helping with munition supplies for the army. After the war, they had become engaged in western trade in the Illinois and Kentucky country. Admired, respected, important men in the Philadelphia business community, they were equally welcomed in the social life of the city. Michael's sons and daughters enjoyed all the diversions of Philadelphian youth and his two younger daughters, Rebecca and Rachel, had been the belles of the Assemblies from the time they began going to dances. Both of them were so beautiful that they were generally known not as the Gratzes but "The Graces." No, Christian prejudice had played no part in what had happened. Rebecca was the one who had made the decision, and Maria, in whom she had confided some of her emotions, knew something of what it had cost her. Rebecca was the one who felt that the difference in faith between her and Samuel created a gulf that would make a happy marriage impossible. For two years Samuel had argued and pleaded with her and Rebecca had seemed at times to waver. But finally she had told Samuel it was no use. She loved him but she would never marry him. He must cease hoping and begin to plan his life without her. That Samuel had at last begun to do so and was courting another young lady of Philadelphia, Maria also knew. She sighed for Rebecca, and she sighed for Samuel too for she was sure he truly loved Rebecca.

The story was one that touched Washington's romantic sensibilities, and though he spoke no word about the subject he looked at Rebecca with even greater admiration. And somehow his knowledge, though unspoken, strengthened the ties of friendship that were growing between the two of them. Rebecca was becoming a very special sort of woman friend, a beautiful, sympathetic woman about whom there was no impulse to weave fantasies of courtship—simply a woman whom he could admire and talk to and like.

Rebecca's company was a pleasure, but Washington let himself be caught up in Philadelphia's social whirl as well, filling his evenings with dances and parties. He wrote long, extravagant letters to Mary Fairlie, in New York, reporting on these activities and on their mutual friends in Philadelphia, and received equally extravagant answers from her.

Nothing had changed. What aspect of his personality he showed depended very much on whom he was with. He sounded new depths in his nature with Rebecca. He took off to new heights of frivolity with Mary Fairlie. And the law remained a dragging, nagging burden from which he saw no way to shake himself free.

Back in New York there was no postponing one hurdle in that career any longer. Washington had to face his bar examination. He was fortunate in having examiners who liked him. Later, he repeated an old story about what one examiner had said to another after testing someone similarly ill-equipped with legal knowledge. "I think he knows a little of the law," one had said.

"Make it stronger," the other replied. "Damned little."

His judges passed him just the same. He was a member of the New York bar by the end of November. He left Judge Hoffman's offices to join his brother John at 3 Wall Street and to await whatever legal chores might come his way and to hope, rather vaguely, that some political appointment might materialize and enable him make a livelihood without undue strain.

No one seemed to see it as part of a pattern that Washington now began to cough again and to show some of the same symptoms that had alarmed his family three years before. A general depression settled over him. His family tried to believe that the poor health was brought on by the gray, cold, scudding weather of a New York December. Washing-

ton met with the Lads and drank with them, though the
sunny interludes at Cockloft Hall were over till spring came
again. He danced and laughed with Mary Fairlie and Ann
Hoffman at the balls and Assemblies. But everyone could see
that something was wrong. Word of it reached Philadelphia
and Rebecca Gratz.

"What is the matter with your favorite Washington?" she
wrote to Maria Hoffman. "I heard he was dejected and in
bad health. 'Does he pine in seclusion and let the queen of
yellow melancholy prey on his cheek?' or is the subtle and
lurking enemy which is said to make such depredations in
your climate undermining his constitution? I should be first
among his lamenting friends if any serious calamity befell him.
But as report generally makes bad, worse, I hope it has proved
so in this instance."

Fortunately, just about this time Washington and Jim
Paulding remembered their summer whim of a little magazine to parody *The Town*. They spoke about it to Washington's brother, William, and William was not only amused
but encouraged them to go ahead with the idea. He even
declared that he would join with them, write light verses
now and then and help with criticism and suggestions.

The whim suddenly expanded into a real project. Washington, Jim, and William considered who might print and
publish their magazine, and the answer was right at hand.
New York's most popular bookstore, The Sentimental Epi-
cure's Ordinary, was run by their friend, David Longworth,
who was also a printer. Longworth's chief printing endeavor
was the annual City Directory, that metropolitan necessity
in the days before telephone directories provided a handy
reference for everyone's address; but he was a high-spirited
fellow, as the name of his bookstore implied, and enjoyed
any opportunity to print something imaginative or entertain-

ing. David, or "Dusky Davy," as Washington generally
called him, after the name of a currently popular song, was
delighted to join in the venture as printer and publisher of
the new magazine and was even convinced he would make
money from it.

Washington, Jim, and William were not thinking of profits.
They were simply taking off on a whim. They met in Dusky
Davy's back parlor, hung with richly framed illustrations
from Shakespearean plays. Dusky Davy served them cake
and wine and urged them on as they planned the outrages
they would include in their first issue.

Quite suddenly, the "dejection and bad health" that had
depressed Washington for a month and more were gone. He
and Jim and William were going to be completely "incog"
as they launched their tease on the town. No one, except
Dusky Davy, was to know who in New York, or elsewhere
for that matter, was responsible for the publication. Involved
in inventing a host of new pseudonyms—Anthony Evergreen,
Will Wizard, Launcelot Langstaff, Esquire, even a name for
a Mohammedan contributor, Mustapha Rub-a-dub Keli Khan
—Washington was once again in tearing spirits.

# 8

# In Hoc Est Hoax

THE FIRST issue of "*Salmagundi*—Or—the Whim-Whams and Opinions of Launcelot Langstaff, Esq. and Others" appeared on January 24, 1807. It was a small, seven-by-four–inch pamphlet with a bright yellow cover. Just below the masthead was its motto.

> "In hoc est hoax, cum quiz et jokeses,
> Et smokem, toastem, roastem folkses,
> Fee, faw, fum.
> With baked and broiled, and stewed and toasted;
> And fried and broiled, and smoked and roasted,
> We treat the town."

The town reacted to the treat quite promptly. The odd size and bright color of the little magazine caught attention and so did its name, which was the popular label for a hash dish made of pickled herrings, onions, green peppers and other oddments. But, "As everybody knows, or ought to know what a SALMAGUND is," the first issue led off, "we shall spare ourselves the trouble of an explanation; besides, we despise trouble as we do everything low and mean. . . ."

Further challenges followed at once. The editors refused
to give any account of themselves, and readers were dared
to guess the identity of Launcelot Langstaff, Esq. and Others.
"As we care for nobody, and as we are not yet at the bar, we
do not feel bound to hold up our hands and answer to our
names." The same disdain was expressed in regard to money:
"We hold it in supreme contempt. The public is welcome to
buy this work or not, just as they choose. So much the better
for the public—and the publisher—we gain not a stiver."
Readers were warned that they were not to look for any
regular schedule of publication. *Salmagundi* would appear
when its editors felt like it, and "so soon as we get tired of
reading our own works, we shall discontinue them without
the least remorse."

The editors did condescend to state their aims in the publication. "Our intention is simply to instruct the young, reform the old, correct the town, and castigate the age; this is
an arduous task and therefore we undertake it with confidence. . . . Like all true and able editors, we consider ourselves infallible. . . .we beg the public particularly to
understand that we solicit no patronage. We are determined
on the contrary, that the patronage shall be entirely on our
side. . . ."

The first New Yorkers to pick up copies seemed delighted
with such arrogance, and even more irresistible was the
promise that the editors were going to "paint a picture of the
town," with a "vast variety of figures" drawn from life. A
piece of theatrical criticism, signed by William Wizard, Esq.,
and another about the New York Assemblies, signed Anthony
Evergreen, Gent. (both actually written by Washington),
made good on this promise at once. A number of personalities were mentioned, some mockingly, a few flatteringly.
Some, like New York's rival dressmakers, Mrs. Toole and
Madame Bouchard, and a well-known French dancing master,

Duport, appeared under their real names. Others were veiled in allusion: "a blooming nymph lately come from the country"; or given fantastic names such as 'Sbidlikens, the cockney.

Washington, James, and William had only to look about them to see how their first issue was being received. Everyone they knew was talking about *Salmagundi*, laughing at its presumption, trying to guess the identities of some of the personalities who had been mentioned, and above all, trying to guess who the editors might be. The three editors themselves, and Washington especially, were pleased to join in the speculation and confess themselves as mystified as anyone or else to throw out wild surmises. For Washington, it was the masquerade of Jonathan Oldstyle all over again only more so, partly because he had collaborators in the joke this time, and chiefly because the little magazine fired its shots over a far greater range than Oldstyle had ever attempted.

Inspired by the success of the first issue, the editors quickly put out a second, third, and fourth, all within the space of a month. Their variety of material widened as they continued. The imaginary Cockloft family, invented during the summer days at Cockloft Hall, made its appearance. Father, maiden sisters, and bachelor brother—a cheerful group of eccentrics— wandered through one essay after another, making various points or none at all, as it struck the editors' fancy. Cockloft Hall itself came to be accepted as home base for most of the variously named contributors to the magazine. William, signing himself Pindar Cockloft, made his first solo contribution with a long jingle of light verse, congratulating Launcelot Langstaff for "taking the quill / To put our gay town and its fair under drill." Mustapha Rub-a-dub-Keli Khan made his appearance. Purporting to be a Mohammedan captive of the Tripolitan wars who had been held in custody in New York for some time, Keli Khan had written long letters to a friend at home in Tripoli and copies of the letters had somehow come into the possession of Will Wizard. In these letters (sometimes written by Washington, sometimes by Paulding), the same innocent bewilderment that Jonathan Oldstyle had brought to the theater was used to comment on the sights of New York and the behavior of its inhabitants.

Sales increased. Dusky Davy, in one of his secret conferences with the editors, reported that during the course of one day alone the fourth issue had sold 800 copies. New York's population had grown to nearly 80,000 inhabitants by this year of 1807. Even so, 800 copies in one day was not bad.

The talk over tea tables and in the coffee houses buzzed louder. The little magazine was something new. Easy though it might be to trace its descent from the *Spectator*, especially since the *Salmagundi* editors openly parodied the famous forerunner from time to time, the magazine had a brash and peppery quality of its own. It was, moreover, directed wholly to the American scene, singling out places, people, and types recognizable and familiar to its readers. By spring, Dusky Davy was distributing the magazine in Boston, Philadelphia, and other cities, where it was also selling well and stirring speculation. A further element in its popularity was its breezy, conversational style which appealed to women readers as well as men. The belles and "Belindas" of New York and the other cities were carrying copies of *Salmagundi* in their reticules, as indeed the editors had planned that they should, having arranged for it to be "printed on hot-pressed vellum paper, as that is held in highest estimation for buckling up young ladies' hair. . . ." and to be small and neat enough so that it could "form a volume sufficiently portable to be carried in old ladies' pockets and young ladies' workbags."

Of all New York's young ladies, Mary Fairlie professed herself in the most constant state of agitation as to whom the editors could be. She had probably guessed quite accurately within a few weeks because she then began directing most of her teasing and questioning at Washington or her assurances that she was keeping his secret safe. By March, she had herself appeared in one of Anthony Evergreen's reports on a ball, in the guise of Miss Sophy Sparkle, "a young lady unrivalled for playful wit and innocent vivacity, and who, like a brilliant adds lustre to the front of fashion." Whether or not she knew that Washington had written that particular piece, most readers in New York, and also in Philadelphia, guessed at once that Mary Fairlie was the original of Sophy Sparkle. Maria Hoffman, on the other hand, did not appear in any guise in *Salmagundi*, nor did Rebecca Gratz, but both of them, like Mary, soon guessed who the magazine's creators were.

Critical opinion began to appear in other magazines. A serious little journal called the *Weekly Inspector* was outraged by *Salmagundi* and offered several paragraphs of displeasure. "Salmagundi—alias Bubble and Squeak," the notice was headed, and a further suggested name was "Sillykickaby." The editors of *Salmagundi* were stimulated by such jibes and quickly replied with much livelier insults of their own. Other critics had more valid points when they complained that *Salmagundi* was hardly classic satire in the tradition of Jonathan Swift, and that nowhere could they perceive any single, deadly point of view. They pointed out that there really were no "moral reflections and instructive lessons" in the magazine, ignoring, one and all, the warning under the masthead, "In hoc est hoax."

(Curiously enough, in the years and generations that followed, literary critics continued to ignore that reminder. Few were able to see that in the very inconsistency of *Salmagundi*'s writers and in their tendency to make fools of themselves as well as their targets they were making fun of the naive belief that people in general would either listen to or profit from "moral reflections and instructive lessons." Many critics read the magazine's statement that it "meant to

instruct the young, reform the old, and castigate the age"
quite literally, and labored on with their charges that it had
not done so, forgetting that "In hoc est hoax.")

The three perpetrators of the hoax, somehow preserving
their anonymity, went on with their usual lives, William busy
in the importing business with Ebenezer, James clerking in
the United States Loan Office, Washington presenting himself most days at John's law office. But they seemed to have
no trouble remaining prolific and inventive as one issue followed another. A new travel feature appeared. "Memoran-
dums for a Tour," mocked the way visitors from abroad
came to America with the sole purpose of taking notes on
that curious country and later writing a book. "The Stranger
in New Jersey" led off the series and included these items:

"Newark—noted for its fine breed of fat mosquitoes—sting
through the thickest boots. . . . Bridge-town, vulgarly called
Spank-town, from a story of a quondam parson and his wife—
real name, according to Linkum Fidelius, Bridge-town, from
*bridge*, a contrivance to get dry shod over a river or brook;
and *town*, an appellation given in America to the accidental
assemblage of a church, a tavern, and a blacksmith's shop. . . .

"Princeton—college—professors wear boots! students famous for their love of a jest—set the college on fire and burnt
out the professors; an excellent joke, but not worth repeating—mem. American students very much addicted to burning
down colleges. . . ."

Life's other activities went on. Judge Hoffman had to take
a trip to Albany and Washington was asked to act as a male
protector for the Hoffman family in the house where they
now lived, on Greenwich Street. Washington wrote to the
Judge after he had been absent a few days to report on the
tranquil state of things at home.

"Dear Sir:—I am writing this letter from your parlor, and
have the pleasure of informing you that the family, at this

moment, are perfectly well; the girls all out in the sunshine, Mrs. H. sewing like a good housewife; little Charles sleeping upstairs, and little old fashion by my side, most studiously turning over the leaves of the family Bible. . . ." He gave some more domestic news and then, showing an unwonted interest in his professional career, asked the Judge to remember him if he should hear of any small political appointment that might be suitable for him. Washington admitted that there were few offices for which he was qualified, but reminded the Judge that John was his partner and learned in the law as he was not, and concluded by saying that he would appreciate "a word in season."

Such efforts to be businesslike were sporadic. By March, Washington had left New York for another visit to Philadelphia. He stayed at the Gratz house as a matter of course. The big bedroom on the second floor was "Washington Irving's room" now. Rebecca's young brother, Joseph, was spellbound by the conversation of this witty young man from New York. Rebecca and he found the same pleasure in each other's company that they had known the year before, and when their talk turned to *Salmagundi* it was impossible for him to withhold from her the fact that he was one of its moving spirits. With Rebecca, he never seemed to have the same teasing need for masquerade that he had with other young women.

He wrote to Mary Fairlie in his more usual style. "You need not be under any apprehensions of my forgetting New York while you are in it (very like a compliment); but I have so many engagements on hand, am so intolerably admired, and have still so much money in my pocket, that I really can fix on no time when I shall return to my New York insignificance." Despite his engagements, however, he managed some writing for *Salmagundi*. More travel notes from "A Stranger at Home" offered a staccato report on a journey to Philadelphia and enlarged on the passion that

Philadelphians had for punning. This was a conceit which Washington, James, and William, all addicted to punning themselves, were constantly elaborating in their magazine, since it allowed them to print outrageous examples of their own concoction while blaming them on the Philadelphians.

A brief excursion into electioneering engaged Washington when he returned to New York. He had never been serious about his politics, being content to trail along after the opinions of William, Ebenezer, and Peter. If they were Republicans (as Burr, not Jefferson, defined the term), so was he. If they were Federalists (Burr's influence having waned after his duel with Hamilton and his abortive attempt to become New York's governor in 1804), so was he. Undoubtedly his vagrant hopes for a political appointment inspired his volunteer work in getting out the Federalist vote in the spring elections of 1807. When his efforts were over, he wrote some of his reactions to Mary Fairlie, currently visiting in Boston.

"Well . . . we have toiled through the purgatory of an election, and may the day stand for aye accursed on the Kalendar, for never were poor devils more intolerably beaten and discomfited than my forlorn brethren, the Federalists. What makes me the more outrageous is, that I got fairly drawn into the vortex, and before the third day was expired, I was as deep in mud and politics as ever a moderate gentleman would wish to be. . . ."

Mary answered cheerily. "How my heart joyed to hear of your defeat! Never did I receive a letter which gave me so much pleasure. I cannot say, however, that it was unexpected, as I am too good a Republican to have thought of leaving New York without being perfectly aware of our victory. . . ."

The absurdity of violent partisanship was what really exercised Washington and he relieved his feelings about this in a Mustapha Rub-a-dub Keli Kahn letter in *Salmagundi*. In a previous letter, Mustapha had already defined the American

government for his Tripolitan friend; it was not an aristoc-
racy, as some declared, not a democracy, nor yet a moboc-
racy. "To let thee at once into a secret, which is unknown to
these people themselves, their government is pure unadul-
terated LOGOCRACY, or government of words," Mustapha
had written. Now he tried to explain American politics.

"Oh Asem! I almost shrink at the recollection of the
scenes of confusion, of licentious disorganization which I
have witnessed during the last three days. I have beheld this
whole city, nay, this whole State, given up to the tongue and
the pen; to the puffers, the bawlers, the babblers, and the
slang-whangers. I have beheld the community convulsed with
a civil war, or civil talk; individuals verbally massacred, families annihilated by whole sheets full, and slang-whangers
coolly bathing their pens in ink and rioting in the slaughter
of thousands. . . . I have seen liberty; I have seen equality;
I have seen fraternity! I have seen that great political puppet
show—an ELECTION!"

Since Washington could not help revealing in his everyday
life his inability to join wholeheartedly in that "great political
puppet show," perhaps it was no wonder that his various
hesitant appeals for a political appointment went unheeded.
However, in May of 1807, he did get an assignment of sorts.
Aaron Burr, whose star had begun declining after his duel
with Hamilton, had been engaged in some more curiously
self-destructive behavior during 1806. He was, it seemed,
first trying to detach the Western states from the union and
sell them to England, then plotting to conquer Mexico and
become its emperor, then planning some other project in
Louisiana. Everything about what he had been doing was
vague, but a former associate, General Wilkinson, suddenly
decided to denounce him to President Jefferson. Jefferson,
not averse to having a public distraction from some of his
own difficulties, and not too upset at having Burr the scape-
goat, had ordered Burr's arrest. Burr had been apprehended

and taken to Richmond, Virginia, for trial on a charge of treason. One of Colonel Burr's friends in New York, interested in getting firsthand reports of the trial, suggested that Washington Irving attend it. Washington's services as a lawyer were not in question, but if he saw any way to help Burr through his writing he was urged to do so.

Washington made the journey to Baltimore a social junket. He lingered in Baltimore where, as he wrote Mary, he "was toted about town and introduced to everybody," stopped off at Fredericksburg for more visiting, and halted again at Williamsburg for a reunion with Joseph Cabell, his companion through Italy and France.

Finally arrived in Richmond, he made his way through the turmoil attendant to the trial, discovered that there was little he could do to aid Burr, and so gave himself up to observing the spectacle while court was in session and to social diversion when it was not. His actor friend, Thomas Cooper, was in the city, playing an engagement, and he dined and drank with him and also lent him a pair of his breeches when Cooper found he did not have the kind he needed for one role. That there was a souvenir in one of the pockets, a brooch which Washington had acquired somehow during one of his "trivial attachments" abroad, caused a good deal of merriment between the two young men.

Inevitably, Washington met Burr's daughter, Theodosia, who was in Richmond using all her charm and intelligence to win sympathy and support for her father. She was a beautiful and witty young married woman. He was a good-looking and amusing young man whose Oldstyle letters she remembered. The two soon were spending a good deal of time together, dancing, chatting, and talking about her father's plight. Years later, there would be rumors that Theodosia Burr Alston and Washington Irving were lovers in the summer of 1807. No letters, no scraps of any documentary evidence have ever been found to substantiate such rumors.

They enjoyed each other's company and Washington, already somewhat sympathetic to Burr, grew more so as Theodosia argued his case.

Little that pointed to actual treason was proved against Burr. Chief Justice John Marshall, who presided at the trial, was at pains to make sure that the prevailing emotionalism did not rule the jury. After two months of trial, Burr was acquitted of the charges against him, but broken in spirit, he was ready for exile. Washington was granted a final interview with him in his cell. He wrote of some of his musings afterward to Mary. "I bid him farewell with a heavy heart and he expressed with peculiar warmth and feeling his sense of the interest I had taken in his fate. . . . Such is the last interview I had with poor Burr, and I shall never ferget it."

Still, *Salmagundi* was not neglected. Washington forwarded several pieces from Richmond to New York. He wrote to James making various suggestions and, once, to regret the appearance of an essay of his that he did not think worthy of publication. He also inquired if Dusky Davy did not have some profits to distribute by this time. "I shall stand much in need of a little sum of money when I return."

The query sounded logical enough. Perhaps he, and James and William too, had forgotten the great scorn for money which they had expressed in the first issue. "As for us—we gain not a stiver." Or perhaps, with the magazine selling so well, they believed Longworth would be willing to laugh off that early disclaimer as a joke. However, when Washington did return to New York in August he found this was not the case. Longworth had obtained copyright for the *Salmagundi* material in his own name and expressed surprise at the suggestion that he should distribute any of the profits. Vague feelings of distrust and misuse began to simmer in the hearts of *Salmagundi's* creators.

That such feelings should arise just now was unfortunate,

since Washington and James both had begun gradually to feel a greater personal commitment to their writing for the magazine. At first, they had paid little attention to who wrote what. They had rewritten each other's materials and William had added his revisions until much of the copy was a joint production. Recently, however, both Washington and James had been inspired to write some pieces quite definitely their own. During the summer, James had written a quiet, sentimental essay about an uncle of his who had courted many a girl but remained a bachelor, comforting himself with the doubtful assurance, "I might have had her." Later in the year, Washington took off on a historical fantasy which held the seeds of something much larger in scope. In this mocking spoof of the way a dancing craze had overtaken the citizens of New York, he called the city, for the first time in its history, Gotham, after the ancient nursery rhyme city, and even more anciently, the city of Gotham in England, which was proverbial for the stupidity of its inhabitants. Washington did not elaborate on the history of America's Gotham. The burden of his tale was an account of how Gotham had been conquered by a fiddler and a dancer, Pirouet and Rigadoon, who finally "put all ages, sexes and conditions to the fiddle and the dance; and in a word, compelled and enforced them to become absolute Hoppingtots." But the name of Gotham for New York lingered in his mind, accumulating other fancies around it.

He seemed little affected by the death of his father in October, 1807. Deacon William Irving had been almost totally paralyzed for the last year. His death was, in a measure, a release. Still, Sarah Sanders Irving, his wife for forty-six years, grieved, and his older sons and daughters felt sorrow at their father's passing. Washington went through the formalities of the funeral with decent gravity, avoiding any charge of coldness by devoting himself to comforting his mother. Unlike the others, however, he could summon no eulogistic remarks about his father's character and integrity. He had buried his father in his own way and for his own reasons long before.

And yet, the next month Washington was represented in *Salmagundi* by a hauntingly melancholy essay titled "The Little Man in Black." The story had to do with a shy and lonely old fellow who appeared in a small town and unwittingly gave his neighbors the superstitious impression that he was versed in the black arts. Shunned by all, he fell ill and before long was near death from starvation because none of his neighbors came near enough to know that he was sick. At the very last, he was befriended by the squire of Cockloft Hall, and dying, he bequeathed to this one sympathetic fellow human his sole possession, an esoteric work of history and philosophy.

"The Little Man in Black" was an even more curious fragment amidst the burlesque of *Salmagundi* than James' "Uncle John" had been. He was, actually, the precursor of a great number of old fellows who would haunt Washington's imagination in years to come—some of them bachelors, some miserably married to shrews, but all of them bewitched in some way by the past, its legends or philosophies, and cut off from the bustling life of the present. Perhaps Washington was groping toward some understanding of his father in this study of an estranged little man. Or perhaps, equally possible, he was trying to express some baffling and hungry aspect of himself that was hidden under his social exterior. He never made any comments on the story. It was not his way to look for deeper meanings in what he wrote or did, and troubling emotions were best buried.

The disagreements that Washington, James, and William

were having with David Longworth over some financial re-
wards for them from the profits he was making on their
magazine came to a climax at the end of the year, and the
three editors decided to suspend publication of *Salmagundi*.
None of them seemed to find anything especially ironic in
the situation. They were the ones who had written for whim
alone, but when the magazine proved unexpectedly popular
and Dusky Davy pocketed all the profits except for a token
one hundred dollars which he allotted to each of them, they
were aggrieved.

The last issue of *Salmagundi* appeared on January 25, 1808,
almost a year to the day from the first issue. As was customary, there was a letter "From the Elbow Chair of Launcelot Langstaff." This last letter discoursed briefly on Saint
Nicholas, or Santa Claus, whom Langstaff put forward as the
proper patron saint for the "antient ciy of Gotham." Then
Langstaff was bidding the readers of the magazine farewell
with an admonition that they read diligently "the Bible and
almanac, the newspaper and *Salmagundi*, which is all the
reading an honest citizen has occasion for."

The abrupt termination of the magazine when it was still
at the height of its popularity and when both Washington
and James had further ideas for it was not as dismaying as it
might have been to Washington. Peter had returned from a
year and a half of travel in Europe. He was as full of the
sense of being "a travelled man," as Washington had been
two years before, and he had been home hardly a week before he and Washington were making enthusiastic plans for
yet another satirical writing project.

Besides, during the months that followed the demise of
*Salmagundi*, Washington was falling in love.

# 9

# Matilinda-dinda-dinda

It is likely that Washington—given to nicknames as he was—invented the nickname by which she sometimes referred to herself, Matilinda-dinda-dinda, a gay little name, ringing like a small silver bell. She had been a quiet part of his life ever since he first became a familiar of the Hoffman house in 1802. He had given her drawing lessons and brought her engravings from Italy as he promised.

Many years later, he wrote of meeting her again after his return from Europe and memory had charged the scene with significance. "She came home from school to see me," he recalled. "She entered full of eagerness, yet shy from her natural timidity, from the time that had elapsed since we parted, and from the idea of my being a *travelled man*,—instead of a stripling student—However what a difference the interval had made. She was but between fifteen and sixteen, just growing up, there was a softness and delicacy in her form and look, a countenance of that eloquent expression, yet that mantling modesty—I thought I had never beheld anything so lovely—."

But that was in retrospect. Through 1806 and 1807, other

loveliness engaged most of his attention. Mary Fairlie's charms amused and pleased him. Rebecca Gratz's beauty seemed more haunting than any he had ever seen. Becoming acquainted with an aspiring young artist, Thomas Sully, he was quick to give Sully a letter of introduction to Rebecca Gratz when Sully moved to Philadelphia in the fall. Washington knew the Gratzes would enable the young man to meet the most helpful and encouraging people in the city, but he also hoped that Sully would paint Rebecca's portrait— which he did, several times, over the course of the next years.

To any casual observer, it must have seemed that if either Hoffman daughter had a special appeal for Washington Irving, it was Ann, dark and volatile. Ann and Mary Fairlie were so frequently together and Washington was so often with them both it could have been difficult to guess which one he preferred. Ann and Mary were an extravagant pair. Their fondness for learning the latest dance steps from France helped inspire Washington's fantasy about the capture of Gotham by Pirouet and Rigadoon, especially since they insisted on teaching the new steps to the young men of their acquaintance.

In one of his letters to Joseph Gratz, Washington told of a "crazy party" Mary had given and how Ann and Mary had "insisted upon shewing us a new way of coming into a room, but we disappointed them by displaying an old way of going out—and actually made a safe retreat to our own homes; since when I have foresworn and abandoned their society; until they shall have regained their understandings (meaning a pun)." With Ann Hoffman he teased almost as much as he did with Mary Fairlie.

But during the spring and summer of 1808, he was looking more and more frequently toward Matilda in his quieter moments. Her face was small, too small for a rather prominent nose, but great dark eyes and a smooth rounded forehead drew attention away from that. Often when he turned his glance toward her he found her eyes fixed on him. All the secret side of his nature responded, the same depths which Rebecca Gratz could stir. He began to talk with her more than before or perhaps it was that he paid more attention to their conversation. He spoke to her of books that he was reading and was pleased by her shy comments. He read poetry to her and found a satisfaction that was lacking when he read to Maria Hoffman or Rebecca. Matilda, so much younger, was so fresh in her perceptions. He could play upon her emotions as he could never do with the older women.

Matilda had her own flashing humor beyond her shyness and a pleasure in life's amusements and trivialities. A letter that she wrote to Ann when the older sister was out of the city on a visit began with a solemn tease about a family locket which an aunt might bequeath to Ann instead of her. Matilda then went on to report on dresses, tea parties, and the progress that was being made in the renovation of the Park Theater. "We went over to the Theatre yesterday with Mrs. Fairlie and Mary, it is totally altered the whole inside has been pulled down and four rows of boxes instead of three put up with pillars between every box burnished with silver, there are three private boxes on each side directly on the stage in the place of the immense pillars which used to be there, with a *number* of other improvements too *numerous* to *enumerate*. . . . Washington says he saw a beautiful girl at Coldenham whose name is Ellen. Tell her that. . . ." Casually spelled and punctuated, the whole letter contained such a cheerful mixture of news, jokes, and underlinings that Matilda added a postscript: "Burn this letter as soon as you have read it, I beg of you I cannot bear that such nonsense should be seen by anyone."

But Washington saw her talent for nonsense and was pleased by that also. If Maria, who knew him so well, began to notice that he showed a new awareness of Matilda during this spring and summer, she held her peace, content to let the situation develop as it would. And to everyone else Washington remained the beau about town, gallant to all the girls and serious with none.

The writing project which he was concocting with Peter occupied much of his free time. The inspiration for it had come in a way very similar to the whim that had led him and Paulding to *Salmagundi*, from a newly published work that seemed to cry out for parody. *The Picture of New-York; or The Traveller's Guide through the Commercial Metropolis of the United States* was the weighty title of a small volume that had been written by one of New York's most respected and public-spirited citizens, Dr. Samuel Latham Mitchell. All his life, it seemed, Washington had been hearing about Dr. Mitchell's educational lectures or other labors in behalf of good causes, but that could not prevent him and Peter from finding the doctor's book the ultimate in pretentious absurdity. In it, the doctor solemnly traced the city's history from the days of the aborigines to the glories of the present, including insurance companies, reservoirs, lighted streets, and other marvels.

The spoofing spirit of *Salmagundi* was still strong in Washington. Peter, having missed out on the fun of that joke, wanted a fling at something in the same vein. A parody of *The Picture of New-York* was all that they had in mind at first. Surely, they told each other, New York's history should begin with the creation of the world, no less. Every cataclysm of nature and humankind should play its part in the eventual rising of a little city at the tip of Manhattan Island. They decided to survey that vast panorama, quoting from obscure and ancient sources, dragging in every possible world convulsion, to lead up to that miracle of man's endeavor— New York.

Research was a game. Tracking down old and dusty tomes that might include passages to suit their purpose had no connection with study as it pertained to the law or to school in Washington's mind. The New York Historical Society had been founded in the same year that he went to Europe. He found his way there now to become a member and browse among the books in its little library. Peter also read, and they shared their choicest discoveries. Each one wrote segments— on the various theories about the creation of the world, on the Flood, on the first Dutch adventurers to reach the New World. They laughed till their sides ached as they read each other's passages, so high-flown, so foolish, so sprinkled with references—*op.cit.*; *idem; et al.*

*Esta obra*, "our work," they called their project as the notes piled up and the chapter fragments and reminders about further items to be researched accumulated. The pile of papers grew immense, and the larger it grew the more formless the project became. Drawn on by their enthusiasm for the bizarre, and the temptation to draw far-flung analogies with current events and indulge in satirical asides, they were collecting a vast kitchen midden of fact, fancy, and legend. Most of the summer, Washington was concerned with the problem of how he and Peter were going to organize the material, how they could give their history some shape, and from what point of view it should be told.

A trip to Canada did not wholly take his mind off the problem. Ebenezer, following the lead of Judge Hoffman, had bought some land along the Canadian border. Washington had already journeyed to that wilderness and was detailed to go again to inspect Ebenezer's holdings and analyze the prospects for developing them. He persuaded Peter to postpone a planned visit to sisters Ann and Catherine in Johnstown and accompany him. Traveling through the forests and down the rivers to the north, they whiled away many hours talking about their project. Perhaps their history should not try to encompass everything from the creation to the present day but merely follow New York's story through the years of Dutch settlement and rule. Certainly they had enough material on the Dutch period to fill a large book, and it amused them both to contemplate burlesquing the glories of the little village of New Amsterdam.

They heard of the death of their sister Ann on their return trip. Both of them were shocked and almost overcome by the unexpected event. Washington felt guilt in addition to his grief because he had prevented Peter from making a visit to Nancy before she died.

Matilda said little, yet she seemed to give him a comfort no one else could. Her youthful sincerity inspired in him a need to act with greater maturity in her presence. He found excuses to spend more time alone with her, and for them to go walking together. Perhaps she would like to go to the Historical Society with him and wait just a moment while he made a few notes for a project on which he was working. *Esta obra*, of course, but it was vaguely cheering to keep it a mystery even from her. Perhaps she would like to walk in the Battery. Ann was being courted by a young man from Philadelphia. Mary Fairlie's most attentive admirer these days was the actor, Thomas Cooper, who was "laying close siege to her." There was no one to tease or pay special notice. So they walked here and there, or sat on a green bank and looked out at the Hudson River and the boats flitting up and down.

Social life became more active when the renovated Park Theater was finally reopened in the fall. Washington had been asked to write a celebratory ode for the opening night. He obliged with a long, dull effort, but nobody paid much attention when it was read, since everyone was much more concerned with the changes in the auditorium, the pillars of "burnished silver," and the boxes on stage which Matilda had described in her letter to Ann.

At another performance, a week or so after opening night, Ann created a sensation of her own when a false fire alarm was given. Washington described it in a letter. The alarm "threw the whole audience in confusion—the Ladies were all in a panic—and Ann who was in box no 3, made a tremendous leap from the front of the next box on the stage—clearing the spikes of the orchestra &c and landing with great decency and considerable grace. The actors, you may easily imagine were astonished by so brilliant a 'first appearance.' But as the new performer seemed excessively frightened & embarrassed Cooper advanced from the other side of the stage, led her to the prompter & directed him to conduct her to Mrs. Prices box—where the little heroine had a most tragic fainting fit."

Laughter to be shared, ludicrous episodes to enjoy—life continued to offer these distractions, but Washington was steadily growing more serious. Day by day, the young man who had followed and observed pretty girls across Italy, Sicily, and France and who had flirted with New York's most popular belles, was coming to the realization that he was really in love at last and with the shy seventeen-year-old Matilda—Matilinda-dinda-dinda. Just how he declared his love, just how she responded, hardly mattered. Suddenly, they were hand in hand, quite sure of each other and the need for a future together.

Equally suddenly, a subject that had never bothered Washington Irving before loomed with an appalling immediacy—money. How was he to go to Judge Hoffman and ask for his daughter's hand when he had no idea of how he would support a wife?

How he had supported himself in the years since he returned from Europe may have seemed as much a mystery to him as it does to anyone looking back at his life from another century. He lived at home, in the house his father had bought in 1802, on William Street at the corner of Ann Street. But where did he get the money that he spent so cheerily on champagne suppers at Dyde's, the money for the trips to Philadelphia, for the evenings at the theater, for the clothes he wore, which, if not lavish, were always of the latest cut and fabric? He made no notes and kept no account books to help explain the matter. He may have earned a small sum as Judge Hoffman's apprentice. Later, he undoubtedly had some share in the income from John's law practice, and William and Ebenezer may well have continued, almost as though he were still the child of the family, to help him financially from time to time.

Whatever his resources, he knew they were totally insufficient for undertaking marriage and the support of a wife. As a result, he fell into a sort of panic, revolving in his mind wild schemes for making more money. He thought of the comic history on which he and Peter had been working for months. Recently Peter had begun preparing for a return to England at the beginning of the year to supervise an English purchasing branch of the Irving import business. He was more than willing for Washington to take over *esta obra* and finish it. But suppose he did? How much money would that mean, even assuming the cumbrous thing could be worked into the shape of a book? No, he had to think in larger terms. Perhaps he should sign on some ship for a voyage to India and make a fortune there. He had no idea of how fortunes were made in India but he knew some people made them. Perhaps he should involve himself somehow in the fur trade. Henry Brevoort was doing very well working for John Jacob Astor.

At some point Judge Hoffman made a suggestion. He had not been formally notified of any understanding between Washington and Matilda, but he was not blind and saw the growing attachment. The ambivalent feelings he had had toward the younger man when Washington had been his wife's devoted knight had vanished. He liked Washington, and could think of no objections to him as a suitor for his younger daughter's hand. And yet he now proposed that if Washington was serious about establishing himself in a career he should apply himself to the study of the law in a much more earnest fashion than he had done so far. If Washington could finally show the ability to handle some of the simpler cases that came into the Hoffman office, Judge Hoffman would take him into partnership with him. Washington would then have no difficulty in supporting a wife, and the Judge would give him Matilda as a bride.

What could Washington say to such an eminently logical offer? Years later, in the same fragmentary memoir in which he recalled his meeting with Matilda on his return from Europe, he wrote of his response. "I set to work with zeal to study anew, and I considered myself bound in honour not to make further advances with the daughter until I should feel satisfied with my proficience in the law—It was all in vain. I had an insuperable repugnance to the study—my mind would not take hold of it; or rather by long despondency had become for the time incapable of dry application. I was in a wretched state of doubt and self distrust. I tried to finish the work which I was secretly writing, hoping it would give me reputation and gain me some public appointment. In the mean time I saw Matilda every day and that helped distract me. . . ."

So Washington flung himself at the law books through December, January, and February and was miserable and saw Matilda and was happy. Shy Matilinda-dinda-dinda had bound him in a spell that no more sophisticated woman had managed to weave. "Her mind seemed to unfold itself, leaf by leaf." Or perhaps, in her quietness, she allowed his mind to unfold itself, with no need for mocking self-doubt. "I in a manner studied her excellence. Never did I meet with more intuitive rectitude of mind, more native delicacy, more exquisite propriety in thought word and action than in this young creature. I am not exaggerating—what I say was acknowledged by all that knew her. Her brilliant little sister used to say that people began by admiring her but ended by loving Matilda. For my part I idolized her."

In February of 1809, Matilda took ill with a cold. No one was unduly concerned. Winter colds were taken for granted in the Hoffman house as well as in most other New York homes. Rebecca Gratz's letters to Maria Hoffman repeated the same refrain every winter. "I hope all your children have quite recovered . . ."

But suddenly this cold of Matilda's turned into something else. She grew worse. The doctor was called. The diagnosis was the one more feared than any other, consumption, the apt nineteenth-century name for tuberculosis, which in those years did consume life in a swift, fierce blaze. The word clanged in the ears of those who loved the girl. She was so young—not yet eighteen. They insisted on hope. She was small and delicate but she had never been really ill before and would recover. But the fire, having caught, blew higher and higher.

Washington had evaded much and denied much in his twenty-six years. He had determined that life should be pleasing, or if not pleasing, amusing. In this crisis, he did not hide or evade. He was at the Hoffman house every day. As many of the hours as he was allowed to be, he was at Matilda's bedside in the girlish room with its spool bed, its dimity hangings, a room that had suddenly become a capsule of destruction.

"I saw her fade rapidly away beautiful and more beautiful and more angelical to the very last. I was often by her bed side and in her wandering state of mind she would talk to me with a sweet natural and affecting eloquence that was overpowering. I saw more of the beauty of her mind in that delirious state than I had ever known before. . . ."

The progress of the disease was incredibly swift. Taken ill in February, she was dying by mid-April. The time seemed endless to those who knew her and watched over her.

"Her dying struggles were painful & protracted. For three days & nights I did not leave the house and scarcely slept," Washington recalled, years later. "I was by her when she died—all the family were assembled around her, some praying, others weeping, for she was adored by them all. I was the last one she looked upon . . ."

April 26, 1809, was the date of her death. Washington did not break down, run away, or blank out what had happened. Instead, he did what he could to help Judge Hoffman, Maria Hoffman, Ann, and the younger children. He helped to write the letters that had to be written, to Rebecca Gratz and to Matilda's other friends in Philadelphia and elsewhere. He stood in the cemetery and saw the coffin lowered and heard the earth dropped on it.

Matilinda-dinda-dinda—a sound like a small silver bell.

After the funeral, he left New York for a stay at the farm of a family friend, Judge William P. Van Ness, who lived in Kinderhook, New York, near the Sleepy Hollow region which he had known since childhood.

# 10

# Diedrich Knickerbocker

WASHINGTON had long since rejected his father's explanations for the mysteries of life and death. He did not turn to them now in his extremity and neither tried to comfort himself with visions of Matilda joining some celestial band of angels nor to further his anguish with questions as to whether or not Matilda had been "saved." The mystery itself confronted him in its flat, plain inexplicability. She had been there, near him, young, breathing, merry. She was gone.

"There was a dismal horror continually in my mind that made me fear to be alone—I had often to get up in the night & seek the bedroom of my brother, as if the having of a human being by me would relieve me from the frightful gloom of my own thoughts . . ."

He did not have the analytic turn of mind that might have led him to reading philosophers or religious writers in search of answers to his grief. He did have a dim, flickering feeling that Matilda's spirit could not have fled utterly, that it lingered somewhere—in the woods he loved, in the shadows over the river or the highlands, in every view that had stirred him before to romantic or melancholy dreaming. This feeling caused him to dip briefly into various writings by members of the Rosicrucian sect, but whatever glimpses of comfort he found there were not convincing for long. All, all was theory, and only the mystery and fact remained. She was gone.

He did not roam the woods around the Van Ness farm seeking her, or at least not often. If he had no discipline of religion or philosophy to give him strength, he found his own way to fight off the "dismal horror" by day. He had brought with him from New York the great pile of notes, memoranda, and manuscript pages which represented the project called *esta obra*. For a while, in the city, when it had seemed there was still hope for Matilda, he had fled from his anxiety about her by working on that manuscript. At some time during those troubled, feverish weeks, he had caught at a solution to give form to the chaotic mass of material that he and Peter had collected. Not only would the comic history of New York be carried no further than the period of its Dutch domination, but he would have the whole story told by an eccentric old Dutch historian whose one goal in life was to record the ancient and "poetic age" of the city before all was lost in dust and oblivion.

The old Dutch historian appeared before his eyes, "a small, brisk looking old gentleman, dressed in a rusty black coat, a pair of olive velvet breeches, and a small cocked hat," carrying as his only luggage two saddlebags stuffed with voluminous notes pertaining to his life's work. The curious figure was already somewhat familiar to Washington's imagination—something like that cranky commentator, Jonathan Oldstyle, something like the "Little Man in Black." But the minute Washington, with the old historian in mind as the narrator, began to sort out the notes and the pages that had been written, everything began to fall into place, and the author-figure took on a reality and vitality that the other eccentrics had never achieved. Diedrich Knickerbocker, Washington named him, choosing a couple of Dutch names at random. Diedrich Knickerbocker, a fine old monomaniac, now erudite, now satirical, often given to digression, sometimes to jokes, sometimes to profundities, but always—first to last— devoted to his task of enshrining New York in the annals of history.

In his room at the Van Ness farmhouse, Washington embraced Diedrich Knickerbocker, he *was* Diedrich Knickerbocker, holding the "dismal horror" at bay while he wrote, revised, and corrected page after page after page. He was not mocking his grief. He was simply keeping it from destroying him when he had Diedrich Knickerbocker swing into almost Rabelaisian humor, describing Dutch ships as built to honor the belles of Amsterdam, "full in the bows, with a pair of enormous cat-heads, a copper bottom, and withal a most prodigious poop!" Diedrich Knickerbocker had much fascinating lore about the first Dutch settlers in the New World. The men indicated their varying degrees of importance by the number of breeches they wore, hence the name Ten Broeck, or Ten Breeches, plainly labeled a man of importance. For the women, the number of petticoats they wore provided the same sort of identification.

Knickerbocker wrote of the first timid explorations of the island of Mannahatoes by Oloffe, the Dreamer, who laid his finger alongside of his nose (the sign of Saint Nicholas), closed his eyes, and was lost in visions of a great city that would arise on the wild site. Knickerbocker described the purchase of the land from the savages, the land included in the sale to be measured by the extent of a man's nethergarments. He wrote then of the astonishment of the natives when the "bulbous-bottomed" Ten Broeck "peeled like an onion, and breeches after breeches spread forth over the land until they covered the actual site of this venerable city."

Sometimes the flow of writing, revising, collecting, and

collating stopped suddenly and the fact that Matilda was dead presented itself to his mind again. On the margin of his manuscript he wrote, as though unbelieving, "MH—died April 26." When Diedrich Knickerbocker's inspiration flagged he had to face it. Then he wrote long letters to Maria Hoffman, who answered promptly and lovingly. He wrote to Brevoort and other friends and made an effort to be courteous to his hosts, the Van Nesses. Even in his numbed state, he was amused by the local school teacher, Jesse Merwin, and made a note somewhere in his mind that some day he must write a character sketch of him.

But the only real forgetfulness lay in Diedrich Knickerbocker's *History of New—York*. The pages drifted around him as he condensed or expanded what had already been written—about the establishment of the grand council of New Amsterdam, where important questions were measured in terms of how many pipefulls of tobacco had to be smoked before they were settled and where a profound peace hung over everything. "Who ever hears of fat men heading a riot, or herding together in turbulent mobs?—no—no it is your lean hungry men who are continually worrying society, and setting the whole community by the ears." The "Golden Reign" of Governor Wouter Van Twiller was described and the difficulties with the English who were taking over Connecticut. (Odd facts that had caught Washington's attention in long-gone school days returned to aid him with his comedy. There had been a geography, for instance, written by a Connecticut clergyman, Jedidiah Morse, which had praised everything about Connecticut without restraint. Washington had never forgotten the book's claim that Wethersfield was noted for "beautiful maidens and bounteous onion crops." Connecticut's pretty girls and bushels of onions played a running part in his comedy.)

Wouter Van Twiller's reign gave way to that of Wilhelm

Kieft, or Wilhelm the Testy, who was, for all the old Dutch setting, very like Thomas Jefferson. Much in the fashion of the President, Wilhelm preserved the peace and banished enemies by proclamation, created curious and impractical inventions, and then, dressed in his red corduroy small clothes, mounted his raw-boned charger to ride to his rural retreat, Dog's Misery.

Finally Knickerbocker's hero, Peter Stuyvesant, appeared on the scene. Under the leadership of Peter, known as the Headstrong, the Dutch challenged the Swedes in Delaware to battles which Knickerbocker grieved to report since there were no casualties, only warriors falling among cabbage stalks and into cow-pies. Still, glory surrounded Stuyvesant in Knickerbocker's saga, even when he was at last forced to surrender his little empire to the English. Knickerbocker's tone became lofty and elegiac as the story came to its close: "In your interesting and authentic history, there is none that occasions such deep and heart-rending grief as the decline and fall of your renowned and mighty empires. . . ." Grievous as the downfall was, Knickerbocker congratulated himself on having completed his record, such as it was, and made his farewell to the reader, praying that from his dust might spring "many a sweet wild-flower, to adorn my beloved island of Manna-hata!"

By the end of June Washington felt that the manuscript was almost in shape at last. He never seemed to think of it as a prodigious accomplishment. *Esta obra*, begun so casually a year and a half before, compiled on whim through the months, was now a completed work of five hundred and more pages that actually did follow the outline of early Dutch history in New York, however that history was embellished now and then with contemporary allusion and caricature, five hundred and more pages that gave New York City what it had never had—a long, fantastic record of a legendary past.

When Washington returned to the city in the heat of July the worst shock of his grief was over. He was only profoundly weary and depressed. He saw almost no one but his family, the Hoffmans and his closest friends. His sister, Sally, three years older than he, had been married two years before to her suitor, Henry Van Wart. Now, in the summer of 1809, Sally and Van Wart were going to Liverpool to make their home there. Peter had been in that English city for the last few months; so Washington gave Sally and Hal his main budget of news for Peter, telling them, for Peter's information, of the changes he had made in *esta obra*. In a note to Peter which he sent along with them, he had little more to add except that his health had been feeble and his spirits depressed. He did, however, "propose setting out on an expedition to Canada with Brevoort on Saturday next, to be absent sixteen days. There is a steamboat on the lake which makes the journey sure and pleasant. I trust the jaunt will perfectly renovate me. On my return I shall go to Mr. Hoffman's retreat at Hellgate, and prepare *esta obra* for a launch. . . ."

Voyaging by steamboat was a novelty, offering a variety of sensations—a chugging of engines and flow of smoke and sparks from the smokestacks that were in sharp contrast to the old placid sailing trip up the river. But it did shorten the journey to Albany amazingly. Brevoort's company was satisfying as always and the wilderness offered its distractions, but Washington was hardly "perfectly renovated" when he returned. He went to the Hoffman's summer place on the East River as planned. Brevoort, again traveling out of the city, left his sailboat for Washington's use. Washington sailed down to the city and back again on errands and visits. On one such sail the boat capsized. Washington clung to its overturned hull for several hours before a passing fishing boat rescued him. He seemed indifferent to both accident and rescue.

Indifferent to almost everything, he could not give up Diedrich Knickerbocker and continued to rewrite, polish, and interpolate new facts into the manuscript. He was also evolving a truly extraordinary "launch" for the old fellow's life work. Practiced in masquerades and hoaxes, he was working out the details of a campaign to arouse and tease public interest in the elderly historian long before the appearance of his book. A century and a half before skilled advertising men developed similar techniques, he had an instinct in these matters. Besides, he seemed to have a need for them.

Confronted with the real mysteries of life and death, he had no explanations or theories to comfort or sustain him. His only answer was what it had been since he was very young—to fling back at life a small mystery of his own. He had no need to be cruel or violent. The mysteries were innocent or amusing. But the gesture seemed to relieve him. By mid-October of 1809, he was ready, with the help of James and Brevoort, to set his newest mystery in motion.

"DISTRESSING," read the heading of a Personal Notice in the *Evening Post* of October 25. "Left his lodgings some time since, and has not since been heard of, a small elderly gentleman, dressed in an old black coat and cocked hat, by the name of KNICKERBOCKER. As there are some reasons for believing he is not entirely in his right mind, and as great anxiety is entertained about him, any information concerning him left either at the Columbian Hotel, Mulberry Street, or at the office of this paper, will be thankfully received. P.S. Printers of newspapers would be aiding the cause of humanity in giving an insert to the above."

Two weeks passed before a response to the "DISTRESSING" notice appeared in the *Post*. "*To the Editor of the Evening Post:* Sir,—Having read in your paper of the 26th October last a paragraph respecting an old gentleman by the name of Knickerbocker who was missing from his lodgings; if it would be any relief to his friends, or furnish them with any clue to discover where he is, you may inform them that a person answering to the description was seen by the passengers of the Albany stage early in the morning about four or five weeks since, resting himself by the side of the road a little above Kingsbridge. He had in his hands a small bundle tied in a red bandana handkerchief; he appeared to be travelling northward, and was very much fatigued and exhausted. A TRAVELLER."

Ten days later, November 16th, still another notice appeared in the *Post*. "Sir:—You have been good enough to publish in your paper a paragraph about Mr. Diedrich Knickerbocker, who was missing so strangely from his lodgings some time since. Nothing satisfactory has been heard of the old gentleman since; but *a very curious kind of written book* has been found in his room in his own handwriting. Now I wish you to notice him, if he is still alive, that if he does not return and pay off his bill, for board and lodging, I shall have to dispose of his Book, to satisfy me for the same. I am, Sir, your humble servant, SETH HANDASIDE, Landlord of the Independent Columbian Hotel, Mulberry-Street."

An air of verisimilitude marked all three of these notices (if one disregarded the fact that the City Directory listed no Independent Columbian Hotel or Seth Handaside either), and readers were attracted. Newspapers were generally four-page affairs; they contained a minimum of local news except for political reports and shipping notices. These queries about an old gentleman in a black coat and cocked hat injected an oddly personal note in the *Post's* pages. A city official read them and became concerned enough to visit a lawyer's office to discuss whether or not the city should offer a reward for the missing man's discovery. The lawyer he visited was John Treat Irving, or so the Irving family legend maintained—which might only mean that the report of the visit was also part of the hoax.

By that time Washington was in Philadelphia where he

had arranged to have the manuscript printed, but for a while it seemed he could not finally relinquish it. He fretted about small facts—when exactly did Peter Stuyvesant travel to Hartford? He worried as to how clearly he had fixed the boundary between the historical and the imaginative. Had he been wise to mingle the two at all? He flipped through the piles of tired-looking sheets, covered with his fine, slanted handwriting, and kept making changes. At last, in a sort of despair, he gave it to the printer.

On December 6, there was a straightforward literary notice in the *American Citizen:*

> Is this day published
> By Inskeep & Bradford, No. 128 Broadway,
> A HISTORY OF NEW—YORK
> In two volumes, duedecimo. Price three dollars.
> Containing an account of its discovery and settlement, with its internal policies, manners, customs, wars, &c. &c. under the Dutch government, furnishing many curious and interesting particulars never before published, and which are gathered from various manuscript and other authenticated sources, the whole being interspersed with philosophical speculations and moral precepts.
> This work was found in the chamber of Mr. Diedrich Knickerbocker, the old gentleman whose sudden and mysterious disappearance has been noticed. It is published in order to discharge certain debts he has left behind.

Just when the first purchasers of the new work, in two volumes duodecimo, began to guess that they had been caught up in an elaborate joke must have varied with each reader. The solemn acknowledgment of debt to the New York Historical Society, the tags of verse in old Dutch which followed the title, gave no real clue. A glance at the table of contents might have given an inkling: "Book I—Containing divers ingenious theories and philosophic speculations, concerning the creation and population of the world, as connected with the history of New-York." But perhaps New Yorkers who had enjoyed Dr. Mitchell's *Picture of New-York* could accept that. The entry for Chapter II, "How that famous navigator, Noah, was shamefully nicknamed; and how he committed an unpardonable oversight in not having four sons. With the great trouble of philosophers caused thereby, and the discovery of America," may have caused suspicion to dawn.

Wherever the clue fell, the first readers were the only ones to pick the book up in ignorance, for the word spread swiftly. Here was a strange, long, unwieldy new book that was a wonderfully funny burlesque of everything—history, geography, and philosophy as well as the early days of New York, with all the mockery, jokes, and satire strung on a thread of sober fact, documented from time to time by decorative footnotes which turned out, if anyone troubled to investigate, to be absolutely authentic.

Washington had been successful with everything he wrote so far. The letters of Jonathan Oldstyle had caused a mild stir. *Salmagundi* had delighted citizens up and down the eastern seaboard. But those successes were as nothing compared to the instant triumph of Diedrich Knickerbocker's *A History of New-York*. There had never been a book in America like this one. It was a humorous epic, a Homeric saga, an Elizabethan masque and bawdy joke, a mélange that borrowed from everything that literate Americans had ever read, Smollett and Cervantes, Ben Jonson, Fielding, Swift, and Rabelais—and yet somehow remained uniquely American.

Literary commentators for the country's various magazines did not exactly recognize a masterpiece of sorts, a book that would endure far beyond its own day, but they did praise it lavishly. *The Monthly Anthology and Boston Review* called it "this amusing book, which is certainly the wittiest our press has ever produced," and went on to note how the historical facts served as "the coarse network of the texture of the cloth, in which the author has embroidered a rich collection of wit and humor. The account of these honest Dutch governors has been made subservient to a lively flow of good-natured satire on the follies and blunders of the present day, and the perplexities they have caused."

Speculation as to the identity of Diedrich Knickerbocker began as soon as the book was recognized as a comedy. Washington had made a real effort to maintain the mystery of Jonathan Oldstyle. He and James and William had gone to great lengths to preserve their anonymity as the creators of *Salmagundi*. With this book, however, Washington seemed not to mind becoming known as its author. A few weeks after the book's publication when he was out of the city for a few days, Maria Hoffman wrote to him about a conversation with her mother-in-law. "Your good friend, the old lady, came home in a great stew this evening. Such a scandalous story had got about town,—a book had come out, called a 'History of New-York;' nothing but a satire and ridicule of the old Dutch people—and they said you was the author; but from this foul slander, I'll venture to say, she has defended you."

A certain atmosphere of scandalized disapproval was indeed helping the book's popularity. Some of the old Dutch families of New York, Albany, and other centers of Dutch settlement, who had long been insulated from the everyday life of the city by their wealth, their land holdings, and their proud sense of descending from city founders, were outraged by the book's indiscriminate use of hallowed Dutch names—Knickerbocker, Ten Broeck, Verplanck, and so on—and the burlesque fashion in which the bearers of such names conducted themselves. Washington, always uneasy at the thought of hurting anyone's feelings, did some apologizing and explaining, but even he could see that this small tempest was all to the good. And the burlesquing of names and events of the past was making those names and events familiar as they had never been before, giving New York a history that it had never thought about in its rush toward the future but which it now grasped eagerly.

Irving's authorship of the comic history was generally known within a month or so. By February 1810, a correspondent to a Baltimore paper wrote that, "If it be true, as Sterne says, that man draws a nail out of his coffin every time he laughs, after reading Irving's book, your coffin will certainly fall to pieces."

His authorship known, he was praised, flattered, admired, and invited everywhere. The joke that he had flung back at life in exchange for the blow he had suffered exploded gently to shower on him fame and money as well, for the book was selling everywhere.

No one could have said that Washington did not enjoy these attentions. He went from engagement to engagement and was amusing or gallant as the occasion required. But beneath the surface gaiety and his social manner, the great mystery still loomed like a dark abyss, a fathomless pool, a "dismal horror" that mocked all his laughter.

# II

# The Heart That Would Not Hold

ONE BURDEN was gone. He no longer had to concern himself with the law. If Washington felt some deep, confused guilt about this, some inner shock that Matilda's death had been the means of releasing him from a profession that repelled him, he fled the recognition of that guilt even as he fled from his grief during the next years. He was free of the law. He felt no inclination to write anything more. So he flung himself into social life as though it were a necessity, a drug to dull emotion and an excitement to absorb his time and energies.

He had no trouble finding all the partying he wanted. Knickerbocker's *History of New—York* increased in popularity as the months went by. Brevoort reported on men reading it in frontier trading posts, passing it eagerly from hand to hand. Washington had earned over two thousand dollars from it before it had been published a year, a good sum for the times. A second edition was required and then a third. And everywhere, people wanted to meet the good-looking, clever young man who had written this monstrously funny book.

"Wherever I went I was overwhelmed by attention," he

wrote years later. "I was full of youth and animation, far different from the being I now am, and I was quite flushed with this early taste of public favour. . . ."

William and Ebenezer maintained their concern for him. They accepted his rejection of the law, understood his inability to write except when the whim was on him, and chiefly wanted to find him some post that would give his life a modicum of security. Sister Catherine's husband, Daniel Paris, had recently been made a member of the council for appointments for New York courts. William and Ebenezer urged Washington to apply for some judiciary appointment. Surely with Daniel's influence the council could find something for him. So for a while Washington was in Albany, presenting his application and waiting for the council to act on it. In the end his application was refused. His two-month stay in Albany had resulted only in a great deal of party-going and some success in mollifying the Dutch families of the city whose feelings had been ruffled by Knickerbocker's satire.

Returned from Albany, he was soon off for Philadelphia, escorting the two youngest Hoffman children on a visit to Ann, who had married her Philadelphia beau, Charles Nicholas, the year before. Philadelphia allowed him another whirl of festivities as well as some quieter times with Rebecca Gratz. His publishers persuaded him to a small writing chore. They wished to publish a collection of poetry by the English writer, Thomas Campbell, and asked Washington to make a selection of Campbell's verse and write an introduction. Washington went at the task half-heartedly and wrote a tepid appreciation of Campbell. He was not especially taken by Campbell's poetry even though the poet had used an American setting for one of his longer works, *Gertrude of Wyoming*. Much more exciting to Washington was a long verse tale, *The Lady of the Lake*, by Walter Scott, which

Bradford and Inskeep were also about to publish in America. Washington borrowed the publishers' copy of the Scott work to read and reread at his leisure.

He was still reading Scott's poem and memorizing passages later in the summer when he spent a week or so in his favorite region, the Hudson highlands. A new friend, Philipse, lived there "in a royal bachelor style," as he wrote to Brevoort, and was a "true Lad of Kilkenny."

Forging ahead in his business career, Brevoort had lost none of his humor or affection for Washington. Letters between the two, when one or the other was away from New York, gave one thread of continuity to Washington's erratic course.

In the fall of 1810, William and Ebenezer decided to provide a sinecure for Washington themselves. Peter was doing well with the purchasing operations in Liverpool, and so a new firm was established, called P. and E. Irving. Washington was given a fifth interest in it, his duties to be minimal and only what suited him best.

A journey to Washington, D.C., to be on hand for the opening sessions of the new Congress at the start of the year, was his first assignment. American difficulties with Great Britain, which had begun back in Jefferson's administration, were increasing. The young war hawks in Congress were pressing for a military confrontation and talking boldly about annexing Canada as well as forcing the British from the western territories. Whatever political or military actions were in the wind, businessmen wanted to be prepared. Washington was to mingle with everyone, find out what he could and report on the situation to William and Ebenezer.

Washington related the livelier aspects of the assignment in long letters to Brevoort. The stagecoach ride to Baltimore was "terrible and sublime," Washington wrote, "as full of adventurous matter and direful peril as one of Walter Scott's pantomimic, melodramatic, romantic tales. . . ." But then, after several days of conviviality in Baltimore, he had arrived at an inn in Georgetown only to learn that the president's lady was holding her levee that very evening.

"I swore by all my gods, I would be there, but how? was the question. I had got away down into Georgetown, & the persons to whom my letters of introduction were directed lived all upon Capitol Hill about three miles off—while the President's house was exactly half way. Here was a nonplus, enough to startle any man of less enterprising spirit—but I had sworn to be there—." So he rattled on telling of how he had mounted to his room, "resolved to put on my pease blossoms & silk stockings," how he had learned from the landlord that a party of gentlemen staying at the inn was just about to leave for the fete and would sponsor him, how he had been shaved by a resident and "Jacobinical barber, who . . . mowed down all the beard on one of my cheeks and laid the other in blood."

At last he had emerged into the blazing splendor of Mrs. Madison's drawing room. "Here I was most graciously received—found a crowded collection of great and little men, of ugly old women, and beautiful young ones—and in ten minutes was hand in glove with half the people in the assemblage. Mrs. Madison is a fine, portly, buxom dame—who has a smile & pleasant word for everybody. Her sisters, Mrs. Cutts & Mrs. Washington are like two Merry Wives of Windsor— but as to Jemmy Madison—ah! poor Jemmy! he is but a withered little apple-John. But of this no more—perish the thought that would militate against sacred things . . ."

In the days following the levee Washington became engaged in "a constant round of banquetting, revelling and dancing," and found "enough matter for observation & entertainment to last me a handful of months. I only want a chosen fellow like yourself to help me wonder, admire and laugh—as it is I must endeavor to do these things as well as I can by myself. . . ."

"To wonder, admire and laugh": this had become the pendant credo to Washington's philosophy of being pleased with everything, or if not pleased, amused. And Brevoort was more than ready to share in those emotions of the detached and mocking observer. Even before receiving Washington's letter from Washington, D.C., Brevoort was writing to him, leading off in the high-flown style it often amused them both to effect. "As the day is uncommonly genial and my spirits at a more than ordinary elevation, I cannot possibly start off without prancing in the air like a high-mettled racer. I look upon you in the light of an eastern sovereign travelling through his vast dominions & collecting from his loveing subjects their tributary caresses. . . ." After which Brevoort settled down to pages of news and gossip—items about new books, business affairs, social events: "I attended the assembly last evening which was numerous and brilliant. Hen was there in all the simple majesty of her charms. . . ." Items about family and friends: "Yr. Mother I understand is well; I have neglected what I firmly intended, I mean to call upon her. . . ." Finally, "I stop the Press to announce the receipt of your welcome letter from Washington City. I admire your undaunted resolution, rejoice in your safety and am inexpressibly diverted with your adventures. God Bless you my dear boy, and send you home soon and safe."

Further letters were exchanged as Washington stayed on at the capital. He wrote to Brevoort of how his lack of partisan feelings allowed him to associate with both parties, and of how he had found "worthy and intelligent men in both— with honest hearts, enlightened minds, generous feelings and bitter prejudices. . . . One day I am dining with a knot of honest furious Federalists, who are damning all their opponents as a set of consummate scoundrels, panders of Bonaparte, &c. &c. The next day I dine perhaps with some of the very men I have heard anathematized, and find them equally honest, warm & indignant—and if I take their word for it, I had been dining the day before with some of the greatest knaves in the nation, men absolutely paid & suborned by the British government."

Brevoort applauded this "plan of mingling freely with the good of all parties, for it is the most bigotted opinion that was ever begotten to maintain that the principles on which the one side found their political creed, are so immaculate & wise as to leave their opposers no other choice than the characters of fools & knaves. . . ."

Washington's nonpartisan attitude probably made him as good an ambassador at the capital as his brothers could have wanted. He sent them bulletins from time to time until Congress adjourned in the spring. Then he also left the capital, journeying northward to Baltimore where he enjoyed "three days & nights' stout carousal, and a fourth's sickness, sorrow, and repentance," and thence went on to Philadelphia and finally New York.

Twenty-eight years old that spring of 1811, Washington made his first break from living at home with his mother in the family house on William Street. Brevoort had been living for some time in bachelor quarters in Mrs. Rumsey's boardinghouse, on Broadway near Bowling Green. When Brevoort left on one of his periodic trips to Canada, Washington moved into his rooms and found the situation so much to his liking that he stayed on after Brevoort's return. Living in a boardinghouse had become quite the fashion, for families with children as well as for single men and women. It not only offered families freedom from housekeeping duties but, in the better boardinghouses at least, a pleasant communal social life at meals and after dinner in the downstairs parlor, where guests could entertain themselves with conversation or music. Washington liked the sociability and also the alternate quiet that he and Brevoort could enjoy in their suite upstairs, which consisted of a parlor with a fireplace, sofa, chairs, writing desks, and two bedrooms.

Life was pleasant. He buried grief and buried guilt and had a chosen fellow with whom to "wonder, admire and laugh" at the world. The two men had a host of female friends. Both Irving and Brevoort had become admirers of Mrs. Jane Jeffrey Renwick, a charming widow who lived not far from Mrs. Rumsey's boardinghouse, and they were often at her home. Mrs. Renwick was a native of Scotland and had known Robert Burns when she was a girl. Burns had composed a poem in her honor, "The Blue-Eyed Lassie." "She's aye sae neat, sae trim and tight, / All grace does round her hover," Burns had written, and twenty years and more later Jane Renwick still had a slim grace and brightness of spirit that made her a delight to know. There were rumors that both Irving and Brevoort were courting her, Brevoort being especially attentive. But she was nine or ten years older than either of them. She had a son, James, nine years younger than Irving, a brilliant youth who was already teaching at Columbia College. If romantic fantasies did rise in either Irving's or Brevoort's hearts, Jane Renwick discouraged them gently and was a good friend to them both.

As for younger women, they drifted through Washington's life by the score, like birds. As if they were birds, he admired them, flirted with them, and sometimes wondered briefly if he was in love with them.

". . . my heart wanted anchorage," he recalled, years later. "I was naturally susceptible and tried to form other attachments, but my heart would not hold on; it would continually recur to what it had lost; and whenever there was a pause in the hurry of novelty & excitement I would sink into dismal dejection. . . ."

The fateful combination that Matilda had presented—the young, so very young, creature who still seemed to hold all the promise of depth and understanding that he knew with women like Maria Hoffman and Rebecca Gratz—did not appear again.

The threat of war with England was closer than ever in the spring of 1812, but Washington seemed indifferent. The lack of partisanship that had enabled him to dine with both Federalists and Democrats at the capital kept him curiously ambivalent now. True, the United States had real grudges against Great Britain. On the other hand, was it quite fair to challenge England when she was already caught in what seemed like a death struggle with Napoleon, who had only been checked, not stopped, at Trafalgar? Or did it matter? William Irving seemed to think so, and had foresworn his long allegiance to Federalist policies to support the goals of the war party, beginning an involvement in politics that would take him to Congress as a Representative in 1814.

Of much more immediate concern to Washington was the fact that Brevoort, undeterred by news of ship seizures at sea and the French-English conflict abroad, was leaving for an extended tour of England and the continent. Brevoort departed and Washington stayed on at the boardinghouse, missed his friend and worked sporadically on a revised edition of Knickerbocker's *History*. For the rest, he continued his drifting.

In June of 1812, war was declared and New York echoed with talk of enlistments, battle strategies, national defense, and the drilling of militia. Writing to Brevoort who was in Paris, Washington commented that the "times were unsettled," and devoted the main part of his letters to social news. "The marriage has at last taken place between Mary F[airlie] and Cooper," he told his friend. "They were married at his new house. Neither Mr. nor Mrs. F. were present. . . . The old Major was worried into a kind of half consent. That is to say, if the girl could not be happy without it, why, he supposed it must take place. Cooper has been applying for a Lieut. Colonelcy or a Majority in the army but I believe he's not succeeded." Washington had nothing further to say about the marriage of the young woman who had once seemed very near to being the object of his own love except, "Such is the end of a dismal courtship and the commencement I fear of an unhappy union."

Further gossip had an oddly cynical edge to it. "The little Taylor has been here and passed some time since your departure. She is a delightful little creature, but alas, my dear Hal, she has not the *pewter*, as the sage Peter says. As to beauty, what is it 'but a flower!' Handsome is that handsome has,—is the modern maxim. Therefore, little Taylor, 'though thy little finger be armed in a thimble' yet will I set thee at defiance. In a word, she is like an ortolan, too rare and costly a dainty for a poor man to afford, but were I a nabob, 'fore George, ortolans should be my only food."

He also mentioned a young woman named Maria for whom Brevoort had once acquired a "sudden admiration . . . which seemed to spring up rather late in the season, like strawberries in the fall. . . ." But his comment now was that the fair Maria had begun to look "d———d stringy. She has been acting very much the part of the dog in the manger— she cannot enjoy her own chastity but seems unwilling to let anybody else do it."

The tone, so different from the delicately romantic one he had always used in the past when speaking of women, may have reflected a growing weariness with his life of sociability. Or perhaps he had become involved at last in some less romantic and more physical relationships which satisfied some needs while outraging others. Brevoort, replying from Paris, also toyed with sexual humor. He was perfecting his French, he wrote, and had "an excellent master, & shall soon have an excellent ———."

A literary project of sorts came along in the fall. A Philadelphia publisher, Moses Thomas, persuaded him to become the editor of a little magazine that reprinted foreign essays, poems, and reviews. The job sounded easy to Washington.

He did not think it would interfere with his periodic excursions to the capital to deal with the shipping difficulties his brothers were experiencing because of the war. "I have undertaken to conduct the Select Reviews," he wrote Brevoort, "for the sake of pastime & employment of idle hours. I am handsomely paid & the work is no trouble."

Brevoort had been in England by this time, visiting with Peter in Liverpool, and then had taken off with Peter on a tour of Scotland. Wherever he went abroad, Brevoort presented copies of Irving's *History of New-York* to anyone he met in literary or critical circles. In Edinburgh, he had an introduction to Walter Scott, spent some pleasant hours with him, and gave Scott a copy of his friend's comic history. Now Brevoort wrote to Washington that he would do all he could to help with the new review and forward as many different periodicals from the continent and the British Isles as possible.

*The Analectic Magazine,* as the review was renamed, turned out to require a good deal more effort than Irving had anticipated. In spite of the material forwarded by Brevoort and Peter from abroad, in spite of material forwarded from other sources, he soon found that each issue required more copy than snipping and pasting could provide. Essays, reviews, poems by England's new literary sensation, George Gordon, Lord Byron, were not enough. He added a column that gave intelligence of American artists living abroad, reporting on the latest works exhibited by such friends as Washington Allston, who was now in London. Still he needed more material. He pressed James Paulding and other writers whom he knew into service to write original material, and he began writing original material himself.

The war was pursuing its lopsided course through 1813. Every American land effort seemed to meet with humiliating defeat. Only engagements on water brought the American cause success and hope. So Washington began a series of biographies of America's outstanding naval men in the *Ana-lectic*. James Paulding wrote a number of these and Washington wrote several, discovering that he rather liked writing biographical sketches. He was less successful with the critical essays with which he further padded out the magazine from time to time. His talents lay with descriptive, humorous, or sentimental writing. Washington knew what he liked in literature—the work of Walter Scott, the poems of Byron and of Thomas Moore, but he could not explain why. Neither could he analyze why he disliked the works of two other contemporary English poets, William Wordsworth and Samuel Coleridge. Whether he liked or disliked the work of a new English novelist who signed herself simply "A Lady," and whose first published novel, *Sense and Sensibility*, had appeared two years before, it is impossible to know. The *Analectic* never mentioned the book.

Tedious as some of the work on the *Analectic* was, definite employment was good for Irving. Brevoort's younger sister, Margaret, wrote to her brother in the summer of 1813 and reported, "Mr. Irving has grown quite a beauty, I told him so the other day at our house thinking it would have a tendency to make him very civil but I was mistaken, he's not a bit better than before his face is not clouded with care as formerly he says he would be perfectly happy if his wife was here; who do you think that is?"

"His mistress" was what he had once called Maria Hoffman, in all love and innocence. "His wife" was what he now called Brevoort, no doubt just as innocently. Such phrases were used more recklessly in the century before psychoanalysis made them suspect. But Washington did miss Brevoort and told him so in every letter; Brevoort responded with equal affection. "I charge you," Brevoort closed one letter, "to write to me immediately upon receipt of this Letter—and unless you write at great length, I do not care about what, I

shall construe it into a disrelish for my long epistles.—God
bless you my dr. fellow! H.B."

The change in the course of the war came early in 1814,
after Napoleon's defeat at Leipzig, the subsequent taking of
Paris by the English, and Napoleon's abdication. By spring,
the English were free at last to deal with the war in America
that had been such an irritating side-issue when their main
concern was with France. Fresh English troops began arriving in Canada. A British fleet began roving the Atlantic coast
from Maine to the Chesapeake. New York City's harbor was
blockaded, and there were fears that the city would be invaded from the north. Meantime, to the south, more British
troops were making their way up the Patuxent River toward
the capital. Inadequate American troops marshaled to defend
Washington, D.C., were running in panic. The British were
entering Washington and setting fire to the public buildings.

Washington was on a Hudson River steamboat, returning
from a stay in the highlands, when the boat put into a small
landing and the local residents excitedly reported on this
latest American disaster. Washington had heard of previous
defeats with philosophic detachment but the news of the
capital in flames roused him from his apathy. When his ship
docked in New York, he went directly to the headquarters
of Daniel Tompkins, the Governor of New York, but more
importantly at the moment, Major General Tompkins, in
command of the defense of New York City, to offer his services. In a space of hours Washington became Colonel Washington Irving, a member of the Iron Greys of the New York
State Militia and a military secretary to Major General
Tompkins.

Brevoort, who had returned to the United States the previous fall, was already in uniform. What letters the young
men exchanged now as they pursued their various military

duties had a new briskness about them. Irving was suddenly wide awake, traveling northward with Tompkins, writing orders and despatches, calling up recruits, dealing with quartermasters, chaplains, scouts, and newspapermen.

Eager for action, Irving obtained a dispensation to go to the front, which was, at the moment, near Sackett's Harbor. His way led along the route he had traveled with the Hoffmans in 1803, through Utica toward the north, and he encountered soldiers, scouts, and Indians as he rode. However, by the time he arrived at what had been the front, the English had been dispersed at Plattsburg by Macdonough and the fighting in the north was over. Even so, he found much to observe in the aftermath of battle. "This was the first thing that had roused and stimulated me," he wrote later.

But it did not last long. Almost as suddenly as Washington's military career had begun it was over. The peace negotiations which has been underway for almost a year were concluded on Christmas Eve, 1814. Major General Tompkins left the field to resume his duties as Governor for the opening of the New York Legislature. Colonel Washington Irving was released from duty.

Back in New York City, his role as editor of the Analectic magazine also slipped away from him. Moses Thomas had become involved with Irving's original publishers, Bradford and Inskeep. The publishers went bankrupt and Thomas was caught in the undertow. The magazine was in receivership. Irving was asked to continue as editor under the new management but he declined. His experiences in editing had ended any desire to make a career of such activity, and he vowed that he "would never again undertake the editorship of that or any other periodical work."

Brevoort and he had moved their bachelor quarters from Mrs. Rumsey's boardinghouse to the establishment of a Mrs. Bradish, a comfortable woman with attractive daughters.

Among Mrs. Bradish's boarders were the naval hero, Stephen Decatur and his wife, already Irving's friends from the days when he was making regular visits to the capital. Evening after evening now, Irving sympathized with Decatur as the Commodore brooded on the events which had led to the capture of his ship, the *President*, by the English when he was trying to run their blockade of New York City. Decatur was sensitive about his honor to the point of obsession and felt that the loss of the ship, unavoidable as it had been, was a disgrace for which he must atone, one way or another. His current hope lay with a plan he had submitted to Congress for him to lead a squadron against the Barbary pirates who were still harassing American ships in the Mediterranean.

When word came that Congress had accepted the plan, Irving sympathized with Decatur's joy. In the general mood of celebration, Decatur suggested that Irving might like to accompany him on this mission against the pirates.

Irving hardly hesitated. He was "weary of every thing and of myself." Here was a chance to break with "idle habits and idle associates," to move into new and invigorating scenes and then return strengthened for a more meaningful life. He packed his trunks and they were carried aboard Decatur's ship, the *Guerriere*.

Then came the news that Napoleon had escaped from his little kingdom of exile, Elba, and had marched on Paris. Louis XVIII had fled before his coming and men of Bonaparte's old army were rallying to him from every part of France, acclaiming him still their emperor. Speculation as to what Napoleon's next move would be and how he would proceed in his new, inevitable confrontation with England agitated Americans as well as Europeans. Decatur decided to postpone his sailing date until he had some further hint as to where Napoleon would mount his attack.

Washington found this prospect of delay unbearable. He was packed and ready to voyage somewhere. Peter was in

Liverpool, managing the firm of P. and E. Irving, of which Washington himself was a partner. Sister Sarah and her family lived in Birmingham now. Perhaps it was more reasonable in every way that he should go to England and visit the family and the business there rather than be a supernumerary on a warship in the Mediterranean.

He had his trunks moved from the warship to a passenger vessel, the *Mexico*, bound for Liverpool. He said good-bye to his mother, who was growing old and somewhat frail. She had been fretting about his listlessness during the past months, but now he reassured her. He was going to England for a while to refresh himself, "refill his sails," and give his "weathercock mind a new direction." Then he would return to America "quite another being." To further comfort the fragile old lady whose eyes shone with a puzzled love as she looked at him, he promised that when he returned he would give up his bachelor boardinghouse life to live with her once again in the house on William Street.

Brevoort was out of the city when his ship was ready to sail. Irving had to send him a farewell note by a tender from Sandy Hook, May 25, 1815:

"Dear Brevoort:—I was extremely sorry to leave New York, without taking you by the hand. Unsettled and almost joyless as has been my life for some time past, yet when I came to the last moment of parting from home, I confess it wrung my heart. But all is for the best and I am satisfied that a little absence will be greatly to my advantage. . . ."

He asked Brevoort to give his remembrances to all their friends, said that he would write from England, and begged Brevoort to write whenever he had "a scribbling fit & leisure moment to spare to an old and constant friend." "God bless you," he wrote, and signed himself, "W. I." Then, in a postcript, he added, "The wind is springing up from the west and I trust we shall clear at sea before morning."

# Part Two

"Quite Another Being"

# 12

# Wind Due East

THERE WAS never any doubt as to what he felt about bankruptcy. It was an experience so immediate, shameful, and horrifying that it drove him as nothing else had to reshape his life. Comparing his feelings about it with what he had suffered after Matilda's death, he said that he had preferred the purifying grief of bereavement to the humiliation of declaring oneself insolvent.

Few hints of any impending financial disaster were evident to Irving when he arrived in Liverpool. Peter was not at the pier to meet him, but Washington soon found him at his lodgings. Peter had been ill, suffering from an unhappy combination of erisypelas and rheumatism, but he rose eagerly from his bed to welcome his youngest brother. Seven years had passed since the two had seen each other—seven years that had encompassed wild extremes of emotion and experience for the younger man, love, grief, success, and finally ennui. Long letters had, of course, kept Peter apprised of the events that had led to such emotions, but still there might have been some constraint between the brothers. Washington had been twenty-five when they parted. He was now thirty-two. Peter was forty-six and he no longer had quite the same fresh, young look that once had caused such a resemblance between him and Washington. But both discovered that the bond of understanding between them had not changed. They could still communicate in the same shorthand fashion with their old humor, alternating exaggeration and understatement.

Washington spoke of his dismay at seeing the mailcoaches decked in laurel branches as he drove across the city to Peter's lodgings. One of the chief reasons he had left America and sailed for England, he said, was so as to be on hand to witness the great massing of armies and the tremendous battles that would ensue when the English again flung themselves against Napoleon and his regrouped forces. But alas, no sooner had he landed than he realized he had come too late. The bedecked mailcoaches thundering into the city were bearing the news that the fateful encounter had already taken place at some spot called Waterloo. The English had been victorious. Napoleon was in flight. So now what great events were there for him to witness? What excitements would force him out of his lethargy and dullness?

Peter consoled him, reminding him that there would be the national rejoicing to observe—bonfires, illuminations, spectaculars of all kinds—as the English celebrated the end of the well-nigh interminable struggle with the French. Bonaparte also had to be apprehended, a decision made as to what to do with him once he was captured, and it would be interesting also to see what course the French nation would take now that the days of *la gloire* were definitely at an end. Washington admitted that Peter was right. There should be much to witness of an enlivening nature.

So they talked and brought each other up to date on past matters as well as current affairs. Washington admired Peter's bachelor quarters, handsomely furnished and situated on Bold Street in a convenient and stylish part of the city. He approved of the efficient and silent servant, Thomas, whom Peter kept, and the neat horse and rig that he maintained. Peter was "not indulging in any extravagance or dash," he wrote to Ebenezer soon after his arrival. "He lives like a man of sense, who knows he can but enjoy his money while he is alive, and would not be a whit the better though he was buried under a mountain of it when dead." There were no hints of financial worry then, not even a whisper from Peter that all might not be as well with the P. and E. Irving Company as appearances indicated.

Washington spent a week with Peter in Liverpool, going to the theater, witnessing the various celebrations held there for the victory at Waterloo, and then took off by stagecoach for Birmingham to visit sister Sally and her family. Sally and Hal had four children now, two boys and two girls. Matilda, who was his godchild, and the baby, Marianne. The Van Wart house, large and comfortable with well-kept grounds, was on the outskirts of the city. Following his penchant for nick-names, Washington had transformed the Van Wart name to Van Tromp and referred to his brother-in-law and sister as the Baron and Baroness and their home as the Castle Van Tromp. When he wrote from the Castle Van Tromp to Brevoort, he declared that he was already "like another being from what I was in that listless period of existence that preceded my departure from America. It seems as if my whole nature had changed—a thousand kind feelings and affections that had lain torpid, are aroused within me—my very blood seems to flow more warm and sprightly."

From Henry Van Wart, the hospitable Baron, who was almost as involved as Peter with the Irving interests in England, there were no words that Washington could interpret to mean that the Baron was worried about money. The recent war between England and America had naturally caused Americans engaged in the exporting business many difficulties. But that war was over and American merchants in England were cheering themselves with thoughts of an eager market in the United States, awaiting the arrival of British woolens, tools, pots and pans, and other necessities and luxuries. Van Wart may have mentioned that some of the English firms with whom he dealt were having trouble in the confusions attendant on the long war with France. But there was nothing in that to alarm Washington.

He went on to London, a city even more welcoming than it had been nine years before, since he knew various residents now, chief among them Washington Allston. He and Allston greeted each other with joy and soon Irving was friendly with other American artists in London who were part of Allston's circle—especially Gilbert Stuart Newton and Charles R. Leslie, both talented and lively young men. With them Irving found the same quick rapport that he aways knew with artists. He had an eye for what they were trying to do, and they sensed it and asked for his comments and criticisms, while he, in turn, seemed far happier talking about art than about writing. When the talk did turn to Knickerbocker's *History*, which they had all read and admired, it quickly centered on the possibility of an illustrated edition. Allston and Leslie both were eager to try their skill at picturing some of its more dramatic or comic scenes.

Meantime, London was still celebrating the triumph over Napoleon, and Washington amused himself by listening to comments on what should be done with the defeated French leader. "They have disposed of him in a thousand ways," he wrote to Ebenezer. "Every fat-sided John Bull has him dished up in a way to please his own palate, excepting that as yet they have not observed that the first direction in the famous receipt to cook a turbot—first catch your turbot.' "

But before he had dispatched the letter he had to add a postcript. "The bells are ringing, and this moment news is brought that poor Boney is a prisoner at Plymouth. *John has caught the turbot."* Romantically, he regretted that Napoleon had not fallen like a hero at Waterloo, and considered that the English government ultimately acted toward its prisoner with a poor spirit. To Washington, it was bitterly ironic that Napoleon should be brought to the feet of the Prince Regent —"this bloated sensualist, this inflation of sack and sugar." "Nothing shows more completely the caprices of fortune," he wrote to Brevoort later in the summer, after Napoleon had been taken to exile on the lonely island of St. Helena, "and how truly she delights in reversing the relative situations of persons, and baffling the flights of intellect and enterprise."

Before he left London he made an excursion to Sydenham to visit Thomas Campbell, the poet, for whose first book to be published in America he had written the introduction. Campbell was not at home so Washington chatted for a time with his wife. Mrs. Campbell fretted because her husband was such a slow and meticulous worker that long intervals separated his published works. Encouraged by Irving's sympathetic manner, she cried out, "Oh, it is unfortunate for Campbell that he lives in the same age with Scott and Byron. They write so much and so rapidly, but Campbell writes slowly, and it takes him some time to get under way; and just as he has fairly begun, out comes one of their poems that sets the world agog, and quite daunts him, so that he throws by his pen in despair." Washington tried to comfort her but he was, in fact, far more interested in anything she could tell him about Scott. A good deal of gossip was current about the difficulties the poet was experiencing owing to the failure of the Ballantyne's publishing firm, and there was also much speculation as to whether or not he was the author of two novels that were creating a great stir, *Waverley* and *Guy Mannering.* Mrs. Campbell's guess was that he was not, and she had little more to say about the Scottish bard except that in spite of all reverses he was as "merry and unconcerned to all appearance as ever; one of the happiest fellows that ever wrote poetry."

James Renwick, son of the charming widow, Mrs. Jane Renwick, arrived in England. He and Washington met at the Castle Van Tromp in Birmingham and set out together for a sightseeing junket through the English summer weather. Their first excursion took them to Kenilworth, Warwick, and Stratford-on-Avon, where Washington experienced the proper emotions but wrote nothing. Instead he carried a sketch book with him in which he made pencil drawings of the cottages, towers, old walls, or trees that pleased him. Returned to Birmingham, Irving and Renwick rested a few days and then took off on a tour of Wales which finally led them back to Liverpool. On this jaunt also, Washington made few notes and relied less on guidebooks than on James, whose "uncommon memory" made him "an exceeding good book of reference."

In Liverpool, Washington found Peter less well than he had been and quite crippled by rheumatism. There seemed but one solution. Peter must go take the baths at one of England's spas. "Solemn Silence" packed for his master, then Washington rode in the coach with Peter and his servant as far as Manchester. There he saw Peter off in a chaise for Harrowgate, "loaded with conveniences . . . and attended by his faithful, discreet, and taciturn man." Washington hoped the waters at Harrowgate would "completely restore both skin & bone, which is nearly all that remain of him."

Then, as September's sun and mists enveloped Liverpool, Washington found himself alone with the family business of P. and E. Irving Company. The chief clerk of the company had died in the spring. Peter had been ill ever since and no one with any authority had been paying attention to the company's affairs. Someone had to make some order out of the piled bills, orders, statements, queries, and drafts that tumbled across the desks in the counting house.

Washington approached the task with a sigh of reluctance and at first was simply confused by the papers he tried to sort. There seemed to be so many bills, inscribed with increasingly sharp demands for payment. He found few receipts. Where were the remittances for shipments of those pots, pans, nails, hats, yard goods, and so on for which P. and E. Irving were being dunned?

Baffled and distrusting his understanding of business methods, Washington enrolled in a course on bookkeeping and attended it faithfully through October. But even as he clung to the hope that once accounting's mysteries were somewhat revealed to him everything would make sense, he realized that he had to do something immediately about the more clamorous creditors who were threatening the firm. The money he had with him, the profits from Knickerbocker's *History* with which he had planned to finance a tour of the continent, he reallocated at once to paying some of the company's bills, but the sum hardly made an impression on the total debt. Desperately, he wrote to his traveling companion of the summer, James Renwick, with a request that he winced to make. Could Renwick possibly make some funds available to him to pay some of the more pressing accounts? Renwick responded immediately and generously and this brought a surcease in pressure, but only a brief one.

In spite of himself Washington was learning some bookkeeping, and as the books made more sense he began to see that the firm had been making unusually large purchases in the last year or so. This seemed reasonable. It was logical to think that the restrictions on imports from England during the war would have built up a great backload of demand in America for British products. Of course Peter had bought enormously. So where were the remittances for the goods shipped?

Washington took a brief holiday in December and tried to put his worries in the back of his mind as he went to London to see the latest plays and then journeyed to Birmingham to spend Christmas at Castle Van Tromp. Peter, returned from his spa, was also in Birmingham, and though he had been little improved by his "cure," the holidays were cheerful. One way and another Washington began to get glimpses of some of the old ways of celebrating Christmas in England—or hear tales of Yule logs, mummers, roasted pigs, and wassails. Fascinated as he always was by lore and legend, he absorbed the colorful details, and they gave a new charm to spending Christmas in England.

Then he was back in Liverpool, facing a mounting concern about the affairs of P. and E. Irving. The situation had grown clearer. The demand in America for British goods was not nearly so large as had been anticipated. The drop in imports during the war had driven Americans into experiments in manufacturing for their needs themselves. They were no longer so dependent on England as they had been. Added to this difficulty, great enough in itself, since it left large shipments unwanted in New York warehouses, shipping to America had been plagued by contrary winds all through the last fall and winter so that what shipments left England were delayed beyond the time when their arrival could have meant a profitable sale.

"I have never passed so anxious a time in my life," Irving wrote to Brevoort in March, "my rest has been broken & my health & spirits almost prostrated; but thank heavens we have weathered the storm & got into smooth waters."

The smooth waters were a delusion. Within a month the firm was facing greater difficulties than before. Bills came in from new quarters. No remittances were reaching the company from the United States, and with Peter still crippled by his rheumatism, Washington faced the crisis by himself. "I am here alone attending to business," he wrote Brevoort in May, "and the times are so hard that they sicken my very soul."

Later, he did not care to write or say much about that year of 1816 and the year that followed. For now, in the summer of 1816, the winds shifted, only to become again contrary for the needs of the business. Washington was desperate for remittances from America, but in the age of sailing ships, everything depended on the wind, and now the wind blew unremittingly from the east, holding off the longed-for ships from shore.

"There it was, day after day, work hard all day and then to bed late, a troubled sleep, for three hours perhaps, and then wake up; thump, thump, thump, at the heart comes the care. No more sleep for that night; then up and off to the coffee-house to see the wind dial; wind due east, due east, day after day, no ship can come in, payments must be made, and nowhere for remittances to come from. . . ."

Much of Washington's anxiety was for his brothers in New York. He had been thoughtless of money all his life except for the months when he had hoped to marry Matilda, and he told himself he could live on bread and water if it came to that. But what of William and Ebenezer who had invested so many years in buiding up the business? William had eight children now, and Ebenezer seven. Their plight was what Washington thought of when he woke after three hours' sleep. What ships did manage to come in at Liverpool brought not remittances but letters that told why the brothers had nothing to send and of how grim the situation was in New York.

The habit of presenting a cheerful front was strong and Washington tried to maintain it. He made trips to Birmingham to see Sally, Hal, and the children. Henry Van Wart was having business worries also, but the children were a distraction to Washington. He told them fantastic stories and played his flute for them to dance. He accompanied Peter to another spa where he hoped the water would be more helpful than Harrowgate's had been for his rheumatism. He visited booksellers in Liverpool and Birmingham, looking for books that Brevoort had requested. He had some clothes tailored for his brothers and also ordered a coat and a waistcoat for Brevoort. He had met friendly people in both Liverpool and Birmingham by this time and now and then he accepted a dinner invitation.

Sometimes he even thought about doing some writing. Writing had been a shield and an escape in the months after Matilda's death, but the work on which he was engaged then had been already more than half complete and its genesis had come from a whim in happier days. No whims were catching at his somber imagination in this year of 1816.

"Thump, thump, thump, at the heart comes the care . . ."

He wrote only erratically to Brevoort and his other friends in New York. He apologized: "My mind is in a sickly state and my imagination so blighted that it cannot put forth a blossom or even a green leaf—."

And still what communications arrived from America brought nothing to lighten the gloom. Washington was grateful to hear that Brevoort had been aiding Ebenezer through his financial difficulties and wrote to thank his friend for this. But other news seemed to emphasize his exile from a world where some people's lives, at least, moved onward happily and optimistically. In July he heard that James Paulding, friend and collaborator of so many years, had married Gouverneur Kemble's sister, Gertrude. Something in Brevoort's letter announcing that marriage hinted to Washington that Brevoort was also thinking of marriage. Washington tried to answer sympathetically. "I rejoice in the confidence you express of your future prospects, and in the intention you seem to entertain of forming a matrimonial connexion. I am sure it will be a worthy one; and though as a Bachelor I might lament you as lost to the fraternity, and feel conscious that some of those links were broken which as bachelors bound us together, yet I could not suffer myself to regret a change of situation which would give you so large an accession of domestic homeful enjoyment. . . ." In the fall came the news that James Renwick was marrying Brevoort's young sister, Margaret. All Washington's friends at home were getting on with their lives, it seemed, taking on new responsibilities, reaching for new happiness.

Caught in his backwater of anxiety and care, he became more aware of others who were suffering. He had paid little heed to social or economic conditions in America, however they varied from year to year. Now, in Liverpool and and Birmingham, he saw the effects of the business recession on the poor of those cities. "You have no idea of the distress and misery that prevails in this country!" he wrote Brevoort. "It is beyond the power of description. In America you have financial difficulties, the embarrassment of trade and the distress of merchants but here you have what is far worse, the distress of the poor—not merely mental sufferings—but the absolute miseries of nature, hunger, nakedness, wretchedness of all kinds that the labouring people in this country are liable to. In the best of times they do but subsist, but in adverse times they starve. How this country is to extricate itself from its present embarrassments . . . how the government is to quiet the multitudes that are already turbulent and clamourous . . . I cannot conceive."

Once again there was a Christmas interlude of family cheer at Castle Van Tromp in Birmingham. Then the dismal days and nights in Liverpool began again, as he and Peter watched over the disintegration of the firm of P. and E. Irving. By now there was little they could do except put off as long as possible the ultimate bankruptcy.

As spring came, homesickness began to assail Washington. He thought of his mother, who had been ailing for the last year, and he had almost determined to return to America to see her again before it was too late when word came that she had died April 9, 1817. "Shall I say it then, I heard of her death with a momentary satisfaction"; he wrote later, "for she died ignorant of my misfortunes and escaped the pang of seeing the child she was so fond & proud of ruined and degraded."

With the news of that death, however, inevitable memories of another April death, eight years before, were revived to add to his sense of grief. He changed his mind about returning to America. Why should he return? To whom would he bring any special happiness or pleasure? He would stay on in Liverpool, giving what lift he could to Peter's spirits as the inevitable bore down on them.

In this melancholy mood, caught by no whim at all but only by the simple need to do something constructive, he began to spend some time each day thinking about a writing project, making notes and then actually writing.

Nothing really took shape. He merely sketched lightly with his pen as he had sketched with his pencil on his various tours, making outlines of scenes or of quaint, curious figures against a landscape. He had no glimmering of what he could make of these fragments. They did not seem to be the seeds of anything larger nor was there anything comic about them as there always had been in his writings before. The tone of what he wrote now was gently appreciative of the beauties of rural England, or melancholy, as in the notes he made on a country funeral he had watched, or almost elegiac, as he composed a character sketch of William Roscoe, one of England's well-known historians, whose home was in Liverpool. What was the use of such bits and pieces? Could he send them off to be published in some American magazine? Which one? He deepened the tones here and there on some of the sketches, smoothed the lines, and then threw down his pen, sure that he was wasting his time.

The wind still blew due east, due east.

# 13

# A Golden-Hearted Man

A YOUNG American, William Campbell Preston, who was touring England in 1817, was taken ill with a fever when he arrived in Liverpool. Sick, half-delirous, he tossed on his bed in a strange room in a strange city. One afternoon, he awoke from a doze to see a "small gentleman dressed in black" standing by his bed.

"I am your countryman, Washington Irving," the gentleman said when Preston showed no signs of recognition. Vaguely then, the sick man remembered having met the visitor several years before in Washington, D.C., but he was too ill to make much response, too ill, in fact, to notice that his visitor was proceeding quietly to restore order to the disheveled room, to depart and then return with a doctor, and then later, to depart and return again with food and drink.

Through the next few days, as Preston's fever gradually waned, Irving came in daily to check the invalid's progress and to take charge of whatever of his affairs seemed to need attention. Later, looking back on that time, Preston would recall a "man of grave, indeed a melancholy aspect, of very staid manners, his kindness rather the offspring of principle and cultivated taste than emotion. There was an unfailing air of moderation about him, his dress was punctilious, his tone of talking, soft and firm, and in general over subdued. . . ."

After Preston recovered and when he began to know Irving better and to become friendly with Peter as well, his view of Washington lightened. He took several short trips out of Liverpool with the brothers, and though Washington had a way of quietly discouraging what he called "boisterous Americanism," still his conversation would "occasionally run into humor, and laughable delineation of character or events."

That Irving had changed from the young man who had laughed at life, finding it all vaguely ridiculous, was undeniable. Washington Allston was aware of the change when his friend visited London that August. He was not fooled, as Preston had been, by an "air of moderation." Allston had always sensed the buried emotions in Irving, his search for some ideal which he hid behind a screen of self-mockery. Now seeing him so quiet Allston knew that the events in Liverpool had precipitated a sort of crisis. He was not altogether sorry. If Irving were ever to commit himself to the talents that were his he had to learn to take himself at least a little seriously.

Allston, and Leslie and Newton also, offered Irving the usual distractions—hours in their studios looking at and commenting on their various works in progress, and the sketches that Allston and Leslie had been working on for an illustrated *Knickerbocker*. Allston arranged to have Irving accompany him to a dinner party given by the eminent English publisher, John Murray, who published Byron, Campbell, and other leading literary figures. He was pleased when Irving was inspired to suggest a sort of literary exchange between England

and America to Murray. Even though nothing came of it eventually, Allston thought it a good sign to have Irving thrusting about for ways to rescue himself financially. He took Irving with him on a visit to his friend, Samuel Coleridge. Allston was accustomed to Coleridge's eccentricities, but Irving noted later his surprise at the poet's volubility and the way he walked about with his right hand over his head, moving the thumb and finger of his hand "as if sprinkling snuff upon his crown."

Finally, Allston was happy to learn that Irving was working seriously, if somewhat diffidently, on some sort of writing. Irving did not say much about the nature of his project— he was just doing some short pieces, he said, little essays on various English scenes or characters that interested him; but Allston saw that in his hours alone Irving was spending time in the British Museum, doing research of some sort, or wandering about in odd corners of London, looking for material. Allston did what he could to encourage his friend in this new commitment to writing and told him that the failure of P. and E. Irving Company might well be a blessing in disguise, if it forced him to a serious exercise of his talents. Such assurances were not especially helpful, however, and Allston wished for some unexpected circumstance—some scene, some meeting, some event—that would really lift Irving's spirits. He was enthusiastic therefore when he learned that Irving was planning a tour of the Scottish highlands in September, accompanied by his new friend, William Preston, whom he was to meet in Edinburgh. He was also pleased to hear that Irving was, rather shyly, hoping to meet Walter Scott and had obtained a letter of introduction to him from Thomas Campbell. Of course he should plan to visit Scott, Allston told Irving, and there was no reason to feel so diffident about calling on him. Brevoort had presented Scott with a copy of Knickerbocker's *History* when he visited him several years before, had he not? And Scott had written a letter of warm appreciation to Brevoort later confessing that he and his family had enjoyed the book immoderately. Of course Scott would welcome him. Perhaps, Allston thought privately, a meeting with "the mighty minstrel of the north" would give Irving some of the encouragement he needed.

Traveling northward by sea to Berwick-on-Tweed, Irving was happy as he always was when on the water, and thrilled as the little vessel on which he was a passenger skirted the storied cliffs of the Northumbrian shore. From Berwick, he went by coach to Edinburgh where he was to meet Preston. The city looked beautiful to him as he approached it, the towers and battlements that crowned its hill rising dreamlike against the sky above the morning mist of the valley. He met Preston as planned and for several days they drifted about the city together, visiting the sites enshrined by history —Arthur's seat and Holyrood and the paths and halls once trod by Mary, Queen of Scots. Irving had a few letters of introduction to the socially prominent citizens of Edinburgh, among them one to Francis Jeffrey, editor of the *Edinburgh Review* and a powerful literary and legal figure in the city. Jeffrey was gracious and invited Irving to visit him at his ancient country estate, Craigcrook, outside the city. Irving had heard reports of Jeffrey's opinionated manner from Brevoort. Now he experienced it for himself as Jeffrey commented on a recent trip he had made to the United States with a variety of sharp observations on American politics, American women, and other aspects of the new nation across the sea.

At last came the day when Irving had arranged to take off on his own from Edinburgh for a visit to Melrose Abbey, on the way to which he planned to stop at Abbotsford and present to Scott his letter of introduction from Campbell.

The first day of the journey he traveled south as far as the border town of Selkirk, where he stopped for the night. The next morning he rose early, had breakfast, and hired a post chaise to take him to the Abbey.

The day was cool and bright. The road led among the Scottish hills, bare of trees but covered with the gray-green mist of heather. Irving gazed at the landscape in a sort of disbelief. Somehow he had imagined that the hills of which Scott and Burns had sung would be more like the forested highlands of the Hudson. The chaise rolled along at a good clip as he gazed and mused. The horse's hooves thudded briskly on the packed dirt of the road. Then the driver was pulling the horse to a stop.

The road which they had been following ran along the side of a hill. On the slope below it, which stretched down to the glittering waters of the Tweed, Irving saw an unpretentious but comfortable-looking country house, its environs somewhat confused by construction activities attending the building of a structure which promised to be much larger. Walls had been laid to the height of several feet, scaffolding surrounded them, and shaped stones were tumbled here and there in great piles. This was Abbotsford?

Nervously, Irving took Campbell's letter from his pocket, along with his own card on which he had already written a short message. He gave the letter and card to the coachman, and then, as the coachman made his way down the driveway that led to the house, sat in the chaise staring at the scene below him. A greyhound, which had heard the approach of the chaise, came bounding around the house and began to bark. More dogs appeared and joined the chorus. The coachman rounded the house to its entrance, the dogs following.

Very shortly, a new figure was stumping up the driveway toward the road, limping and using a cane, but moving

rapidly all the same. Irving knew at once that it was Walter
Scott from descriptions he had heard. He was "tall, and of a
large and powerful frame. His dress was simple, and almost
rustic. An old green shooting-coat, with a dog-whistle at the
button hole, brown linen pantaloons, stout shoes that tied at
the ankle, and a white hat that had evidently seen service."

Irving jumped from the chaise and went forward to meet
Scott. Scott's free hand was out to clasp his. "Come, drive
down, drive down to the house," he said. "Ye're just in time
for breakfast, and afterwards ye shall see all the wonders of
the Abbey."

Irving's protestations that he had already had his breakfast
were brushed aside. The keen air of the highlands prepared
anyone for a second breakfast, Scott said. Within minutes
the chaise had carried both Scott and Irving to the door of
the house, and Irving had been ushered inside, where he met
Mrs. Scott and Scott's four children. He was seated at a
sunny breakfast table, food was being pressed upon him, and
Scott's jovial, burring voice was running on and on, repeating
his welcome, referring to the pleasure he and his family had
had in Knickerbocker, and suggesting a dozen sights and
diversions Irving must see and enjoy now that he had arrived
at Abbotsford.

So began a visit that would last almost a week, a visit that
would ultimately take on the aspects of a legend in Washington's mind, while Scott became a magical figure to him,
a "genial, golden-hearted man," filled with almost limitless
energy, imagination, and genius. It was very much as though
Washington had at last found in this man twelve years his
senior the sort of father he had never known—a father who
understood, encouraged, pointed the way and was both a
towering inspiration and kindly friend.

There were, in fact, many points of resemblance between
the two men, some of which Washington noted with delight,

some of which he seemed not to notice. He never remarked later, for instance, on the fact that both he and Scott had studied the law and though Scott had practiced for many years with some success, he had never cared for it much more than Irving did. More surprisingly, Washington saw no parallel between his own long fondness for mystery and anonymity as a writer and the mystery which Scott was currently keeping alive as to whether or not he was the author of the "Waverley" novels. During the time that Washington was at Abbotsford, Scott made dozens of references to local characters and surrounding scenes which were obviously linked to characters and scenes in *The Antiquary* and *Old Mortality*. "He gave me several anecdotes of a noted pauper named Andrew Gemmells," Irving would write later, ". . . whom he had seen and talked and joked with when a boy; and I instantly recognized the likeness of that mirror of philosophic vagabonds and Nestor of beggars, Edie Ochiltree. I was on the point of pronouncing the name and recognizing the portrait, when I recollected the incognito observed by Scott with respect to novels, and checked myself. . . ." Washington never intruded any further on another person's life than he seemed to be invited.

Subjects of common interest on which they could and did talk were more than sufficient to keep the conversation spinning hour after hour. Both men were lovers of legends, of antique tales, traditions, and superstitions. Scott, the host, taking Irving on rambles through the countryside, showing him the local wonders and curiosities, was the one who talked the most, pouring out a flood of history, anecdote, and lore. Still, Washington was soon enough at ease with the man whom he had come to visit with such trepidation, so that he talked freely also.

On their first day together they stood on a hill commanding a wide view, and Scott pointed out Lammermueir, Gallawater, and the Braes of Yarrow. Washington was already confident enough to confess that he had been a little disappointed by the sight of "gray waving hills, line beyond line," as far his eye could reach, hills "so destitute of trees that one could almost see a stout fly walking along their profile." But he quickly added that Scott and Burns had both thrown such a "magic web of poetry and romance" over the country that bare as it was he found it had a greater charm than the richest scenery of England.

Scott was silent a moment, looking out over the hills. Then he said gravely, "I like the very nakedness of the land; it has something bold and stern and solitary about it. When I have been for some time in the rich scenery about Edinburgh, which is like ornamented garden land, I begin to wish myself back again among my own honest gray hills, and if I did not see heather at least once a year, I think I should die!"

Washington understood the claims that arose from early associations and spoke of the landscapes that he had known since childhood, the hills crowned with forests, and streams breaking their way through a wilderness of trees. Scott was sympathetic.

"There is nothing I should like more," he said, "than to be in the midst of one of your grand, wild, original forests." He remembered once having seen, at Leith, an immense piece of timber, just landed from America. He could hardly imagine the tree it must have been at its full height, with all its branches. "In fact," Scott said, "those vast aboriginal trees, that have sheltered the Indians before the intrustion of the white men, are the monuments and antiquities of your country."

They talked of Thomas Campbell's poem with an American setting, *Gertrude of Wyoming*, and Scott, praising the work, spoke of how much poetic material there must be in American scenes. Soon the conversation was turning to what Irving was writing now.

Caught up in a sort of euphoria by the interest of his companion, feeling surer of himself as a writer than he had for a long time, Washington mentioned the fragments in his portfolio, and the "light tales" that he wanted to write, in the manner of the German author, Wieland. He spoke of some of the legends and superstitions he had collected in his own country, tales the Dutch had been telling around their firesides for two centuries, that he wanted to use somehow.

Scott was delighted by the stories Washington related. They reminded him of other tales from his own Highlands, reminded him also of various German legends which he had not only read but translated for publication in England. He asked Washington if he had read much of the material collected by Bürgler. Washington said that he did not read German very well. Scott insisted that he must learn German. The Germans were collecting a positive treasury of legend, stories, and tales that helped one to see the basic and universal themes that underlay the legends of all lands.

The talk between the two ran on and on. They came back across the hills to dinner, at which the whole family was gathered again. After dinner, everyone repaired, along with what appeared to be a customary entourage of dogs and cats, to the drawing room which was also a sort of study and library. There they sat around the great fireplace and Scott continued to entertain his guest, showing him bits of armor and other curios, reading to him from old black letter manuscripts, asking his oldest daughter, Sophia, to sing some of the old Scottish ballads she had learned.

Washington went to bed that night with his head in a whirl. He had found his way into many places that had become "homes away from home"—the Hoffman house in New York, Rebecca Gratz's home in Philadelphia, Castle Van Tromp in Birmingham, but never had he been so totally the center of concern and attention as in the home of this writer whom he admired more than any other living author. Sleep

was a long time in coming as he recalled the way Scott spoke
to him as a fellow writer and an equal. Words he must not
forget, promises he was making to himself filled his mind.

The days that followed were equally full of good talk, of
rambles across the countryside and meetings with local characters. Scott and Irving were caught in a sudden Highlands downpour in the course of one walk and Scott held
out his plaidie so that Washington also might take shelter
under it. They rowed on the lake. Neighbors were asked to
dinner so that Washington might meet some of the "good
plain Scottish folk." Two English tourists arrived, "a gentleman of fortune" and his traveling companion. Scott's behavior to them, perfectly polite, but quickly dismissive, gave
further proof, if any was needed, of what a special guest he
considered Washington Irving to be.

Washington talked more and more. Not only about his
own writing and future hopes for it but of friends and
family who had helped to shape his life. He spoke of his
brother William and of Henry Brevoort whom Scott remembered with pleasure. He talked of the women he had
known, describing Maria Hoffman who had been his early
ideal. In a rare mood of confidence, he took out the small
miniature of Matilda Hoffman which he carried with him
always, and showed that to Scott, telling him of his love for
her and her early, tragic death. Then, pulling the talk away
from those memories, Washington spoke of yet another
woman he had known and admired, Rebecca Gratz of Philadelphia. Scott was interested in what he said about Rebecca.
Scott knew few Jewish people and wanted to hear more
about the young woman. Washington told him of the rich
and productive life that the Gratzes knew in Philadelphia.
He went on to tell of Rebecca's unhappy romance, of how
she had loved and been loved by Samuel Ewing, and of her

final decision that she and Samuel should not marry. The story impressed Scott, and he was silent for a while after Washington had concluded, turning it over in his mind and pondering it.

(A few years later, after Scott's novel, *Ivanhoe*, was published, a rumor would arise that the secondary heroine of the book, Rebecca, had been inspired by Washington Irving's talk with Scott about Rebecca Gratz. Before long the rumor spread until it became a legend, both in England and America. Scholars tend to discount the story since neither Scott nor Irving ever acknowledged the legend, either to affirm or deny it.

If the legend is apocryphal, however, one may ask what started it. Irving had found a new success of his own when *Ivanhoe* appeared. *The Sketch Book* which brought him acclaim opened with a preface acknowledging his gratitude to Walter Scott, by that time Sir Walter, for Scott's help in getting the book published. Did some sentimental soul who knew of Irving's friendship for Rebecca Gratz invent a nicely balanced exchange of favors between the two authors? Scott had helped and encouraged Irving. How pleasant then to believe that Irving had also helped and inspired Scott. There is no way, it seems, to know for sure how direct any inspiration was, but that Irving spoke of Rebecca to Scott seems more than credible in the light of the many topics they did discuss.

Rebecca Gratz herself had heard that she was supposed to have been the inspiration for Scott's heroine when she read *Ivanhoe* in 1824. All through her long, busy, and distinguished life a general belief that this was so added a vaguely romantic aura to her presence. When she was asked directly if she was the original Rebecca she only shook her head. "They say so," was her response.)

Washington's visit with Scott and his family, so long protracted, came to its end. He had made arrangements to meet Preston for their further tour of the Highlands which could not be postponed any longer. Scott walked Irving up the gravel path to the road where his chaise waited, told him how much he had enjoyed his visit, and wished him good fortune in his writing. He added a further fatherly note by hoping that Irving would marry and have a family of "young bairns" after his return to America. "If you are happy, there they are to share your happiness—if you are otherwise, there they are to comfort you."

They came to the gate and Scott took Irving's hand. "I will not say farewell," he said, "for it is always a painful word, but I will say, come again. When you have made your tour to the Highlands, come here and give me a few more days—but come when you please, you will always find Abbotsford open to you, and a hearty welcome."

When Washington stopped again at Abbotsford on his way back to Edinburgh, he found Scott away on business; so he was not to see him again for some time. But the light that the days of his visit with Scott had shed over his ambitions, his future, his very sense of himself gave a glow to everything that he saw in Scotland. Preston found his friend far less melancholy than he had been before and exhibiting much more of the bubbling humor that had been his in the past.

Returned at last to Liverpool, Irving's mood changed rather abruptly. A letter from Brevoort was waiting for him. It announced Brevoort's marriage to Miss Laura Elizabeth Carson of South Carolina. This news gave Washington a pensive hour or so as he reflected that marriage was bound to end the bachelors' freedom which they had shared. But that was only the most fleeting of shadows in the midst of a far greater gloom.

A declaration of the bankruptcy of P. and E. Irving Company could no longer be postponed. This meant testifying before the Court of Chancery that the firm was wholly unable to satisfy its creditors. Because as many payments as possible had been made on accounts, the Court was enabled to release the Irvings from the rest of their indebtedness. But the experience was agony for Washington.

"I underwent ruin in all its bitterness & humiliation," he recalled in later years, "in a strange land—among strangers. I went through the horrible ordeal of Bankruptcy." (The actual proceedings began on January 8, 1818. They were not completed until March.) "It is true I was treated with indulgence—even with courtesy; for they perceived that I was a mere nominal party in the concern—But to me it was a cruel blow—I felt cast down—abased—I had lost my *cast*—I had always been proud of Spirit, and in my own country had been, as it were, a being of the air—I felt the force of the text 'a wounded spirit who can bear?' . . ."

In the midst of this misery, he looked back almost incredulously to the September days at Abbotsford, days he was already remembering as "among the very happiest in my life; for I was conscious at the time of being happy."

Plunging from the "happiest" time of his life to the most miserable, he clung to the advice and encouragement Scott had given him and refused to despair utterly.

"Guter Wein, gute Milch, gutes Bier," he wrote in his notebook, furiously concentrating on German grammar when it was impossible to think of working on his sketches . . . "ein thaler, eine Frau. . . ." He *would* learn German as Scott had suggested, and he *would* go on with his writing just as soon as he was able, "not so much for support . . . but to reinstate myself in the world's thoughts—to raise myself from the degradation into which I considered myself fallen."

# 14

# You Will Return Immediately

IT WAS A warm day of early fall in Washington, D.C. No breeze cooled the air on Capitol Hill where the government buildings were still in a state of reconstruction after the fires lit by the British in the summer of 1814. But Representative William Irving did not notice the heat or the unfinished look of the buildings around him. He walked rapidly down the hill toward his boardinghouse, eager to pack his trunk and get aboard the stagecoach for New York. He had won a definite commitment from Stephen Decatur at last.

Jolting along in the coach toward Baltimore a few hours later, he relaxed with a sense of satisfaction that he had not felt since the business troubles had started three years before. He had never doubted that Decatur would do what he could, but in spite of his high post as Naval Commissioner to which he had been appointed after returning in triumph from his expedition against the Tripolitans in 1815, Decatur had to work within the same constricting political mazes as everyone else at the capital. William knew that for months Decatur had been trying to do something about his request, but every move Decatur might make seemed contingent on some move or moves that others must make first. But now all the moves had been made. The thing was set.

Arrived in New York the next afternoon, William found Ebenezer just sealing a letter to Washington and a boy waiting to hurry it to a ship setting sail for Liverpool within the hour. Quickly telling Ebenezer his news, he took the letter from him and scribbled a postscript. The full story would have to be told to Washington later, in a longer letter to go by the next ship to Liverpool. Meantime, he could at least give Washington a hint that everything was going to be all right now.

It was late November when Washington, in Liverpool, received the letter that told the story.

"My dear Brother," William had written on October 24, 1818. "I added a postscript to a letter of Br. Ebenezer to you, written a few days ago. The purport of the letter was to inform you that Commodore Decatur informed me that he had made such arrangements & such steps would further be made by the Navy Board, as that you will be able to obtain the office of first Clerk in the Navy Department, which is indeed similar to that of under secretary in England. The salary is equal to 2400 Dollars pr. annum, which as the Commodore says, is sufficient to enable you to live in Washington like a prince. . . ."

Washington stopped reading for a moment. Had a hush fallen through the lodgings he had shared with Peter for so long now?

"It is a berth highly respectable—Very comfortable in its income, light in its duties, and will afford you a very ample leisure to pursue the bent of your literary inclinations. It may also be a mere stepping stone to higher station & may be considered at any rate permanent.

"If you think it will suit, you will return immediately.

Leave your present engagement with the Doctor, it will provide for him a present support, until it is in our power to do better. My dear brother, how happy I will be to see you all in a comfortable way once more. It will take the only load remaining, from my heart."

A moment of decision had come for Washington, perhaps the first real moment of decision in his life. Everything before had been whim, or a submissive acceptance of some plan put forward by his brothers.

Now indeed he was presented with still another plan, the finest his brothers had yet managed to arrange. Certainly the offer of the post of first Navy Clerk was more than he had ever hoped for when he had been making vague efforts to find a political position in previous years. If only William's letter had come ten months earlier, when Washington had been at the nadir of his despair, declining German nouns to keep from thinking about the disgrace of bankruptcy. If only it had come before he had at last "taken up his pen" to restore his honor by that means since no other was open.

"If you think it will suit, you will return immediately. . . ." The words echoed in Washington's mind as he thought of the recent months. He recalled the gray springtime after the bankruptcy decree became final, his struggles to read some of the German authors whom Scott had recommended, the faint glimmers of interest that he had felt from time to time as he caught the similarity between some German legends and those of his own Hudson River, and then the fading of that interest in the weight of his depression. He remembered his flight to Birmingham to spend some weeks with Sally, Hal, and the little Van Warts. But not even their welcome had been able to rouse him from his lethargy. He had known times of melancholy before but nothing had compared to those days, uniformly gray in color, no matter how the sun shone or how the green began to show on the trees and lawns of Birmingham. He had seen, as from a distance, the children shocked by his remoteness and then gradually withdrawing to stare at him from time to time, baffled by the change in the uncle who had always been such a good playfellow before. April had passed and May and part of June, and though he had sat day after day in his room, paper and notes spread before him, he wrote almost nothing.

Then had come the evening when Hal, never wearying of trying to cheer his brother-in-law, had urged Washington out for an evening walk. Strolling in the quiet dark, Hal had turned the conversation to bygone days in Sleepy Hollow. Washington's mood had lifted somewhat as he recalled the little villages with their red brick houses and the talks he had had with the Dutch villagers.

Suddenly—who knows how inspiration comes—a picture was in his mind. He saw a lazy, ne'er do-well Dutchman, who preferred hunting and fishing to any other work, stealing away from the scoldings of his shrewish wife for a day in the hills with his dog and gun. But that was not all. Suddenly Washington was aware that this good-natured fellow was on his way to being whisked into a curious enchantment. A dozen tales that he had heard in America, a German legend he had read recently, an old Scottish story that Scott had told him, had somehow collided and blended in Washington's mind and then vanished, each having cast some part of its glow over a mystery that could only have its setting in America's Catskill Mountains.

Six months later, Washington sat in the Liverpool parlor with William's letter in his hand and remembered the excitement that had risen in him and the way he had turned to Hal Van Wart and he said he wanted to go back to the house. Hal had not questioned him but turned as Washington did and hurried to keep pace with Washington's quickened steps toward the house. Inside the door, Washington called to Sally in a new, vibrant voice that he was going up to his room to write and then he had leaped up the stairs. Settled down at the table in his room, he had begun to scribble out the tale that had come to him in such a flash, the details of which were now unfolding easily and almost inevitably. No moments of blankness assailed him nor any fretting need to reread, polish, and rephrase such as he had felt in attempts at writing in recent months. The hours passed. The family went to bed. Still he sat writing. Dawn began to lighten the windows, then full morning came. At last he was finished. With no sense of weariness for having sat up all night, he dashed sand across the last page, gathered the sheets together, and went downstairs to the dining room where the family was gathered at breakfast.

He remembered how Sally and Hal and the children had looked at him with surprise as though some electricity in his manner had communicated itself to them. Then he had sat down and read them the opening pages of the story of "Rip Van Winkle."

It had been the turning of the tide for him, or like the wakening from a long, disturbed sleep, a sleep perhaps a little like the enchanted slumber into which the hero of his tale had fallen. Except that once awakened, Washington had felt none of the bewilderment that Rip knew after his twenty year's nap. He was exhilarated, eager now to finish the sketches in his portfolio and plunge on to new themes.

All his writing after that had not gone so effortlessly, but he seemed able to be patient and to rewrite without a sense of hopelessness. He could consider calmly the problems inherent in making some sort of finished work out of a group of sketches, widely divergent in their themes and scenes.

Looking back on the summer, Washington remembered the further encouragement he had found when he traveled to London in July. He had been disappointed to learn that Allston was preparing to return to America to live, but in the days before Allston departed Irving read some of his completed stories to him and Leslie and Newton. Their enthusiasm had been a tonic, and the kinship he felt with them as artists had settled something else as well. What did it matter if the material he had written was a diverse collection of stories, essays, character sketches, and mood pieces? That was how artists filled their sketchbooks, with a detail on one page, a finished drawing on another, a suggestion of a composition on another.

A title—"The Sketch Book"—presented itself to Washington's mind. It was so simple and right that he accepted it as inevitable. He began to think of a pseudonym for himself, a name to emphasize further the fact that these sketches were to be thought of as the works of a draughtsman rather than a writer. Pen? Pencil? Crayon? Crayon—that was it. Now a first name, perhaps one with a hint of Englishness about it, since so many of the sketches were of English scenes. George? Sidney? Geoffrey? Geoffrey! He had it. He would be Geoffrey Crayon,—Gent.

Allston departed for America and Irving, Leslie and Newton saw him off with a sense of loss. But after his departure, Irving had walked about London purposefully, not just vaguely looking for material, but seeking to verify certain details of scenes he was describing. He and Leslie took a brief trip out into the country and he was aware and responsive as he had not been in months, taking notes and finding inspiration for further sketches.

It came to him that he did not have to have a thick folio of sketches before he could present them to the public. He could publish them in small groups, almost like the issues of a magazine. He was not aware of anyone having used that method of publication for stories before, but what did that matter? The periodic appearance of another group of sketches might build cumulative interest in the work.

Washington had returned to Liverpool in September, his program clear in his mind, his hopes rising that he might indeed reinstate himself in the world's thoughts by the exercise of his pen. He had set himself to a final polishing of four or five sketches which he thought would make a fair sampling for a first issue of a "Sketch Book."

Now here was William's letter, offering him ease, respectability, security, and proposing that he return to the United States at once. "If you think it will suit, you will return immediately."

He heard the thump of Peter's cane approaching. He would show Peter the letter. He would ask Peter's advice—Peter, who had been exercising his pen also and was working on a novel—Peter, with whom his rapport had grown even deeper these past months as they shared the miseries and joys of composition—Peter, who thought the sketches quite the best things his younger brother had ever written.

Peter came into the room and raised his eyebrows in inquiry. Washington handed him the letter.

Still, he knew that for once in his life he was going to have to make a decision on his own. He was thirty-five years old. Would he take his chances as a writer, or would he please William and go home to be first Clerk in the Navy Department?

# 15

# Geoffrey Crayon

THE REACTION came as soon as he had sent off the letter to William.

"I had offended the best brother a man ever had; given over the chance Providence seemed to have opened, and now my writing hand was palsied; a more miserable, doubting creature than I . . . can hardly ever have lived."

Peter, who had applauded his decision, sympathized with his distress and tried to encourage him to go on with writing the introductory material he had planned for the issue. But Washington could think of nothing but the fact that he had rejected the efforts William had made in his behalf—and Decatur's also. "Decatur is a worthy true hearted fellow," William had written. "His sincere attachment to you has been greatly transferred to me; I have received many kind attentions from him . . ." Decatur's interest too, he had rejected. Washington was actually relieved when William's letter, clearly breathing his disappointment, finally arrived. The worst known, he was able to sit down at his desk and work. By the first of March, 1819, he and Peter were journeying to London. Then Washington was packing up his manuscript to send to New York by the next ship. A long letter to Henry

Brevoort, to go by the same boat, reflected some of his nervousness.

"I have just sent to my brother Ebenr—Mss: for the first number of a work which if successful I hope to continue occasionally. . . . Will you, as you are a literary man and a man of leisure, take it under your care. I wish the copy right secured for me, and the work printed, and then sold to one or more booksellers, who will take the whole impression at a fair discount & give cash or good notes for it. . . .

"I feel great diffidence about this re-appearance in literature. I am conscious of my imperfections—and my mind has been for a long time past so preyed upon and agitated by various cares and anxieties, that I fear it has lost much of its cheerfulness and some of its activity.

"I have attempted no lofty theme nor sought to look wise and learned, which appears to be very much the fashion among our American writers at present. I have preferred addressing myself to the feeling & fancy of the reader, more than to his judgement. My writings may appear therefore light & trifling in our country of philosophers & politicians—but if they possess merit in the class of literature to which they belong it is all to which I aspire in the work. I seek only to blow a flute of accompaniment in the national concert, and leave others to play the fiddle & French horn. . . ."

There was more to the letter—gratitude for Brevoort's offer that Washington draw on him whenever he was in need of money, affectionate greetings to friends in New York, and a few words about Washington's hope to visit the continent briefly before returning to America. "If I can get my mind into full play, and dash off a set of writings that may do me credit; I shall return home with alacrity, and it will hasten my return—but I cannot bear the thoughts of limping home broken down & spiritless, to be received kindly in rememberance of former services. . . . God bless you my dear Brevoort," he concluded, "Your friend, W. I."

In another long letter, to Ebenezer, he tried once again, as he had tried in his first letter to William, to explain the decision he had made. "My talents are merely literary, and all my habits of thinking, reading &c., have been in a different direction from that required for the active politician. . . . I have been for some time past nursing my mind up for literary operations, and collecting materials for the purpose. . . . I now wish to be left for a while entirely to the bent of my own inclinations, and not agitated by new plans for subsistence, or by entreaties to come home."

The statement was blunter than any he had ever made to the brothers who had looked after him and protected him so long. He tried to soften it. "Do not, I beseech you, impute my lingering in Europe to any indifference to my own country or my friends. My greatest desire is to make myself worthy of the good-will of my country, and my greatest anticipation of happiness is the return to my friends. . . ." Then Washington outlined what he wanted Ebenezer to do with the manuscript he would receive with the letter, the way he wanted it printed and distributed, and his hopes that a good price would be asked for it.

It would be a month before Ebenezer received the manuscript and letter, another month before Washington could hope to hear his and Brevoort's reactions to his new project, and who could guess how long before he would hear any news about the actual publication of the first issue of his *Sketch Book* and its reception in America. "Unequal" as his spirits were, he did not allow himself to waste time in apprehension but began to ready material for a second issue to send off to Ebenezer within another month. At the end of the day's work, he and Peter sometimes joined Leslie for dinner, and their talk was light and lively. Only at night, with the candles and lamps blown out, did Washington let himself think of how much he had ventured and how long were the odds that he would be vindicated.

Ebenezer received the bulky parcel containing the material for the first issue in April. He was pleased at this evidence that Washington had been seriously at work, but perhaps even more agitated than Washington as to how this new venture of his would fare. Always a bit of a worrier and never the dabbler in literary affairs that his brothers were, Ebenezer read through the densely covered pages and smiled and then frowned because somehow it was so different from what Washington usually wrote. Perhaps, he suggested to Elizabeth that evening, after the children were in bed, it might not be a bad idea to invite some of Washington's friends over for an evening and read the manuscript to them. William was at the capital. There was no way to get his opinion. But he could read it to Brevoort, Gouverneur Kemble, James Renwick—any other of the Lads who were around. They were clever, witty, literary fellows, all of them, and would know if it was all right. Elizabeth agreed that such a gathering might be a good idea.

There was a fire on the hearth in Ebenezer Irving's parlor the next evening, for the April air was still chill. The candles in the sconces were lighted and so was the lamp on the table by which Ebenezer was sitting with Washington's manuscript. Elizabeth had set out a plate of cakes. Ebenezer brought out a decanter of wine. Seated around the room were the friends he had invited, holding glasses from which they sipped from time to time. They looked both expectant and a little fearful. All of them had received letters from Washington during the last few years telling of his depression, fatigue, and anxiety. They were unsure of what he had been able to achieve in such a mood.

Ebenezer cleared his throat and began to read "The Author's Account of Himself": "I was always fond of visiting new scenes, and observing strange characters and manners," he read. "Even when a mere child I began my travels, and made many tours of discovery into foreign parts and unknown regions of my native city, to the frequent alarm of my parents, and the amolument of the town-crier. . . ." The easy sentences spun on, telling of the increase in the author's propensity for wandering as he grew older and finally of his desire to visit Europe where the "very ruins told the history of times gone by." He wanted also to see the great men of the earth. True, America had her great men, but he had "read in the works of various philosophers, that all animals degenerated in America, and man among the number. A great man of Europe, thought I, must therefore be as superior to a great man of America as a peak of the Alps to a highland of the Hudson. . . . I will visit this land of wonders, thought I, and see the gigantic race from which I am degenerated."

Ebenezer's listeners began to smile and relax. The phrases had a sheen and rhythm like no writing Washington had done before. If he were to keep this up, everything would be all right. Ebenezer concluded the introductory passage with its explanation that the essays which were to follow were like sketches that tourists brought home from abroad for the entertainment of their friends. Here readers would find no grand landscapes, merely sketches of nooks, corners, and byplaces. As Ebenezer paused, his listeners were smiling expectantly. Read on, they urged.

Ebenezer read "The Voyage," in which Washington had caught, in the same easy, colorful way, the special moods that a traveler knew during that long suspension of normal life which the sea passage to Europe entailed. When that sketch was concluded, Ebenezer's listeners, delighted by the way Washington was sustaining his flowing prose, simply asked for more. So Ebenezer read the essay which Washington had placed next in order, a character sketch of the historian William Roscoe. When that grave and touching tribute to a scholar was finished, Ebenezer asked if perhaps his listeners were growing tired. He was answered by a clamor of negatives. A gentle story of a wife's loyalty to her husband when he met financial reverses was the next sketch, and it brought murmurs of appreciation from all the men. Then Ebenezer launched into the last story of the group, a work that Washington introduced as a "posthumous tale from the papers of Diedrich Knickerbocker—the legend of Rip Van Winkle."

"Who ever has made a voyage up the Hudson must remember the Kaatskill mountains," Ebenezer began, and his audience was caught to a still sharper attention. This was their own country that their friend was writing about now, the region he had already made Knickerbocker territory. Ebenezer's breathy voice went on, reading the passages wherein Washington painted the scenes they all knew, the beautiful hills, the little villages. Rip was introduced; that "simple good-natured man" and "obedient hen-pecked husband." His popularity in the village was detailed, and his failure as a farmer. Then Rip was off with his gun and his dog Wolf for a day's hunting in the hills. After a fruitless time of looking for game, Rip had thrown himself down on a high knoll to rest, and then heard a voice hallooing him from a distance. "Rip Van Winkle, Rip Van Winkle!"

A burnt log broke and fell in the fireplace, sending up a shower of sparks, but not one paid it any heed. Glasses were empty but no one got up to refill his glass with more wine. Ebenezer read on and on, his voice growing hoarse. He stumbled now and then over words, or as he squinted at some of Washington's more indecipherable script. No such distractions made any difference. His listeners were as rapt in enchantment as old Rip Van Winkle who now found himself in a glen where solemn little men in old Dutch costumes were playing at ninepins. They were, he learned, Henry Hudson and his ghostly crew. Somewhat dazed, Rip began to try to clear his head by draughts from a keg of excellent Hollands which was near at hand.

After a good deal of such tippling, Rip fell into a deep sleep, but the group in Ebenezer's parlor did not, for almost immediately Rip was waking again. He called vainly for his dog, and was bewildered to see his flintlock rusted. The strange and awful consequences of the enchantment began to unfold. Rip looked for the glen where he had seen the small bowlers. There was a waterfall where the entrance to the glen had been. Puzzled, he made his way down the mountain toward the village. Gradually, as his hand touched and then explored a long beard, as everyone whom he met was a stranger to him, it was borne in on him that his little slumber had been a nap of twenty years. The tale wound to its close. Rip found his place before the new hotel which had once been the village tavern and told his curious story to every new arrival in the town. Most strangers refused to believe his strange adventure. "The old Dutch inhabitants, however, almost universally give it full credit. Even to this day they never hear a thunderstorm of a summer afternoon about the Kaatskill, but they say Hendrick Hudson and his crew are at their game of nine-pins; and it is a common wish of all henpecked husbands in the neighborhood, when life hangs heavy on their hands, that they might have a quieting draught out of Rip Van Winkle's flagon."

There was a hush as Ebenezer finished. Then an almost simultaneous expulsion of breath and of exclamations. In the hubbub of excitement and pleasure, Ebenezer looked around the group and burst into tears.

Meantime, in London, Washington was bundling up the sketches he had made ready for a second issue and sending them off to Ebenezer. He put a letter to Brevoort in the mailbag also, explaining that the second group of sketches was not as large as the first but that he had no concern about the work being regular in any way. He mentioned a report that he had heard of some public criticisms that a New York acquaintance, Gulian Verplanck, had made of *Knickerbocker's History*, and his old mocking humor asserted itself. "I could not help laughing at this burst of filial feeling in Verplanck, on the jokes put upon his ancestors, though I honour the feeling and admire the manner in which it is expressed. It met my eyes just as I had finished the little story of Rip Van Winkle and I could not help noticing it in the introduction to that Bagatelle. I hope Verplanck will not think the article was written in defiance of his Vituperation. Remember me heartily to him, and tell him I mean to grow wiser and better and older every day and to lay the castigation he has given me seriously to heart. . . . Give my best regards to Mrs. Brevoort," he added, "and believe me, my dear Brevoort, Yours affectionately, W.I." In a postcript, he had a further thought. "If you can suggest any hints that will be of service to me in the work—anything that will cheer & excite me, do so I beg of you. Let me know what themes etc. would be popular and striking in America; for I have been so long in England that things cease to strike me here as realities and to wear a commonplace aspect."

The sketches for the second number on their way, he went to work to complete and write new items for a third number. By mid-May he had collected four which he thought would make a balanced issue. One was a romantic account of a visit to the castle where James I of Scotland had been imprisoned, another was a pastoral essay. "The Country Church," a third was a pathetic tale about a widow and her son, and finally he had a humorous sketch reporting on Geoffrey Crayon's attempts to find fresh material on Shakespeare by seeking out the tavern frequented by Falstaff.

"I am extremely anxious to hear from you what you think of the first number," he wrote to Brevoort as he sent off this third group. The suspense was beginning to tell on him, and he was finding it difficult to continue writing new material without any word of how the first had been received.

Not until July did he finally get three letters from Brevoort, two of which had been unaccountably held in Liverpool. Brevoort seemed to approve of the first number, but his chief concern in all the letters was with details of publication. Two weeks later, an actual copy of the first number of *The Sketch Book* arrived.

There it was in Washington's hands at last, real and tangible, a small octavo volume, with gray-brown covers and the title in shaded letters, *The Sketch Book* by Geoffrey Crayon, Gent.

"I cannot but express how much more than ever I feel myself indebted to you," he wrote Brevoort, "for the manner in which you have attended to my concerns. The work is got up in a beautiful style; I should scarcely have ventured to have made so elegant an entree had it been left to myself, for I had lost confidence in my writings."

Pleased as he was by the book's appearance, he soon found half a dozen or more errors in grammar or expression which caused him to wince, and he noted those in his letters for correction in case the first number should ever come to a second edition.

Then he went back to completing the material for the fourth number—a fantasy on "The Mutability of Literature," a sketch about a visit to Westminster Abbey, a gently melancholy account of "Rural Funerals," a cheerful view of "The Inn Kitchen," and finally a mock-gothic story, full of ghosts and terrors, but with a happy ending, "The Spectre Bridegroom."

In August, when he sent off this bundle of manuscript, he still had had no word from America to tell him whether he had been vindicated in his decisions to refuse William's plans for him and stand by Geoffrey Crayon.

# 16

# It Cannot Be Real

REBECCA GRATZ, returned from a visit to Baltimore, found a copy of the first issue of *The Sketch Book* waiting for her on the hall table of the family home in Philadelphia. She opened it eagerly and spent the afternoon reading it. That night, writing her weekly letter to Maria Hoffman, she shared her pleasure in "W. Irving's beautiful little Sketch Book." To Rebecca, it seemed that Washington was "indulging his love of home" in the volume. Perhaps Rebecca, more than many of his friends, sensed the ambivalence in Washington that sent him on long self-imposed wanderings while part of him yearned all the time to be settled. At any rate, she was "charmed" by his "sending such a polished little memorial to announce him among his friends."

In Washington, D.C., James Paulding had his first inkling of Irving's new project when his brother-in-law, Gouverneur Kemble, arrived in the city, bringing him a copy. For sensitive James, the initial reaction was one of embarrassment and dismay. If only he had known that Washington was planning to publish something this summer he would have held off the publication of a new work of his own, nothing less than a revival of *Salmagundi*. A year before he had written to Washington asking if he would like to join him in putting out the magazine again, but when Washington had replied that he thought "Old Sal" a juvenile joke that might well be forgotten, James had decided to try an issue or two on his own. The first copies were even now at the booksellers. Would Washington—would anyone—think that he, James, was trying to compete with his long-time friend and collaborator, and in such a crude way, by reviving just now the magazine with which *both* their names had been associated? To James, it was far more important that Washington's first writing venture after such a long time should do well than that his own should be noticed. Wincing inwardly and planning the letter of explanation he would write to Washington, James delayed some time before settling down to read *The Sketch Book* and make his own evaluation of the work.

Here, there, and everywhere in the United States, Washington's friends were picking up the slim volume and having their varied reactions, while in London Washington still fretted for some word as to its reception. He tried to concentrate on the contents of the fifth issue. Looking at the calendar, he realized that this issue would probably be published some time near Christmas, and he had begun to toy with the idea of having all the sketches in it revolve around descriptions of old-time English Christmas celebrations. He enjoyed writing about traditional festivities and rites and was sure he had collected enough material to work up four or five sketches. But how would such a subject be received at home? Christmas was hardly noticed there except for a few token observances by the Dutch. The Fourth of July was the only holiday that really counted in America—the glorious Fourth that celebrated the flouting of all tradition except the spirit of '76.

He began a sketch describing a stagecoach ride to an old

English manor house on Christmas Eve. But indecision tormented him. If only he knew how the first number was doing.

His long wait was finally ended in early September, 1819. A parcel arrived from Brevoort. It contained not only several copies of both the first and second numbers of *The Sketch Book*, but also a sheaf of reviews from American newspapers and periodicals, reporting reactions of the critics to the first two issues.

Washington's hands trembled as he unfolded the clippings. His eyes skimmed the columns of type, hardly daring to do more than catch a word here and there. Then, gradually, an immense relief was filling him. It was his turn, as it had been Ebenezer's some months before, to feel tears welling in his eyes.

Through tears, he read again some of the comments in the *New York Evening Post:* "This is a new production said to be from the elegant and racy pen of Washington Irving, Esq. . . . The graces of style; the rich, warm tone of benevolent feeling; the freely-flowing vein of hearty and happy humor, and the fine-eyed spirit of observation . . . regulated by a perception of fitness—a tact—wonderfully quick and sure . . . are all exhibited anew in the Sketch Book, with freshened beauty and added charms. . . . Roscoe—a just and noble-spirited eulogium. . . . The 'Wife' . . . beautifully pathetic. . . . But Rip Van Winkle is the master-piece. For that comic spirit which is without any infusion of gall, which delights in what is ludicrous rather than what is ridiculous . . . the story of Rip Van Winkle has few competitors."

Not for some months would Washington learn that the *Post's* review had been written by Brevoort. By then he would have no need to think it was simply praise from a friend and so to be somewhat discredited. It might not have mattered too much if he had known even as he first read it, for Brevoort had included reviews from other magazines and papers that were equally favorable. There was praise in *The Analectic* and still more in *The North American Review*. At last he was able to read Brevoort's letter which led off with business details about paper and booksellers' orders and then went on to report that the first number was selling well with the demand rising everywhere.

Later, when he was calm enough to hold a pen, he wrote to Brevoort.

"The manner in which the work has been received and the eulogiums that have been passed upon it in the American papers and periodical works have completely overwhelmed me. They go far, *far* beyond my most sanguine expectations and indeed are expressed with such peculiar warmth and kindness as to affect me in the tenderest manner. The receipt of your letter and the reading of some of these criticisms this morning have rendered me nervous for the whole day. I feel almost appalled by such success, and fearful that it cannot be real—or that it is not fully merited, or that I shall not set up to the expectations that may be formed. We are whimsically constituted beings. I had got out of conceit of all that I had written, and considered it very questionable stuff—and now that it is so extravagantly bepraised I begin to feel afraid that I shall not do so well again."

"It cannot be real. . ." He had to glance at the clippings again and again. And was the praise "fully merited"? He did not believe it could be. Still, he was reassured enough to take his chances with a fifth number devoted to an English Christmas. Within the next few weeks he completed four sketches on the theme which he then packed up to catch the next mailboat.

Sometime soon after that he learned that some of the material already published in America was finding its way back to England. A Liverpool magazine, *The Kaleidoscope*, had republished the tale of "The Wife," and another periodical, *The Literary Gazette*, in London, had picked up and reprinted several sketches from the early numbers, introducing the first with the rather patronizing and inaccurate comment: "The following production has been handed to us by an able friend, who tells us that it is the work of a very intelligent native of America, just arrived from New York."

Washington might have no head for business as it concerned calico, tinware, or tobacco, but when it came to his own work being republished in England at no profit to himself and with any sort of misprint, omission, or error that the reprinting publisher might be pleased to allow, he felt stirrings of self-preservation. He had already shown John Murray, that chief of English publishers, the first number of *The Sketch Book* and Murray had been complimentary about its appearance. Other London literary men whom he had met through Leslie and Newton had been kind. One had asked why Irving did not collect the numbers published so far in America and have them published in a single volume in England.

A fear of criticism had lain under his nervousness in sending forth any of his works, contributing to his devotion to pseudonyms, but his fear of English criticism was supreme. He knew, by now, how savage that attention could be even when directed at English writers and poets of renown. He knew, as well, that the idea of America being a source of literary talent was almost incomprehensible to most English critics. If he felt any doubt he only had to read again that phrase in the *Gazette*—"the work of a very intelligent native of America." How did he dare expose his little sketches to English criticism?

On the other hand, since his works were being reprinted anyway, how did he dare not risk it?

He gathered up the copies of *The Sketch Book* which he

had received from America and took them to John Murray for his consideration, explaining that if Murray decided to publish that material as a volume he would soon have enough further material to make a companion second volume.

The rebuff he had feared was only a few days in arriving. Murray's letter which accompanied the returned *Sketch Book* was polite but clear.

"If it would not suit me to engage in the publication of your present work, it is only because I do not see that scope in the nature of it which would enable me to make those satisfactory accounts between us, without which I really feel no satisfaction in engaging—but I will do all I can to promote their circulation, and shall be most ready to attend any future plan of your."

"This was," as Washington later wrote, "disheartening." But he refused to give up. He had made a friend, two years before, a friend who had encouraged him in the writing of *The Sketch Book* and whose opinion carried weight in many quarters. He did not know whether Walter Scott was at his country place, Abbotsford, or in Edinburgh. Covering both possibilities he sent his copies of *The Sketch Book* to Scott's address in Edinburgh and an explanatory letter to Abbotsford. In the letter he hinted at the reverses in fortune he had known since his visit with Scott which made the need to exercise his pen all important, and wondered if Scott might query Constable, the Edinburgh publisher, as to his interest in bringing out a British edition of *The Sketch Book*.

Scott, that "golden-hearted man," replied promptly. He had been in the country when the packet of books went to Edinburgh, but he said that he was on his way to town and even without seeing *The Sketch Book* would see Constable, "and do all in my power to forward your views." Picking up the hint of financial difficulties, Scott also offered Washington the editorship of a new magazine which was being started in Edinburgh. The position, which would pay five hundred pounds sterling a year with a prospect of further advantage, was Irving's if he wished it. Scott admitted that the magazine was to have a political slant, "Yet I risk the question because I know no man so well qualified for this important task, and perhaps because it will necessarily bring you to Edinburgh."

Again Washington faced an offer of something secure and responsible as opposed to the uncertain life of an author. But once having made the decision, he did not hesitate in his reply to Scott. Grateful for the offer that both surprised and flattered him, he still had to confess that editorial work was not for him. "My whole course of life," he wrote Scott, "has been desultory, and I am unfitted for any periodically recurring task, or any stipulated labor of body or mind. I have no command of my talents, such as they are, and have to watch the varyings of my mind as I would those of a weathercock."

Meantime, he had a letter from Scott who had now read *The Sketch Book*. "It is positively beautiful, and increases my desire to *crimp* you, if it be possible. Some difficulties there always are in managing such a matter, especially at the outset; but we will obviate them as much as we possibly can." Still another letter from Scott explained to Irving some of the usual arrangements between publishers and authors in England and Scotland and reported that he had given Constable his "earnest recommendation . . . to enter into the negotiation."

Suddenly, however, Washington decided to ask no favors from anyone. He would himself arrange for a volume of the sketches to be published by some printer who had not achieved an exalted reputation, and then send it forth to the public or stand or fall on its own.

The publisher he found was a certain John Miller, who seemed quite agreeable to printing and selling the work—at the author's risk. Early in January of 1820, Irving signed the contract with Miller. Within a month, the volume was ready to appear in the bookstores, nicely printed and handsomely bound. His face still set against begging for attention, Irving refused to send free copies to reviewers or critics of importance and simply let the book appear in various bookstores.

At first the luck that had attended all his writing ventures seemed to be with him again. *The Sketch Book* by Geoffrey Crayon, Gent. was not heralded or advertised, but the excerpts in the periodicals had created some interest. A fair number of copies was sold. In Edinburgh, Scott suggested to John Lockhart, a young contributor to Blackwood's *Edinburgh Magazine,* and his oldest daughter's fiancé, that he write some comments on the works of Scott's "faithful friend Knickerbocker." The resulting columns of appreciation did the sale of *The Sketch Book* no harm.

Then Irving's agreeable publisher suddenly failed and was out of business before *The Sketch Book* had been on sale a month.

With a timeliness worthy of a storybook, Walter Scott appeared in London, whither he had come to be honored by a knighthood. It was only logical that Irving should pay him a congratulatory call, and inevitable that the sad fate of *The Sketch Book* should be revealed during the course of the visit. The trouble barely was outlined before Scott was on his way to Murray's, where the new baronet had no need to press Murray unduly for a personal favor. The publisher had seen for himself that the little volume which he had rejected several months previously had been doing fairly well without any special encouragement. He agreed at once to take over the publication of Geoffrey Crayon's *Sketch Book.*

A few weeks later a new edition of the first volume, bearing the imprint of John Murray, was at the booksellers, and Washington had collected enough material for a second vol-

ume which was about to go to press. He had already sent
sketches for a sixth number to America. By the time he was
ready to send off the seventh and final group of tales, he
could write to Brevoort, "I have recd very flattering compliments from several of the literati and find my circle of acquaintance extending faster than I could wish. Murray's
drawing room is now a frequent resort of mine, where I have
been introduced to several interesting characters."

The book was indeed selling briskly. Signed Geoffrey
Crayon, Gent., just as in America, its real author was unknown to most English readers outside of the literary coterie
with which Washington had become familiar, and this was
causing a certain amount of speculation. Some readers had
even decided that *The Sketch Book* was the work of Sir
Walter Scott, which was as flattering a compliment as Washington could ask.

In America, the seven issues that made up the whole were
in their second and third editions, and Ebenezer and Brevoort
were making plans to collect and publish them in a two-
volume edition as in England. Copies of the American numbers or the English volumes were finding their way to the
continent as well, where they were also winning a certain
small reputation among English readers.

Two and a half years before Irving had been "cast down—
abased." He had "lost his cast," and had made the decision to
reinstate himself in the world's thoughts with his pen. Nine
months before he had been almost "appalled" at an American
success which could not be real. Now Geoffrey Crayon was
being read and talked about on both sides of the Atlantic.

The wind had changed direction for fair.

# 17

## Casting Loose

CHRISTMAS WOULD never again be the half-forgotten holiday that it had been for so long in most of the United States. Washington Irving's four Christmas sketches in the fifth issue of *The Sketch Book* were not wholly responsible for this change, but they did appear just as old Puritan prejudices and prohibitions were weakening throughout New England and a desire for more festivity during the course of the year was beginning to be felt.

"Was that really how things were long ago?" Americans wondered as they read Irving's accounts of the goings on at Bracebridge Hall at Christmas time. A certain wistfulness led, in a surprising number of cases, to some small element of the old English Christmas being introduced into American homes on the next December twenty-fifth and then the next and the next.

The Christmas sketches had an effect in England as well. Irving had romanticized the picture of a hearty country holiday when everyone, from the Squire and his family on through neighbors, local farmers, and servants, had his traditional role to play; but exactly because of that most English readers were comforted to think that this was how life had been in the good old happy times before poverty, unrest, and other modern troubles had agitated the countryside. There were impulses in England, also, to revive some of the old customs.

A few years after *The Sketch Book's* appearance and when the book had attained the status of a minor classic in England as well as America, young Charles Dickens would read it and be charmed not only by its style and flashes of humor but by its evocations of past Christmas times. The pleasure Dickens felt in the Christmas sketches lingered through the years and had a strong influence on him when he came to write his own famous Christmas stories. The Dickens' concept of Christmas, in its turn, deepened and widened the popular feeling for a holiday fraught with tradition and family gatherings. So Irving's Christmas sketches, about which he had felt such uncertainty when he was writing them, became very like the wellspring for a new-old celebration of the holiday for generations to come.

Dickens was not the only youth who would read *The Sketch Book* and feel its influence on his own writings in later years. In America, a young Henry Wadsworth Longfellow was seeking out each issue as it appeared and, as he wrote later, he "read each succeeding number with ever-increasing wonder and delight; spellbound by its pleasant humor, its melancholy tenderness, its atmosphere of reverie." He vowed that when he had finished his studies at Bowdoin College he would try to write like Washington Irving. In America, a whole congregation of youthful scribblers was to fall under Irving's spell, each one hoping that some day he might write as easily, as gracefully as Geoffrey Crayon.

Not every critical reaction was admiring. In England even more than America, there were a few critics who complained that there was nothing especially new in *The Sketch Book* and that it only followed old models of village tales, such as Oliver Goldsmith and William Cowper had already made familiar. Even at the time of its first appearance, when the idealization of women in fiction was almost obligatory and when sentiment was quickly roused by broken hearts or by widows grieving over dead sons, there were those who wrote or spoke rather waspishly about "sentimental twaddle."

Still, some of Irving's truest emotions had been expressed in his essays that touched on mortality, especially when someone young was involved, and his sincerity raised several of these essays above such carping about sentimentality. He had not forgotten, or ever would, the break in his life when Matilda had died at seventeen. And many, many of his readers remembered similar experiences. It was a time when consumption and other diseases did carry off young people in a way that science would later make unusual. Many men and women had followed the coffin of a dead girl or boy to a cemetery, and they found their own grief expressed in haunting phrases, in such an essay as "Rural Funerals."

Besides, balancing the melancholy of that tale, and the other sketches in a somber or sentimental vein, there were a variety of sketches in a merrier mood—happy accounts of a wanderer's experiences at Stratford-on-Avon, in the British Museum, or while looking for the Boar's Head Tavern in Eastcheap. There were, as well, the tales reputedly rescued from the papers of "the late Diedrich Knickerbocker": "Rip Van Winkle" and "The Legend of Sleepy Hollow," with which fine, mysterious, and mocking spoof Irving had concluded the whole series.

Lord Byron, currently living in Italy, received a packet of books from his publisher, Murray. He complained about the books Murray had chosen to send. Byron had wanted Scott's latest novel. "Instead of this, here are Johnny Keats p-ss-a-bed poetry and three novels by God knows whom. However," Byron added, "Crayon is very good." Washington would have been as pleased to hear that as he was by being compared with Scott. Other well-known writers praised him. Robert Southey, England's poet laureate, wrote that he did not wonder at Irving's success. "He is a remarkably agreeable writer, & writes with a feeling & temper which ought to conciliate every reader." William Godwin, the political philosopher and gray eminence of literature, said of the essay on "Rural Life in England," "It is, I believe, all true, and one wonders, while reading, that nobody ever said this before."

But if what Washington had written about England was even partly, romantically true, and if he had indeed helped change the face of Christmas, he had also, with two of his sketches, "Rip Van Winkle" and " The Legend of Sleepy Hollow," enriched the Hudson River highlands far, far more. For generations to come, those highlands would echo with the rumble of the ninepin balls of Hendrick Hudson's ghostly crew. The hills, forests, and streams of the whole Hudson River valley would be overlaid with the magic of a legendary past and peopled for even the idlest tourists with visions of buxom Dutch maidens, or lanky school teachers (somewhat modeled on Jesse Merwin whom Washington had known long before on the Van Ness farm where he went after Matilda's death), or horses ridden wildly through the night.

So—"I am now in all the hurry and bustle of breaking up my encampment," Washington wrote Brevoort from London, "and moving off for the continent. After remaining so long in one place it is painful to cast loose again and turn oneself adrift; but I do not wish to remain long enough in any place in Europe to make it a home."

He went on to tell Brevoort about some of the people he had been meeting since the flurry of his success. There had been the Countess of Besborough at whose home he had met the Duke of Wellington, and Lady Caroline Lamb, who was perfectly willing to boast of some of the more scandalous aspects of her affair with Lord Byron. He wrote also of "Belzoni, the traveller, who is just bringing out a personal narrative of his researches, illustrated with very extraordinary plates." He wrote of "Hallam, whose able & interesting work on the Middle ages you have no doubt seen, and most probably have in your library." Then he checked himself. "But it is useless merely to mention names in this manner, and it is too much like entertaining one with a description of a banquet, by merely naming the dishes."

A surge of homesickness overcame him before he concluded. "Oh my dear Brevoort, how my heart warms towards you all, when I get talking and thinking of past times and past scenes. What would I not give for a few days among the Highlands of the Hudson, with the little knot that was once assembled there! But I shall return home and find all changed, and shall be made sensible how much I have changed myself. It is this idea which continually comes across my mind, when I think of home, and I am continually picturing to myself the dreary state of a poor devil like myself, who after wandering about the world among strangers returns to find himself a still greater stranger in his native place."

> He feels like one that treads alone
> Your Banquet Hall deserted,
> Whose lights are fled, whose garlands dead,
> And all but he departed.

He longed for home, he wrote of home, but he resolutely set himself toward a wandering that was bound to bring him home a Rip Van Winkle at last. Was there some unconscious feeling that if he wandered long enough and far enough he would some day find that cleft in the hills where mystery had its dwelling?

He had money now. He and Peter could take a leisurely journey by coach toward Southampton, stopping off to visit all the "ancient piles" at Winchester—the cathedral where so many kings and great men were buried, and the shell of the palace designed by Sir Christopher Wren. There they could savor also the atmosphere that emanated from reputed relics of England's greatest dream-king, Arthur, and Washington took up his pencil to do some sketching, making a drawing of the Round Table, indicating the seats for two of the knights— Mordred, the traitor, and Sir Launcelot du Lac, Arthur's friend and rival.

Across the Channel and disembarking at Le Havre, they were at once in surroundings which sharply contrasted with the quiet English countryside. Here all was "Clamourous and garrulous. . . . Houses with windows and doors all open instead of the close reserved look of the English—In the evening—people on public walks in groups—women at fountain in the centre of the street—picturesque groups—."

He and Peter checked in at a small, noisy hotel but soon left it to be the guests of the United States consul, a New Yorker, Reuben Beasley, who lived in a richly appointed house on the banks of the Seine. Beasley, wealthy and affable, spent much of his time with his guests discussing his interest in a new steamboat line which ran from Havre to Paris. Both Washington and Peter had been in New York for some of the excitement attendant on Robert Fulton's successful launching of a Hudson River steamboat. Now, listening to Beasley's enthusiastic talk about the new French line, both Peter and Washington felt a flush of investment fever. Peter especially, whose novel had been published with none of the success Washington had found and who really did not know what his future was to be since the failure of P. and E. Irving Company, dwelt with some excitement on the profits that might be made by taking an interest in this French venture.

A few days later, Washington and Peter went aboard the small steamboat, which was the pilot craft of the new company, to travel toward Paris by water. Washington made descriptive notes in his journal of the steamboat chugging past little villages where women in high caps watched the curious craft from the windows of their homes and men cheered and fired guns in its honor. He wrote of puffing past the towers of old churches, the ruins of abbeys, and past wooded hills or willowy banks as the river wound through the verdant countryside between the villages. Peter, however, could think of little except the possibilities of fortune represented by this modern mode of traveling.

And there it was—Washington had money now. If he did not have it all at hand, it was coming and he could draw on the brothers in New York against future profits on his book. He had it in his power to ease the future for Peter as William and Ebenezer had so long smoothed the way for him.

Arrived in Paris, he and Peter settled themselves in an apartment on a small hotel on the Rue du Mont-Thabor, not far from the expanses of the Place de la Concorde and the Rue de Rivoli. Washington at once sat down to write to William, in New York, to tell him about the French steamboat company, its expectations and the decision he and Peter had made to invest in it. He asked that he might count on William to honor a draft that he was going to make on him for two thousand dollars. Then, not entirely sure of William's response (he had been nervewrackingly silent for months after Washington refused the Navy post), he wrote a letter to Brevoort as well. "The purport of this letter is that you will use your exertions to prevent my brothers from disappointing us in this business. I do not doubt their good will; but they are apt to hang fire; and delay would completely frustrate the whole enterprize as far as we are concerned; as there are men of capital here extremely desirous of entering into the scheme. . . . Peter has now been living on hopes, and very feeble ones, for two or three years; it is pretty evident that they are not likely to strike out any thing for him in America; and now that he has struck out something for himself it behooves them to back him like two brothers."

He was right to fear that William and Ebenezer would show some reluctance to encourage the steamboat investment. Two months later, their response reached him in Paris. Bluntly, they went so far as to refuse to honor any drafts Washington might write upon them for investing in the project. All through the winter, the discouraging correspondence continued, with Washington determined to make the investment, for Peter's sake, and William and Ebenezer determined to protect their not-very-businesslike brothers from their own folly.

In the end, Washington had his way. His money, finally drawn on Brevoort, was invested in the steamboat company. But William and Ebenezer proved right in the years that followed. The French, not as speculative as Americans, might cheer the steamboat as it chugged up the Seine, but they were reluctant to support it. Ultimately, the Seine Steamboat Company would sink in failure and with it would be drowned Washington's investment.

But that was all in the future during the winter of 1820–1821. Once the letters to William, Ebenezer, and Brevoort were written, Washington gave little thought to the venture and let Peter handle the details of investment and management.

Washington had regained the good opinion of the world. He no longer was penniless, and he was in Paris, the city that had first charmed him fifteen years before by its beauty, the friendliness of its citizens, and the great gift it offered to everyone—"the perfect liberty of private conduct."

# 18

# Again Taking Pen in Hand

IN THE STORY of "A Royal Poet" in *The Sketch Book* Geoffrey Crayon described wandering through the salons and long-echoing galleries of Windsor Castle and of passing by with indifference whole rows of portraits of warriors and statesmen. But then he came to a chamber where "hang the likenesses of the beauties which graced the gay court of Charles the Second"; and as he gazed upon them, he blessed the pencil of Sir Peter Lely, who had so well depicted the ladies "with amorous, half-dishevelled tresses, and the sleepy eyes of love."

The phrases are not much on which to base the belief that somehow, somewhere, Irving had gazed into such sleepy eyes himself, but the words are almost too easy, too exact, to enable one to think he could have written just such lines if he had never experienced such lazy, satisfied dishevelment.

"She was a blooming lass of fresh eighteen; plump as a partridge; ripe and melting and rosy cheeked as one of her father's peaches. . . . She wore the ornaments of pure yellow gold, which her great-great-grandmother had brought over from Saardam; the tempting stomacher of the olden time;

and withal a provokingly short petticoat. . . ." That was Katrina Van Tassel in "The Legend of Sleepy Hollow."

Not much—but so directly, casually sensuous it seems impossible that it could have been written by a man who truly rejected the enticement of sex however his father had taught him that "everything pleasant was somehow wicked." There had been, as well, the rowdy sexual humor of *Knickerbocker's History*, the descriptions of bundling, whereby young people acquired "that intimate acquaintance with each other's good qualities before marriage, which has been pronounced by philosophers the sure basis of a happy union." There had been the sly account of the amatory feats of Anthony, the Trumpeter, who returned from a diplomatic mission to the Connecticut Yankees, "stopping occasionally in the villages to eat pumpkin-pies, dance at country frolics, and bundle with the Yankee lasses—whom he rejoiced exceedingly with his soul-stirring instrument."

Whatever evidence his published works give of a healthy interest in both the physical and humorous aspects of sex, Irving left no records of any sort of amorous dalliance through the winter of 1820–1821 in Paris. He entered no anecdotes about *filles de joie* in his journal. For once he did not even seem to have a particular female friend, like Maria Hoffman, Rebecca Gratz, or Jane Renwick, to whom he could pay innocent court while idealizing her charms. Nor was there any record of some young beauty with whom he could flirt.

He and Peter walked the boulevards, noting the changes that had come to Paris with the restoration of the monarchy and observing how many restless men there seemed to be, fiercely mustached, black cravated, and vaguely menacing in appearance, hanging about the cafés and other public places. They recognized these men as former soldiers of Napoleon's army, lost and displaced now that peace had come, vainly seeking for the sort of camaraderie they had known under arms.

They stopped in cafés for coffee, or looked in at various shops, and it seemed to them that a certain change had taken place in the French, or at least the Parisian, character. The good humor that had once marked the tone of the city had vanished. Waiters, salespeople, chance acquaintances seemed irritable, quick to fancy affronts. But Washington did not think it remarkable. Who could wonder if the French were a little rude to English visitors? Twice now, they had been subdued by English armies, and whatever they thought of Louis XVIII, how could they forget he had been restored to his throne by English might? Washington pondered on how the English might have reacted had the French army reinstated Charles II to his throne and then come piling into London to enjoy themselves. No, he thought, the wonder was how magnanimous the French were toward the hordes of English who were making themselves so at home in their capital.

With Peter, and various new acquaintances, he went to the theater and opera as he had always done. The talents of France's great tragedian, Talma, impressed him, and he was delighted with the music of a new composer, Rossini, who had charmed Paris with his opera, *The Barber of Seville*. The American ambassador in Paris called upon the Irvings, invited them to dinner, and introduced them to a number of people. Albert Gallatin, the financier and statesman, took an interest in them. Washington also met people in the front room of the publishing offices of Galagnani, where Americans and English alike gathered of a morning to look over the latest newspapers that were always available there. An English merchant, Thomas Wentworth Storrow, resident in Paris with his family, invited both Washington and Peter to his home, where Washington found the sort of family circle that was always appealing to him.

The pattern could very well have begun to repeat the one he had followed for so long in the United States after the success of *Knickerbocker's History*. The English and Americans in Paris all knew *The Sketch Book*. Plans were being made for a French translation of the work and a French edition of *Knickerbocker* as well. Washington was a celebrity of sorts and the invitations came in daily. He could have spent his days and evenings in walks, sighteeing junkets, teas, balls, dinners, or visits to the theater or opera.

But something had changed. Ten years previously, he would hardly have cared that Murray was anxious to have another work from him. He might have been pleased to hear that this difficult publisher was now so sure of Geoffrey Crayon's worth that he was putting out an English edition of *Knickerbocker*, with illustrations by Leslie, and even reaching so far back into the past as to publish an English edition of *Salmagundi*. Ten years before, Washington would not have felt this laid him under any obligation to do something new. But at last, so many years after he had first written on whim, he had committed himself. He had chosen to be a writer as opposed to something else that might have been more secure and less demanding.

What was he going to write next? Underneath the social distractions of Paris the question agitated him. He had worked *The Sketch Book* up out of fragments. He did not even have fragments now. He was still the wanderer, and the observer of this scene and that, but he wondered if he dared another miscellany.

He was at this point when he met Thomas Moore, the Irish poet and ballad singer, one evening when both were dining at the restaurant in Meurice's hotel. Washington had long been familiar with Moore's poems and admired them. He had been interested in Moore's preoccupation with Irish ballads, so much like Scott's concern with the songs of Scotland. But he had felt some reservations about the man ever since Moore had visited the United States in 1808. During the course of that visit Moore had attended a dinner at the White House and not only taken offense at some display of democratic manners by President Jefferson but made an outraged public comment on the episode. Washington and James Paulding had been provoked into some satirical remarks about the Irish visitor in *Salmagundi*, and a vague feeling of displeasure with Moore had lingered in Washington's mind.

Now, in a room full of the soothing aroma of good food and wine, the air humming with the talk of the diners at their various tables, he was introduced to a small man, much shorter than himself, with a cheerful, open face, eager to establish friendly relations. Before long, all Washington's reservations had vanished. Moore ruefully apologized for the long-ago outburst in America. He had spoken out of turn, he confessed, jumping to false conclusions. Soon he was also explaining the reason for his residence in Paris. Some years before, the English government had appointed him to a government post in Bermuda. After a short stay there, he had left a deputy in charge and returned to England to busy himself with his writing. Then news had come that the deputy had defaulted with a huge sum of money. Moore was faced with the alternative of repaying the money or going to prison for the debt. Successful as he had been with some of his writing, he could make only a partial restitution, and so he had fled England with his family to stay away until he could wipe out the whole sum.

It was a form of exile, Moore admitted, then smiled, adding that it was a pleasant one. A great many delightful people came and went in Paris at all seasons. He would see that Irving met those who were in town. He knew Irving would enjoy Sir Sidney Smith and the hospitable Villamils. Above all, he must get to know Lord John Russell. Moore and Lord John had returned only recently from a visit in Italy with Lord Byron.

Byron! The name was almost as magical to Irving as Scott's. He wanted to hear everything that Moore could tell him about that poet and Moore was happy to oblige, finally confessing that Byron had made him the custodian of his memoirs, which were not to be published while the poet lived. However, Moore promised that if Irving would like to read them he could.

After that evening, the friendship deepened rapidly. Moore and his pretty wife, Bessie, and their two children, lived in a cheerful little house on the Champs Elysées. Soon the house was almost as much a "home away from home" to Washington as the Storrows'. Moore was working each morning on a long poem that he had in progress. When Irving stopped by of an afternoon, both he and Moore would talk of their work and Irving was soon revealing his concern because he was not able to seize on a theme for a new book.

Moore reflected a moment and then began to talk about the Christmas pieces in *The Sketch Book* and their fine sense of atmosphere. Why not, he asked, take Bracebridge Hall as the setting for a whole book? The old hall and the characters already introduced in the essays in *The Sketch Book* might provide a framework for Irving to elaborate on various aspects of English country living.

The next day Washington was at his desk in the apartment on the Rue du Mont-Thabor. For ten days Moore did not see him. Then Irving appeared with a thick sheaf of manuscript, eager to read what he had written to Moore.

"A hundred and thirty pages in ten days?" Moore was incredulous. He considered himself fortunate when he could write ten lines of his poem in one day. Then he settled himself to hear the first chapters of *Bracebridge Hall*. Later, in his journal, Moore wrote that he wondered if what Irving was writing now would quite live up to the expectations that *The Sketch Book* had raised, but to Washington himself he spoke only congratulation and encouragement.

Caught up in his theme, a spring wedding at Bracebridge Hall, which allowed him to bring on stage a number of typical English characters and to write about a variety of country activities, from gypsy camps to poachers to fairs, Washington accomplished enough each morning so that he could enjoy a social life in the afternoon and evening with a free conscience.

The fabled Lady Auguste-Marie Holland, who presided over London's most popular and terrifying literary salon, appeared in Paris and Moore took Irving to meet her. Offering a quiet but smiling resistance to her sharp sallies, Irving pleased the autocratic lady sufficiently to be invited again and again. He met the young George Bancroft, who was hopeful of becoming a historian and who listened to Irving's comments on writing as to an oracle. Spring came on and he went with Moore to the countryside to help him look for a summer cottage for his family. He and Moore walked together in the Bois and ate cold dinners which Bessie prepared for them, and Moore walked up and down, declaiming passages from his poem.

Washington was surprised one day, but not unduly so, to run into his old friend, John Howard Payne, on the street. An element of the unexpected had been part of Payne's character ever since Washington had first known him when Payne was a boy wonder of the New York theater in 1806 and 1807. Even before that, while Washington was in Europe on his first tour, the thirteen-year-old Payne had startled the city by writing and publishing a creditable theatrical news magazine. Tiring of that venture, he had written a play which had been produced at the Park Theater to mixed reactions. Many in the audience felt the work was entirely too worldly for a fourteen-year-old to have created. Payne had been downcast by the criticism only briefly and soon had won himself a starring role in an established production. It was at this point that Washington, returned from Europe, had been introduced to the precocious and handsome youth by Henry Brevoort. Irving then joined Brevoort in taking a brotherly interest in the lad's fortunes, counseling him against letting his head be turned by the applause he received not only in New York but on tour in Boston, Philadelphia, Baltimore, and Richmond. But counsel to young Payne, though gratefully received, never had any lasting effect. The youth remained an extravagant mixture of self-confidence, impetuosity, and humility. Finally, in 1811, he had managed to embroil himself in so many difficulties with managers, producers, and other actors that he had left America to try his luck on the English stage.

Washington had not lost track of him through the years that followed. He had heard of Payne's initial success in the London theater and had, while in London himself in 1815 and 1816, seen him perform and then met him after the performances for supper. Ultimately, however, Payne had been no more able to stay out of difficulties in England than in America. Plumper than he had been, which also was an obstacle to acting engagements, he had turned to managing small productions outside of London. For one summer he had presided over the theatrical productions at Sadler's Wells Theater, then an adjunct of an amusement park. Managing, directing, even on occasion writing the plays, Payne had kept the little theater filled. Then, somehow, in spite of every appearance of success, he was bankrupt at the end of the season and in jail for debt. Languishing in his cell, he had been struck by an inspiration for a play. Payne had written the play, and placed it, through obliging go-betweens. He was out of jail, and his play was successfully produced. And then he was in debt again and fleeing England to escape another term in jail.

Now here he was in Paris, as full of bubbling optimism as ever. He took Irving to the lodgings where he had established

himself, a suite of sunny rooms filled with canary birds singing madly. Brushing aside the subject of his insolvency, he
talked eagerly to Irving of the projects which were going to
restore his fortunes. His chief aim, while in Paris, was searching out French plays suitable for English production. These
he would translate and adapt. He was also working on an
original script. Then, veering to another subject, he asked if
Irving knew that Talma, the great tragedian, was a good
friend of his and had given him the freedom of the Théâtre
Nationale? Come, Payne insisted, he and Irving would go to
visit Talma in his apartments right now. Irving protested that
an appointment might be in order, but Payne was not to be
resisted. Irving met Talma that afternoon and had a pleasant
conversation with him about the theater and about Paris in
the days of Napoleon.

Later, Washington found it equally impossible to resist
Payne when he asked humbly for a small loan to tide him
over until some expected funds came in. Nor was Washington able to say no when Payne begged for his advice and help
on the original play he was writing, a work rather aptly titled
*The Borrowers*. Familiar as he was with the theater, Washington was not sure that he had any instinct about writing
for it. Still he took Payne's play with him, when he returned
to the apartment on Rue du Mont-Thabor, to study it after
he laid aside the day's stint on *Bracebridge Hall*.

With the coming of summer, Thomas Moore and Bessie
moved with their children to the cottage they had rented in
Passy. Peter, still hopefully concerned with the activities of
the Seine Steamboat Company, departed for Havre to be near
the headquarters of the business.

Early in July, Washington also prepared to leave Paris. An
immediate excuse for returning to London was his desire to
be present for the coronation of George IV, the dissolute
prince whose long regency had spanned most of the years

during which Irving had known London. Washington wanted
to see the ritual and pageantry of a coronation. He was eager
to see his artist friends, Leslie and Newton, and there was, as
well, a chance of meeting Scott during the festivities. Besides,
he had by now promised Payne that he would try to place
his play, *The Borrowers*, with some producer in London,
Payne being unable to visit London himself for the purpose. And as always in England, there were Sally and her
welcoming family at the Castle Van Tromp in Birmingham.
Perhaps there, in that sheltering atmosphere where he had
written "Rip Van Winkle" almost overnight, he could finish
*Bracebridge Hall.*

The night before his departure he attended a dinner party
given by Lord and Lady Holland. A strange note was struck
after dinner when the actor, Talma, arrived to announce the
news of Napoleon's death on the island of his exile, St.
Helena. Washington saw a certain irony in the death of the
"captured eagle" so near the date of the coronation of the
weak, licentious man to whom Napoleon had pled for his life
a few years before.

The next morning he was on his way to Havre for a visit
with Peter, after which he would take off for England. A
committed writer, with a half-completed manuscript in his
luggage, he was looking for a few distractions perhaps, but
most of all, a quiet place and time to complete *Bracebridge
Hall,* and he was not without some nervousness about the
project. As he would later observe in his preface for the
book, "on again taking pen in hand," he could not but be
sensible of special circumstances. Some of the success of *The
Sketch Book* had come about because it was "a matter of
marvel, to my European readers, that a man from the wilds
of America should express himself in tolerable English." Such
novelty, he knew, was at an end. This time, "taking pen in
hand," he must expect much sterner criticisms.

# 19

# Strange Tenant

PEOPLE WHO thought of themselves as "true Americans" were growing prouder and touchier all the time. Or so it seemed to Henry Brevoort. In New York, in South Carolina, his wife's home where they spent their winters, and in every city, hamlet, or countryside through which their journeyings north and south took them, he seemed to sense a more jealous and aggressive patriotism than ever before. Remembering the days when he and Washington and the other Lads of Kilkenny had listened to the cannonading across the river that celebrated the Fourth of July and rolled with mocking laughter on the lawn of Cockloft Hall, he thought there had been a sort of childish innocence about those earlier displays of patriotism that was vanished now.

Being an American had become a serious business. Suspicion fell on any man or woman who did not so regard it. Look, the true American seemed forever saying, for thirty years and more the republic has not only endured but prospered. Look, we challenged England a second time, didn't we, and if we didn't win all we set out for, we taught John Bull a little respect. Look at the money panics we have survived, look at Florida, wrested from Spain, and look at the roads and canals stretching out in every direction. Pride in it all was supposed to suffuse every native breast. And whatever success or good fortune any individual knew it was expected that he credit it to the inestimable boon of being a "freeborn American."

Brevoort had seen how this pride in everything American had warmed readers in the United States to Washington's *Sketch Book*. How wonderful that an American had at last written a book that was entertaining and affecting to read, beautifully styled, and with all that, lavishly praised in England as well. Brevoort realized that this recognition, so rare for any American work, was really the one which filled hearts to bursting, for it was recognition on a scale quite above British submission to American marksmen.

But as month followed month and America's prize author did not return to his home country and make the announcement that he owed his success to being a "freeborn American," a certain dissatisfaction was beginning to manifest itself. Over and over, Brevoort heard the edgy questions. Why was it that Washington Irving did not come home? Had he grown too fine for his own country? Did the praise he got in England and other foreign parts seem sweeter to him than anything his own countrymen could say?

Washington was still in Paris when Brevoort became enough concerned about the questioning to write to his friend about it. He felt Washington should know his readers' mood, and besides he missed his friend and wondered about his plans. When did he intend to take up a fixed residence and finally, like Brevoort, Paulding, Renwick, and the other companions of his youth, find a wife and raise a family?

The letter had shaken Washington. Once again, as when he had rejected William's offer of the Navy post, he had to justify his wandering course and it was not easy. He had no skill in analyzing himself and no ability to say that perhaps it was only in a wandering course, maintaining a role of detached observer, that he was able to write as he did. Instead, he tried to defend himself as an American.

"You urged me to return to New York; and say, many ask whether I mean to renounce my country. For this last question I have no reply to make, and yet I will make a reply. As far as my precarious and imperfect abilities enable me, I am endeavoring to serve my country. Whatever I have written has been written with the feelings and published as the writing of an American. Is that renouncing my country? How else am I to serve my country? by coming home and begging an office of it? . . ."

He grew almost angry as he continued his defense. "As to the idea you hold out of being provided for *sooner or later* in our *fortunate* city, I can only say that I see no way in which I could be provided for, not being a man of business, a man of science, or, in fact, any thing but a mere belles-lettres writer. And as to the fortunate character of our city; to me and mine it has been a very disastrous one. . . ."

Then he wanted no more of the subject. Somehow, even thinking of America "discomposed" his feelings and revived "many distressing circumstances and trains of thought." He shut them out and held fast to his need to labor on the "various literary materials" which he had on hand and which he needed to "work up" among the scenes where they had been envisioned. He lightened the tone of his letter and wrote of his friendship with "Anacreon" Moore, "a charming, joyous fellow! full of frank, generous manly feelings. . . ." And also of his meetings with George Canning, the British statesman, who had been "very polite in his attentions."

After that he traveled to London, and with Leslie and Newton found a place outside Westminster Abbey from which to watch the coronation—a dazzling display in which even George IV looked splendid thanks to his ermine robes and other rich trappings. The next day Irving called upon Sir

Walter Scott and found him as warmly friendly as ever, but the two could make no plans for a further meeting since Sir Walter was engaged "up to the hub" for his few days in London.

Soon thereafter a sort of gloom fell upon Washington, and he wondered why he had come to England to finish his manuscript. London was "terribly dull and monotonous" after Paris. But he had to linger there, waiting to receive Payne's play, which the erratic young man had kept at the last moment of Irving's departure from Paris to make some more revisions. Washington "fagged hard" at his writing every morning, read aloud what he had written to Leslie and Newton in the afternoon, and then dined with them. Payne's play arrived and Washington had a number of interviews with producers, all of which proved fruitless. Finally, he and Leslie left London together to visit Washington's family in Birmingham.

The trip across England in late summer revived his spirits for a while. Leslie sketched and Washington found an idea for a humorous tale to include in *Bracebridge Hall* which he called "The Stout Gentleman." They lingered at such familiar spots at Stratford-on-Avon, Warwick, and Kenilworth before they arrived to a tumultuous welcome at Castle Van Tromp.

Very soon after arriving in Birmingham, Washington's health began to trouble him. He suffered "bilious attacks," he wrote Ebenezer, "to which I had never before been subject." He had a curious swelling of his ankles which caused him pain in walking. Diagnosing his own case, he decided that he had been too much within doors and not taking exercise enough. It did not occur to him that anxiety might be playing any role in his difficulties. Struggling each day to carry *Bracebridge Hall* nearer to completion, secretly fretting about the "sterner criticism" this new book was sure to face, now that the novelty of an American writing decent English had worn off, he might well have had some "bilious attacks."

The news from home did not cheer him. Sister Catherine had lost her oldest daughter two years before. In November of 1821, Ebenezer wrote that Catherine's second daughter had died suddenly. She had left to her only one child, the eight-year-old Sarah. Washington tried to express his shock and dismay. "The calamities in poor sister Catherine's family are dreadful. She has had her cup of bitterness filled to the brim, and I fear will suffer seriously in health by these repeated trials. . . . It is the after-sorrow that preys upon and undermines the health."

More terrible than the news about Catherine's daughter was the report on William's health. Washington had heard a year or so before that William was not well. Then letters had taken an optimistic tone. Now they were suddenly, gravely, preparing the family in England for the worst. William had consumption. The disease was progressing rapidly.

"Brother William's situation, I perceive, is hopeless," Washington wrote. "I had been persuading myself that there was a reaction in his system, and that he might be induced to make a voyage to France in time to produce a complete renovation; but the tenor of all the letters from New York puts an end to all hopes of the kind. I cannot reconcile myself to the thought. . . ."

William, the brother who more than any other had been like a father to him, was dying. He would not see him again.

"Give my most affectionate remembrances to Brother William," Washington wrote. "I would write to him, but cannot trust my feelings, whenever the thought of him comes over my mind, I feel my heart and eyes overflow."

Washington's bilious attacks did not abate. The pain and inflammation in his ankles grew so severe that he could hardly walk.

The letter bearing the final news came in December. William had died November 8, 1821. He had been "clear and collected to the last, and departed with the composure of a virtuous man to whom death had no terrors."

The family in Birmingham had been expecting the news. Still, for Washington, "It was one of the dismallest blows that I have ever experienced."

The Van Warts spent a very quiet Christmas that year. The next day, Washington, still ailing and barely able to walk, took the coach to London. An American acquaintance from Baltimore was currently living in the city and had given Irving many invitations to be his guest. This time Irving accepted the offer and was soon installed in the comfort of a luxurious London house on Hanover Square. Quiet surrounded him, fires glowed in the fireplace, his meals were brought on trays. He had nothing to concern him but finishing *Bracebridge Hall*.

Three weeks of steady work in such surroundings and he was ready by the end of January, 1822, to pack up the manuscript for the first volume of *Bracebridge Hall, or The Humourists, A Medley in two volumes*.

"I had hoped to have sent both volumes," he wrote Ebenezer, "but I have not been able to get the second volume ready in time. . . . You will receive it, however, by the very next opportunity, and very probably before you can have made the necessary arrangements for printing. At any rate put the first volume to press *immediately* and publish it *as soon as possible* with or without the second volume. . . . it is of the greatest importance that some part of the work should appear as early as possible to give me some chance of securing copyright. I shall have to put it to press here in a very short time, as the season is advancing, and my publisher is very impatient." He further asked that the work be put up in lettered covers like *The Sketch Book* and that Moses Thomas be given preference as publisher. The manuscript was not paged and he apologized, but "I have fagged until the last moment and am now fit to go to bed. My health is still unrestored."

Ill as he felt, he managed to send off the material for the second volume by the end of February, at which point he felt safe enough to offer the complete work to Murray for publication in England.

Limping and leaning on a cane, he made the excursion from his sheltered haven to Murray's offices. Leslie and Newton had stuffed him with advice that he should ask his own price from Murray for this new work, especially since another publisher had already shown interest in it. Accordingly, when Murray asked what he wished as an advance, Washington straightened his shoulders and asked for 1,500 guineas. He saw at once that Murray was startled.

"If you had asked for a thousand guineas," Murray began.

Washington was incapable of bargaining. "You shall have it for a thousand," he said quickly. Murray seized the offer and immediately prepared the notes for the payment of the advance, though Washington was not going to deliver the manuscript for a week or so.

One other matter was on Washington's mind. An American named James Fenimore Cooper had recently written a novel, *The Spy*, which was delighting American readers. Cooper's American publisher had sent a copy to Murray and suggested that if he were interested in publishing it in England he might discuss the terms with Washington Irving. Irving did not know Cooper but he had admired the novel, which the publisher had sent to him with an explanatory letter, and he was eager as always to give help abroad to any of his countrymen however he could. He asked Murray if he had made a decision in regard to *The Spy*, but Murray admitted he had not read it as yet. Washington could only speak of his own faith in the book, hope that Murray would consider it favorably, and take his leave.

Word came from Peter that the steamboat company was

not living up to expectations so far as revenue was concerned. This was disappointing but was balanced by his contract with Murray for a thousand guineas, "a sum that whatever anyone said did have 'a golden sound.'" He wrote to Peter enclosing two hundred pounds. "I beg you won't be squeamish about the thing. If you don't want the money, it may as well lie idle in your hands as mine; and if you do want it, why you must get it from some source or other, and I don't know any one more unexceptionable than from one who has been a great part of his life under such pecuniary obligations to you."

Perhaps relief at having a contract with Murray had something to do with an improvement in his health. He made many changes and improvements in the English copy for *Bracebridge Hall,* and by mid-March the manuscript was at the printers and soon thereafter proof sheets were arriving on which Irving could make further corrections and alterations.

Irving was pleasantly surprised when "Anacreon" Moore arrived in London. Moore had rescued himself from his financial exile by what seemed to him a great coup. He had sold to Murray the memoirs of Lord Byron with which he had been entrusted by the poet on condition that Murray abide by the same agreement he had made. The memoirs were not to be published during Byron's lifetime. Murray had paid two thousand pounds for this long-term investment, and with the two thousand pounds Moore had paid off his debt to the English government. Able to move about freely in London at last, Moore began involving Irving in his daily rounds of walks, calls, and dinners.

Washington dined with Moore at Holland House, the regal London residence of Lord and Lady Holland, and stiffened himself once more against the challenges and commands of Lady Holland. The evenings there had a dream-like quality as he moved, with the other guests, through the paneled rooms and halls, the many-coursed meals, the wines with the gentlemen, and later, the coffee with the ladies. Other days, he "walked about" with Moore and with him called on Lady Blessington and other of Moore's friends.

In May, *Bracebridge Hall* appeared in the bookstores in both America and England and began to sell nicely in both countries. The praise for it was not quite as great as the praise had been for *The Sketch Book*, but Washington's fear of a "sterner criticism" was not really justified. *Bracebridge Hall*, by its very focus on life at one country seat, was not as various, as alternately melancholy or robustly humorous as *The Sketch Book*. Maria Edgeworth, the popular lady novelist and a skilled depicter of English and Irish country life herself, commented that "The fault of the book is that the workmanship surpasses the work. There is too much care and cost depicted on petty objects." *Blackwood's Magazine*'s review expressed the opinion that "*Bracebridge Hall* certainly does not possess the spirit of the *Sketch Book* . . ." But these, and others like them, were minor reservations. For most critics, and readers as well, the book had the same charm as *The Sketch Book*, what Francis Jeffrey, who usually wrote in acid ink, called a "singular sweetness of composition."

"It seems to give satisfaction here," Irving wrote to Brevoort, "and I am nearly killed with kindness. . . . Within these two months past I have given myself up to society more than I have at any time since I have been in Europe, having for the last four or five years been very much shut up and at home. I was determined to give myself a holiday, and make use of the opportunity presented me of seeing fashionable life."

Fashionable life in the spring of 1822, took him "the rounds of routs, dinners, operas, balls and blue-stocking coteries." He met Englishmen and women of fame and importance and he met visiting Americans of importance also, among them John Randolph, the Virginian from Roanoke, who had been left beardless and soprano-voiced from some curious disease but dared anyone to challenge or pity him. Randolph attracted much attention in London, Washington wrote Brevoort, "his eccentricity of appearance and manner makes him the more current and interesting, for in high life here, they are always eager after anything strange and peculiar."

An invitation to dine at Wimbledon with Lord and Lady Spencer came in June. They were the parents of young Lady Lyttleton, who had entered into a brief correspondence with the American Ambassador to London, Richard Rush, two years before, in connection with the speculation as to who was the author of *The Sketch Book*. Lady Lyttleton had delighted in the book and then heard that it was the work of Sir Walter Scott, and she begged Rush to let her know if that were so or if it really was the work of one of his countrymen. Rush had forwarded the letter to Irving who had responded with gratitude for the flattering remarks but begged Rush to tell Lady Lyttleton that "it was written entirely by myself. . . . I speak fully to this point, not from any anxiety of authorship, but because the doubts which her ladyship has heard on the subject seem to have risen from the old notion that it is impossible for an *American to write decent English*. If I have indeed been fortunate enough to do anything, however trifling, to stagger this prejudice, I am too good a patriot to give up even the little ground I have gained."

A consequence of this letter had been an invitation from Lady Lyttleton's parents, Lord and Lady Spencer, to spend Christmas of 1820 with them, but Irving had been in Paris at that time. The invitation in June, 1822, two years later, was a reiteration of their desire to know him. So one June afternoon Irving traveled to their splendid country house, about twelve miles out of London. At the dinner that evening, he met, among others, Samuel Rogers, the pale, balding banker, poet and aesthete, who more than any other man was the autocrat of British literary criticism. Irving, who still presented himself shyly in company, found it reassuring to be greeted by Rogers as though he were an old friend. When Irving spoke during the evening of the number of invitations he received these days, Rogers immediately took on the role of advisor. "Show me your list of invitations," he said, "and let me give you a hint or two."

Just how it was that Irving had such a list on him at the moment is hard to know, but according to his later account, he showed the inventory to Rogers. Pursing his lips, Rogers glanced from name to name. "Accept this one," he said tersely. "Decline this one." And then, at another, "This man avoid by all means; oh! he's a direful bore."

Invitations from Rogers himself were so sought after that Washington felt honored when he was given one of the coveted bids to breakfast at Rogers' elegant little mansion on St. James's Place a few days later. On the appointed day he presented himself on the marble steps. As he was ushered into the perfect hall and thence through the drawing room to the breakfast room, he knew himself surrounded by excellence on every hand. The walls, covered with crimson damask, were hung with paintings by Titian, Raphael, and Giorgione. The bookcases, painted with scenes from the works of Boccaccio, Chaucer, and Shakespeare, were filled with richly bound volumes and what were obviously rare editions. Conversation at the breakfast table was expected to match the same standard of excellence. Epigrams and aphorisms studded the discussion of any subject that was surveyed. Washington, who had once been able to stand off the punsters of Philadelphia with his rejoinders, had grown quieter in the years since then. But with Rogers accepting him and encouraging him, with everyone looking upon him as a fair sort of wonder at best, "an American who could write decent English," he did not do badly in his responses. He had always been skilled in the use of the unexpected adverb or verb. He would never lose his ability to cap an anecdote with a wry or unexpected ending. He did well enough to be asked back again and again to Rogers' breakfasts.

"To be pleased" had been his motto once. "To please in return" was its logical corollary. In late June he was spending a few days at a country house in Sussex. Writing to sister Catherine, he described his host and hostess: "Mr. Thomas Hope, one of the richest and most extraordinary men in England, not more famous for his wealth and magnificence than for being the Author of Anastasius, a work of great merit and curious character. His wife, the Hon. Mrs. Hope, is one of the loveliest women in the kingdom, and one of the reigning deities of fashion. Their country seat is furnished in a style of taste and magnificence of which I can give you no idea. With all this, they are delightfully frank, simple and unpretending in their manners, especially in their country retreat; which is the true place to see English people to advantage."

Green lawns sloping away to the park where the deer could be seen of mornings, gardens filled with summer flowers and statuary—the long, cool corridors of the house leading to rooms appointed with all the graces that taste and money could buy—other guests, casually ready for rambles through the grounds or for idle conversation on the terrace or in the library—with such companions and in such surroundings, he was indeed seeing "English people to advantage."

When his visit came to an end, his host, Mr. Hope, asked him to write something in the Guest Album. Irving was inspired to one of his rare excursions into verse. He had had a delightful time, almost forgetting the trouble with his ankles. The richness of an English summer was a fragrance that permeated everything. Somehow, the transient loveliness he had enjoyed brought forth the truest poetry he was ever to write.

The first two verses were ordinary enough, praising the "fairy shrine," where "worth and loveliness combine." Only in the third and fourth stanzas did he express, almost accidentally, something of his truest self.

> Go plough the wave, and sow the sand;
> Throw seed to every wind that blows;
> Along the highway strew thy hand
> And fatten on the crop that grows.
>
> For even thus the man that roams
> On heedless hearts his feeling spends;
> Strange tenant of a thousand homes,
> And friendless, with ten thousand friends!

Two more stanzas completed his gratitude for "a resting-place," which a "wayworn heart had fondly sought." He signed the entry, Washington Irving, and dated it June 24, 1822.

"Strange tenant of a thousand homes—" had the fate found him or had he sought it out for himself?

Back in London, he continued to accept most of the invitations that arrived. "I have been leading a sad life lately," he wrote Peter, ". . . tossed about 'hither and thither and whither I would not'; have been at the levee and the drawing-room, been at routs, and balls and dinners, and country-seats; been hand-in-glove with nobility and mobility, until like Trim I have satisfied the sentiment, and am now preparing to make my escape from all this splendid confusion."

He was, more exactly, now that *Bracebridge Hall* was launched and doing well, on his way to the continent, to take the baths at Aix-la-Chapelle, in the hope that those waters might cure the misery in his ankles, then planning a short tour through Germany, after which he thought he might spend the winter in Paris.

# 20

# An Intoxication of the Heart

A CURIOUS KIND of romance began to surround this particular journey soon after its beginning. The atmosphere of enchantment deepened as Irving traveled, so that when he had reached the farthest point in his wanderings and halted he was hardly surprised to find himself in the midst of a small mystery. How should he wonder or be surprised? It was all part of a spell that seemed to take him back into the past—a world of ancient castles and costumes and manners—and then, at the heart of it, love.

His physical afflictions bothered him considerably during the first weeks of his travels. But in spite of the pain in his legs and the uneasiness of his digestion, he began noting his surroundings with revived interest from the moment of his arrival in Amsterdam. "My chamber," he wrote in his journal, "one of those high old Dutch rooms with long windows that might serve for a church, looking out upon a narrow street of tall houses, with queer faces at every window. The room has an overhanging chimney with stove under it. Arcadian scene, shepherd in silk breeches on the wall."

At Aix-la-Chapelle, his complaints were not much relieved

by the baths, which were rigorous and tiring. But the old city, seat of Charlemagne's capital, had some fascination. The hotel in which he was staying was not far from the cathedral where Charlemagne was buried under a slab of black marble. Every night he could hear the hours chimed on its bells, and at eleven, twelve, and one o'clock, the watchman on the tower of the cathedral blew as many blasts on a horn as there were strokes of the clock. The sound of those warning notes in the stillness of the night gave Irving an "extremely solemn feeling." But as the baths continued to do him no good and as it seemed to him the town was crowded with a rough and motley type of visitor, he determined to travel eastward into the Rhineland to the more fashionable spa of Wiesbaden.

How odd that just at this moment, a figure from the past should suddenly appear at Aix. None other than the jaunty Thomas Brandram, who had been one of the fellow passengers on the long-ago trip up the Hudson with Judge and Mrs. Hoffman and Ann and the Ogdens—Brandram, who had contributed to the merriment of that journey with the watchwords "luxury and dissipation." Irving and Brandram greeted each other with the pleasure that wanderers in strange places always feel, fell into reminiscence over dinner together, and agreed that it was part of the happy chance of their meeting that Brandram was traveling to Wiesbaden in his own carriage and would much enjoy Irving's company.

"Away then we rolled," Washington wrote to Peter. "He had a charming light open carriage in which I could loll at full length. . . . Though too lame to explore the curious old towns and the romantic ruins which we passed, yet I lolled in the carriage, and banquetted on fine scenery in Brevoort's favorite style."

Wiesbaden was indeed more fashionable than Aix had been. There were fine public walks and a beautiful public garden not far from the hotel where Washington settled.

After Brandram had traveled on, Washington limped to the garden and spent most of his day there. He grew more and more pleased with the Germans whom he saw, "a frank, kind well-meaning people." The daily schedule observed by the health-seekers was strict and primitive, but it seemed to do Irving good. Most hotel guests were up at six, bathing and having breakfast in their rooms. Dinner was served at one o'clock in the grand saloon. After that, there were the preparations for the promenade, theater, ball, concert, or whatever the entertainment of the evening might be. Supper was served about eight o'clock, and most good people went to bed by ten o'clock. Improving under this regime and his daily baths, Washington began taking drives about the neighborhood to admire the views across the fertile Rhine Valley. Soon, however, he was restlessly thinking that the waters at Mayence, still further south along the Rhine, might be even more therapeutic.

Before long he was in Mayence, "a battered old warrior town," but, like Wiesbaden, set in a scene of loveliness. From "a bridge of boats which crosses the river in front of the town, there is a beautiful view down the Rheingau . . . while along the opposite side of the river lie the warm sunny hills which produce the finest Rhine grapes." He took a river excursion to Coblenz and was, to a degree, transported home, but with a difference. "Fancy," he wrote to sister Sally, "some of the finest parts of the Hudson embellished with old towns, castles and convents, and seen under the loveliest weather, and you may have some idea of the magnificence and beauty of the Rhine."

At the hotel in Mayence he became friendly with the innkeeper and whiled away some of his time by taking French and German lessons from one of his daughters, "la belle Katrina." He was still suffering pain in his ankles but he was taking notes seriously on the landscape and characters around him, so evocative of home and yet so overlaid with a sense of the past that home did not have. A strange, new feeling of obligation began to concern him. "I feel the value of life and health now in a degree that I never did before," he wrote Sally. "I have always looked upon myself as a useless being, whose existence was of little moment. I now think, if I live and enjoy my health, I may be of some use to those who are most dear to me."

After a week or so in Mayence, he struck up an acquaintance with a young English officer of the dragoons, Captain Wemyss. Wemyss was planning to travel through Germany toward Vienna and invited Irving to accompany him. Irving accepted at once, eager to travel deeper into this country that seemed to mirror his most romantic dreams.

Frankfort, "bustling and thriving," held them for a few days and then they turned southward toward Heidelberg. "Our road lay along the foot of the mountains of the Odenwald, with vineyards about their skirts, and their summits covered by crests, from which every now and then peeped out the crumbling towers of some old castle, famous in German song and story; to our right spread out a rich plain . . . with a faint line of blue hills marking the course of the distant Rhine. . . . Men, women and children were busy in the vineyards on the side of the hills; the road was alive with peasants laden with baskets of fruit, or tubs in which the grapes were pressed. . . . We bought clusters of delicious grapes for almost nothing as we travelled along, and I drank of the newly pressed wine, which has the sweetness of cider."

Traveling through such bucolic serenity, Irving began to feel stronger. "I do not know whether it is the peculiar fineness of the season, or the general character of the climate, but I never was more sensible to the delicious effect of the atmosphere," he wrote Sally, "perhaps my very malady has made me more susceptible to influences of the kind. I feel a kind of intoxication of the heart, as I draw in the pure air of the mountains; and the clear, transparent atmosphere, the steady, serene, golden sunshine, seems to enter into my very soul."

By the time he and Captain Wemyss had spent several days in Heidelberg under the shadow of its famous castle, he was able to take walks in the hills and scramble about the ruins of other old castles in the neighborhood. And his journal was growing fat with descriptions of landscapes, odd characters, and scraps of legend that he heard in the inns of an evening.

Their route led next to the little duchy of Baden, and it was part of the charm of Germany to Irving that it was no unified nation like England or France, but a patchwork of principalities, each with its own flavor, each ruled over by some potentate who seemed "to have all the sweets of sovereignty without its cares and troubles."

The city of Baden was "one of the most romantically situated watering places" Irving had ever seen. Its ruined castle had mysterious, subterranean apartments "that equalled the fabrications of novelists." In these chambers "the secret tribunal held its sittings . . . its victims were confined, tortured and executed. . . . Its members all sworn to secrecy; all forbidden to make known their being members; and all sworn by the most imposing oaths to inflict the punishment decreed by the tribunal, without regard to any tie of kindred or affection." But such cruelty and bloodthirst were in the past and brought no shudders to Irving.

From damp, underground passages the travelers came out to the sunshine of the road, again to ride past "wagons bearing great pipes of new wine, with branches of flowers and streams of ribbons stuck in the bung."

Turning east from Strasbourg, a gay city that seemed to beckon them back to France, their road led up the narrow valley of the Kenseg into the Black Forest. "Partial moonlight now and then breaking from among the clouds" illuminated their way as they rode through the night to reach an inn where they stopped and entered "a great public room, wainscotted with wood, blackened by smoke, in which were waggoners and rustic travellers, supping and smoking; a huge, rambling staircase led up to a number of old-fashioned wainscotted apartments."

Through the principality of Hohenzollern to Ulm and thence still farther east to Munich they traveled. Munich was "a charming little capital" where they arrived in time for a fete in honor of the King's birthday, and a view of Napoleon's stepson, Eugene Beauharnois. But Irving did not forget that Munich was the city where Mozart had composed several of his best operas.

As the way led farther east across Austria to Salzburg, Irving spent every evening making notes. "These mountain regions are full of fable and elfin story," he wrote to Sally in Birmingham, "and I had some wonderful tales told me which I shall keep in mind against I have another match at story-telling with the children. There is one great mountain that towers into the clouds close by Salzburg, which is called the Untersberg, which the common people believe to be quite hollow, with churches and palaces inside; where the Emperor Charles V. and all his army remain spellbound."

Vienna, capital of Austria, was a shock after the medieval towns and the countryside with its gothic ruins and legends. Here were immense palaces in the new classic mode, art galleries, theaters, and a great, cosmopolitan mingling of people, dressed in French, English, and even Oriental fashion. Washington attended the theaters, visited the galleries, and went to the libraries where no one had heard as yet of any writer named Washington Irving. But it was not being unknown that made him weary of Vienna. He saw it as a city devoted to "sensual gratification," with none of those quiet charms that he had seen in so many German cities. Neither did it seem a place where he could settle down to sort out the notes in his journal and begin on some new book. A letter from Moore in Paris reminded him of his original plan to winter there, but meantime he had heard pleasant things about Dresden, the capital of Saxony, which was reported to be a city of "taste, intellect, and literary feeling," as well as a good place to perfect a knowledge of German. Suddenly, Washington decided not to return to Paris but to make Dresden his headquarters for the winter.

Wemyss did not want to travel so far north as Dresden so late in the season and elected to remain in Vienna. Washington inquired here and there as to other travelers who might be going toward Dresden, but hearing of none, he decided to make the journey northward alone.

An odd incident occurred shortly before he left Vienna. A thick letter was delivered to him and on opening it he saw at once that it was not meant for him but had miscarried in the post. He read it, puzzling over the unknown handwriting, and hoping for some clues as to who the sender might have been, or the addressee. It was a long letter, closely written, with much domestic news. At last he came to some comments about books which the writer had been reading. *The Sketch Book* was mentioned. With a sensation of eavesdropping, Irving read the praise that the writer had for the book and then was launched onto a long quotation from one of his sketches. At the end of the quoted passage, the letter writer had carefully added the author's name in full, "Washington Irving." This had been encircled by some official blue pencil and the mystery of why he had received the letter was solved. The address on the outer part of the letter had been blurred. Some postal authority had read the name Washington Irving and so the letter had been routed to him.

Washington smiled as that much of the mystery unraveled

itself and read again the words of commendation for his writing. Here there was no intent to flatter or please the author, but gratuitous appreciation. Touched, he read the letter yet again, working at the rest of the mystery. The letter writer was obviously a woman, a mother, in Europe somewhere with some of her children, where they were pursuing their education, while an older daughter remained at home—in England, it seemed quite clear. But where in Europe was this woman who had so enjoyed *The Sketch Book?*

Somewhere in the letter was there a hint that her current residence was Dresden? Somewhere in the letter was there a mention of the surname Foster? Irving never explained away the details of the mystery later. He preferred mysteries which were only half-explained and best of all liked mysteries that ended in laughter.

He put the letter with his papers, not knowing whether he would ever learn anything more about the writer than he already knew, but wondering a little. Then he started off on his journey, by way of Prague, to the capital of Saxony, Dresden.

# 21

# Emily

"FOSTER?" Irving repeated the name almost incredulously to his companion at the theater that evening and then turned to gaze again at the occupants of one of the boxes. In the pale and silvery blaze of the candles of the great chandelier, he saw three women, their faces and figures highlighted by the glow of the lamps in their box. One, slim and attractive, was obviously the more mature of the group. The other two were very young, girls who had only recently been wearing their hair high and their necklines low. A mother and her daughters, perhaps?

Yes, said Irving's companion, Colonel Barham Livius, whom he had met shortly after his arrival in Dresden. The lady was Mrs. John Foster, the girls were her daughters, Emily and Flora, and they were by way of being relatives of the Colonel's, some sort of cousins, he said. He apologized for not having introduced Irving to them before.

Irving brushed that aside to ask if the family was from England and if there were two younger boys and a daughter at home named Margaret.

Livius looked at his new friend with surprise, and then admitted that all of that was so, though Margaret actually was Mrs. Foster's stepdaughter, Mrs. Foster being the third wife of Mr. John Foster. Then his bewilderment could not be denied. How did Irving know these details about the Fosters?

Irving smiled, said he would explain later and asked that he might be introduced to the Fosters at the next intermission. A wave of disbelief ran through him and a surge of laughter such as he had not known in years, perhaps not since the days of *Salmagundi*, when half of New York was puzzling over the identity of the authors, and he had solemnly joined in the speculation.

He had been pleased by Dresden from the moment of his arrival, reacting to the city's special charm, a kind of formality mixed with coziness. Around the squares the public buildings presented their clean, classic façades, and yet everywhere along the streets a merry mood seemed to emanate from the citizens as they moved about on their errands. He had found an apartment available very cheaply in the Hotel du Saxe, looking out on one of the main squares. He had discovered that he already knew someone in the city—John Philip Morier, who had been with the British Legation in Washington, D.C., when Irving was a familiar of that city, and now was with the British Legation in Dresden. Morier had introduced him to other members of the English colony, including Colonel Livius, and it had been gratifying to discover that his name and writings were well known in this provincial capital. He was glad also to learn that the old king, Frederick, was indeed a patron of the arts. The well-known composer, Karl Maria von Weber, was musician in residence at the court, and the singers and actors at the opera and Royal Theater were all of high quality. Irving's mood had been anticipatory when he agreed to attend a performance of *La Gazza Ladra* with Colonel Livius.

But he had never anticipated that this evening would see the mystery of the misdirected letter falling open like a magic apple. In all his life of seeking out mysteries, of inventing them and perpetrating them, never had one so neatly turned dropped into his lap. He smiled as he followed Colonel Livius up the aisle, through the foyer, and then up the stairs to the boxes. Colonel Livius held aside the curtains, and they stepped into the box.

"Amelia," the Colonel said, "may I present Mr. Washington Irving? Mrs. John Foster, Mr. Irving. Miss Emily Foster and Miss Flora Foster, Mr. Irving."

Washington bowed over the hand of a woman only a few years older than himself who was even more attractive face to face than she had appeared at a distance. He bowed to the daughters who were lovely in the freshness of their youth, and then all three of the ladies were expressing their pleasure at meeting the famous author of *The Sketch Book* and *Bracebridge Hall*.

Mrs. Foster urged Irving and Colonel Livius to join them in their box for the rest of the performance and both of the men took chairs. Other guests came in and out of the box during the intermission. There were more introductions. Still Washington's eyes sparkled and his new animation brightened the scene for him. The curtain rose for the next act and he stole glances from time to time at his new acquaintances.

At the next intermission, before any visitors had yet arrived, he spoke to Mrs. Foster, asking with a smile, "Have you lately heard from Miss Margaret?"

A faint look of puzzlement crossed Mrs. Foster's face as she pondered how this author, newly arrived in Dresden, could know anything about her stepdaughter. She glanced at Colonel Livius.

Washington went on. "And Mr. Foster's journey to the north. Did he enjoy it as he had hoped?"

Mrs. Foster's look of bewilderment changed to real surprise and she seemed to have no words to answer. At which
point Washington pressed on with the most unlikely query
yet, a question about the health of Mrs. Foster's favorite
horse, Bessie.

"But how—" Mrs. Foster began, "—how did you know?
How could you tell?"

"Ah," said Washington happily. "There's the mystery."

He savored the situation as long as seemed reasonable or
kind and then revealed the story of the letter that had been
delivered to him in Vienna and his own wonder at finding
so soon the solution of the mystery.

Exclamations and gasps from his audience accompanied his
explanation. Then everyone talked and laughed at almost the
same time. Washington promised to return the letter to Mrs.
Foster and thanked her for the kind words she had written
in it about his *Sketch Book*.

It was, without a doubt, the most felicitous of all ways to
begin a friendship. The next day Irving made a call on the
Fosters, who lived in an old rented palace on one of Dresden's
finest streets. In the shabby elegance of the high-ceilinged
room that the Fosters used as a sitting room, a salon subtly
transformed by the arrangement of furniture and draperies
to convey the comfort and coziness of an English drawing
room, Washington saw Mrs. Foster and Emily and Flora by
daylight and found them even more attractive than he had
the night before. They welcomed him warmly. Mrs. Foster's
two young sons and their tutor were called in to meet Irving.
The hour of the visit passed in a flash. There was no doubt
that Irving would be calling again very soon and that they
would be meeting also at this, that, and the other social event
of the city in the near future. Already they felt established
friends, co-observers of the Dresden scene and committed to
knowing each other better and better.

Any realization that he was falling in love was a thought that Irving simply refused to recognize as the days and weeks in Dresden passed and his life began to center more and more on the Fosters. He never seemed to notice that the journey which had taken him so deeply into a fairy-tale landscape had led him also to a group uncannily reminiscent of a group he had known in his youth, one which had left a lasting emotional mark on him. An attractive, sympathetic woman a little older than he, and two daughters, younger than he. Surely the shadows of Maria Hoffman, and of Ann and Matilda, were stirring somewhere in his unconscious as he hurried to the Foster home to relate the amusing details of his presentation at court, or to tell about his dinner with the learned antiquarian, Karl August Bottiger, to whom he had been introduced by Morier, or about other dinners at the homes of the Russian minister, or the French minister, or the Danish, M. de Bergh, whose wife, Mme. de Bergh, was so pretty, flirtatious, and vaguely surrounded by rumors of past indiscretions. He hid from any recognition that the past was somehow repeating itself and hid as well from wondering why he woke each day with such a sense of eagerness and anticipation when he knew that later he would be seeing the Fosters.

Love was an emotion he had buried with Matilda Hoffman. The whole course of his life since her death seemed to have prohibited any resurrection of the feeling. Besides, in his attraction to the Fosters, on whom did his love focus?

With Mrs. Foster he soon began regular sessions of reading aloud from the works of Goethe, Schiller, and other German authors as they worked together to improve their mastery of the language. With Mrs. Foster he talked of his hopes to make something of his notes on German lore, legend, scenery, and history. Mrs. Foster was intelligent and sympathetic as no one had been since Maria Hoffman and Rebecca

Gratz. He found himself telling her of his difficulties in finding any point of view for his German material. So much had been done in that field already, and he did not want to imitate anybody. His daily conversations with her relaxed and stimulated him.

But he could not be in love with her any more than he had been able to be *in* love with Maria Hoffman. She was married. Her husband, in England, was still the center of her life. And Irving, thirty-nine, almost forty, could hardly assume the youthful role of worshiper at a shrine as he once had done with Maria. He could find with Mrs. Foster only a satisfaction he had not known in years.

Still, even as he talked with Mrs. Foster, he could not resist glancing frequently at young Emily. Flora, hardly seventeen, was almost as pretty as Emily, but Flora had a giddiness about her, a childish way of exaggerating her remarks and emotions that amused Irving without really appealing to him. Emily, on the other hand, though she was quick to laugh and guilelessly showed her pleasure in the beaux she had acquired in Dresden, had a kind of purity about her face that wakened echoes of Matilda's "native delicacy" and "exquisite propriety."

But Emily Foster was not yet twenty, half Irving's age. He was old enough to be her father, and had known sorrows, successes, and despairs that created what was surely an impassable gulf between them. It was impossible that he should be in love with Emily Foster, or *Miss* Foster, as he called her in the properly formal address for the oldest daughter of a family.

So he evaded the unanswerable question about love and continued to enjoy the same feelings of buoyancy and expectancy each day.

The cold and snow of winter settled over Dresden. The Elbe froze and there was skating on the river, or ladies in their velvets and furs snuggled into small sledges that were pulled along the frozen river. Out of doors, breath steamed in puffy clouds. Indoors, there was the warmth of fireplaces, porcelain stoves, and the heat generated by many lamps and candles. New Year's Day of 1823 was marked by a variety of social events. Irving was waked at dawn as the military band paraded through the streets before his hotel. At nine-thirty in the morning, he went to court to attend the first of the functions that would star the holiday, a levee with all the princes, princesses, and courtiers of the little kingdom gathered at the palace in full court dress of scarlet and gold lace. At noon, the Queen, richly dressed and adorned with many diamonds, held her levee. She greeted Irving sociably and asked if he was planning to write a book about Germany or Dresden to reflect the special characteristics of those countries as *The Sketch Book* and *Bracebridge Hall* had reflected England's. At six in the evening came a Grand Assembly at court, with everyone in grand toilette, bowing as the King and Queen went around to speak to each one present, after which the royal family and the various guests settled themselves to play whist until eight o'clock when the assembly dispersed.

Irving's involvement in the social life of the Dresden court continued. "January 5th:—from the king's levee went by invitation to the queen's apartment, being to dine at the royal table. . . . Dinner served up in room where there is very good Gobelin tapestry—sat at dinner between Count Vilzthurm and——, a Russian. The latter a very amiable, agreeable young man of great possessions—speaks English—invited me to visit him at his place in the *Crimea*."

"January 7th, evening—Ball at Count Saxburgh's, the Bavarian minister, in honor of the nuptials of Prince John and Princess of Bavaria—staircase lighted up and decorated with evergreens, so as to form a green alley—elegant supper—com-

pany danced until three o'clock—curtain caught fire—pulled
it down, and received the thanks of the princes—made an
arrangement with the Forestmeister to accompany him to the
chase. . . ."

A dream—of fairy-tale royalty, gentle, nodding and benign,
and then a hunt in the snow-covered forests of Saxony. The
King riding out on his stately mount, following the forest
masters, all clad in the ancient hunting costumes of green.
The horns sounding, the dogs baying, and Irving cantering
along on his horse, following the chase down the forest roads
and paths, first in one direction, then another, until finally the
boar was captured and killed. "Qu.?" Irving noted in his
journal that evening. "Does not the continent continually
present pictures of customs and manners, such as formerly
prevailed in England. The king's *chasse* at Dresden is quite
a picture of ancient hunting in Queen Elizabeth's reign."

Meantime, at the heart of the dream was the felicity he
found at the Fosters' home, where another winter amusement
was presently underway. A small, quite usable theater in one
of the wings of the old palace had inspired Colonel Livius,
who had once been connected with the London stage, to
suggest amateur theatricals. A version of *Tom Thumb* was
essayed, with Irving playing King Arthur and Mrs. Foster
Dollalolla. Somehow this play failed to get beyond rehearsal,
but Colonel Livius, undiscouraged, appeared next with a
French opera which he had shortened and felt would be suitable for amateur talents.

One evening, Irving, amused by the Colonel's autocratic
directorial methods and the total lack of progress in the new
rehearsals, drew Mrs. Foster aside and suggested that they,
give the Colonel a dramatic surprise. He, Irving, would find
some simple comedy which was really within the grasp of
amateurs and further adapt it to their needs. They could re-
hearse it secretly, and then, on the night when the dress re-

hearsal of the Colonel's opera was scheduled, they could astound him by presenting instead a polished version of the comedy.

Mrs. Foster professed herself delighted with the plan, as did Emily and Flora. Now Irving's morning hours, instead of being devoted to his German notes, were turned toward finding the proper comedy, which he ultimately decided was a frivolous item called *Three Weeks After Marriage*. He shortened it and wrote out several characters to arrive at a manageable cast. The final version provided roles for five, with Irving playing Sir Charles Rackett opposite Emily as Lady Rackett; Flora as Dimity and Mrs. Foster as Mrs. Druggett, while a young officer named Corkran, who was part of the theatrical group, played Mr. Druggett.

"You cannot imagine the amusement this little theatrical plot furnished us," Irving reported later in a letter to Peter. "We rehearsed in Mrs. Foster's drawing-room, and as the whole was to be kept a profound secret, and as Mrs. Foster's drawing-room is a great place of resort, and as especially our dramatic sovereign, Colonel Livius, was almost an inmate of the family, we were in continued risk of discovery, and had to gather together like a set of conspirators."

In the hushed merriment evoked by the various alarums and excursions connected with this conspiracy, Irving tried to hide for a while longer from the emotions that distracted him inwardly. He was not in love with Mrs. Foster. She was a dear friend who had drawn him in to be almost a member of her family, and his heart was full of gratitude and affection, but that was all. He could not be in love with Emily, so delightful and so young, but the scenes he played with her in the comedy were fraught with a tension he could not control.

The dramatic surprise was finally sprung on Colonel Livius. "The Colonel had ordered a dress rehearsal of his little opera; the scenery was all prepared, the theater lighted up, a few amateurs admitted the Colonel took his seat before the curtain to direct the rehearsal. The curtain rose, and out walked Mr. and Mrs. Druggett in proper costume. The little Colonel was perfectly astonished, and did not recover before the first act was finished; it was a perfect explosion to him. . . ." Washington's letter to Peter, reported that a night or so later the performance was repeated before a full audience of the English residents of Dresden, and those of the nobility who understood English, and the comedy went off with "great spirit and success."

The whole proceedings had been so enlivening that Irving at once began preparing a new play for the same cast, *The Wonder, A Woman Keeps A Secret*. In this he was to play the part of Don Felix to Emily's Violante. "She plays charmingly," he wrote to Peter, but that was as much as he allowed himself to write about her.

Not even in his journal did Irving record anything but the objective events of that winter of 1823 in Dresden. "March 19th.—Evening at Mrs. Foster's. Rehearsal, and then to the soirée of Count Luxbourg, the Bavarian minister. March 23rd.—Make alterations in play. 24th.—Walk along the Elbe with Mrs. and Miss Foster—in evening a party at Mrs. Foster's. 25th.—At home writing letters—in evening rehearsal of 'The Wonder.'

Through the winter, Emily and Flora, well-brought up English girls, also kept journals. In Emily's journal there were frequent references to "Mr. Irving," whom she had described after their first meeting as "neither tall nor slight, but most interesting, dark, hair of a man of genius waving, silky, & black, grey eyes full of varying feeling, & an amiable smile." Her entries showed that she was impressed by this author with "the hair of a man of genius," and she frequently made notes of the stories or anecdotes he told to the family on their quiet evenings together, as one would preserve the sayings of any great man. But as winter gave way to spring in Dresden, Emily's notes began to betray a certain uneasiness. Whatever he was saying, whatever he was admitting even to himself, Irving had begun to show an intensity in his attentions to her that frightened and confused her, although she could hardly admit this directly. Instead, in her journal she scolded herself for falling prey to "capricious coldness fits" when Mr. Irving talked with her. She knew somewhere inside herself what was happening. He was caring too much. She could sense it and feel it when he appeared, always ready at a ball to be her partner, or to sit beside her if she rested a moment.

Others were noticing Irving's attentions to her and this further distracted her. "Party at Friesen's—the report that I am to marry 'certo signor autore'—begins to annoy me—Kleise joking about it—got up when ———— appeared to leave me tête-à-tête with him I was quite angry."

Irving felt her withdrawal and tried to rescue himself from his own emotions. He began a flirtatious relationship with Madame de Bergh who seemed more than willing to co-operate. On April first, she played some sort of April Fool joke on him. April third was his birthday, his fortieth, and everyone in the Dresden circle within which he moved knew it and planned accordingly. The Fosters and Colonel Livius, playing Irving's own game, arranged for a birthday dinner at the Foster house, and after the toasts, the party was summoned to the little theater. The curtains were raised and a surprise series of tableaux from *Knickerbocker's History*, *The Sketch Book* and *Bracebridge Hall* was presented. Irving noted in his journal that "Madame de Bergh took part admirably."

The next evening the theater was lighted again, this time for the première performance of *The Wonder*, in which Irving played Emily's suitor. He did not write much about the success of this production to Peter or in his journal either, but Madame de Bergh was mentioned again and again. He sat next to her at a dinner at Baron Lowenstein's and she was "looking very pretty." After the dinner party had broken up he stopped by the de Bergh home and waltzed with Madame de Bergh until midnight.

But it was all of no avail. The feeling for Emily Foster which he had fled from for so long had become obsessive.

Flora Foster, who had also been making notes on Mr. Irving's stories and anecdotes in her journal and making her own deductions about his attitude toward her older sister, was the only one of the journal writers to chronicle his ultimate revelation of feeling.

"He has written," Flora recorded in her exclamatory style. "He has confessed to my mother, as to a true and dear friend, his love for E————, and his conviction of its utter hopelessness. He finds himself unable to combat it. He thinks he must try, by absence, to bring more peace to his mind. Yet he cannot bear to give up our friendship, an intercourse become so dear to him, and so necessary to his daily happiness. Poor Irving!"

# 22

# My Time Is Now Gone By

How was it that he had never married? Mrs. Foster asked him. He had told them about many of the incidents of his life, spoken of his friends in America and in Europe, spoken of Brevoort, of Tom Moore, John Howard Payne, Sir Walter Scott. But he was a man attracted to women and attractive to them as well. How was it that, forty years old, he was still unmarried? Irving bowed his head at her question, then said that she had a right to know but it was a long story. Perhaps it would be simpler for him to write his answer.

For a day or two he did not make his usual visits to the Foster residence. Then he appeared to give Mrs. Foster a letter that told the story. It was a sheaf of manuscript almost as thick as one of the sketches he sometimes brought to read aloud to her and the girls. But this letter was for her eyes, and her daughters', alone, he told Mrs. Foster. He asked that she take no copy of it and that she return it to him when she was finished.

There was, it would seem, no reason to present the letter with such an air of mystery except that it had always been

Washington's way to hide emotions that were unhappy or fearful and the letter spoke almost wholly of such emotions. Something had happened when he was very young that caused him to lock such feelings inside himself. With an effort, he unlocked the door briefly for Mrs. Foster and her daughters, but once they had learned what was inside, he wanted the doors closed again.

It is only what might be expected then, that this one rare document of self-revelation should have continued shrouded in mystery throughout his life and even afterward. Returned to him by Mrs. Foster, locked into a box marked "Private Mems," the letter was found after his death by the nephew whom he had authorized to write the story of his life. His nephew, respecting all he had learned and sensed of his uncle's desire for privacy, did not mention the letter in his biography and did not indicate that Irving might have known any special emotions in Dresden. That the Fosters were anything more than friends, like any others, was revealed only when an English edition of *The Life and Letters of Washington Irving* was published in 1863. To avoid the need for paying copyright, this edition contained an Appendix of new matter, the new matter being reminiscences obtained from Flora Foster Dawson. Flora, as melodramatic as ever, had culled extracts from her journal to document Irving's love for her sister in the winter of 1823. The publication of this unexpected material forced Irving's nephew, Pierre Munro Irving, to acknowledge and include Flora Foster Dawson's contributions to the story of his uncle's life in a revised American edition. He admitted that there was a letter which Washington Irving had given to Mrs. Foster one day in late April of 1823, and, confounding Flora, who had written that he did not have it, declared that it was in his possession. Or, to be exact, he had sixteen pages of the letter. The first and the last pages were missing. Still, he refrained from publishing the document, and it was not until almost seventy-five years later that the letter was finally printed.

With the first and the last pages missing, the account not only begins in the middle of a sentence but ends in the middle of a phrase—it would, no doubt, have pleased Washington to know that he was leaving behind a mystery that seemingly could never be unraveled. Had he himself destroyed the first and last pages so that this would be so?

Whatever the explanation, to those who came after him and who would try, with prying curiosity, to know all, he left a "Private Mem" which began:

". . . feelings since I entered upon the world, which like severe wounds and maims in the body, leave forever after a morbid sensitiveness, and a quick susceptibility to any new injury. Still there was always a reaction in my spirits; they rose readily of themselves when the immediate pressure was removed; I never soured under sufferings; my disposition which was originally rather impatient, seemed to soften under trials, and I had always a great facility at receiving pleasurable impressions. . . ."

The "Private Mem" ended:

"Do you want some of the *real* causes? While at Dresden I had repeated . . ."

In between this provocative beginning and tantalizing ending, he had reviewed his life as it appeared to him up to the moment of writing the apologia. Many of his summations have already been quoted:

"When I was very young I had an impossible flow of spirits that often went beyond my strength. Everything was fairy land to me. . . ." That had been when he was a boy in the garden of the house on William Street in New York City in 1790 and 1791.

Later: "I read law with a gentleman distinguished both in legal and political concerns, one who took a great part in pub-

lic affairs & was eminent for his talents. He took a fancy to
me, though a very heedless student, and made me almost an
inmate of his house. He had lately married for the second
time; a woman much younger than himself, one of the most
amiable and gentle of human beings. She was like a sister to
me. . . ." And that was his tribute to Maria Hoffman, his
idealized "mistress" in the years when he was nineteen,
twenty, and twenty-one.

He wrote of Judge Hoffman's two daughters by his first
wife, Ann and Matilda. "I saw a great deal of them. I was a
mere stripling, and we were all shy and awkward at first, but
we soon grew sociable and I began to take a great interest in
Matilda, though little more at the time than a mere boyish
fancy." In a sentence or two he disposed of his trips to Europe, necessitated by the "delicate state of my health." Then
he wrote of his return:

"I recollect my meeting with Matilda as if it was yesterday. She came home from school to see me. . . ." He wrote
of his growing awareness of her, and of how her mind
seemed to "unfold itself leaf by leaf." He touched on his
struggles to study for the law, and of the "satirical & humourous work" which he began "in company with one of
my brothers," and of his "wretched state of doubt and self-
mistrust."

Then, "In the midst of this struggle and anxiety she was
taken ill with a cold. Nothing was thought of it at first, but
she grew rapidly worse, and fell into consumption. I cannot
tell you what I suffered."

He recalled how the world had been "a blank" to him for
a while after her death, and then of how he had applied himself to finish the comic history. "The time and circumstances in which it was produced" had rendered him "always
unable to look upon it with satisfaction." But the book had
taken with the public, since "an original work was something

remarkable & uncommon in America." He had been "noticed caressed & for a time elated by the popularity. . . ." "Still however the career of gaiety & notoriety soon palled upon me. I seemed to drift about without aim or object, at the mercy of every breeze; my heart wanted anchorage. I was naturally susceptible and tried to form other attachments, but my heart would not hold on. . . ."

Never before and never afterward would he write of his life in such somber tones. To the world at large he would most often try to present the face of one who was "pleased by everything, or if not pleased, amused." To the Fosters, he bared, at least to a degree, the sadness and despair that underlay the surface amiability. For them he described the torments that the bankruptcy of P. and E. Irving Company had meant, and of how he had decided to reinstate himself in the world's thoughts by writing, and how he had finally produced *The Sketch Book*. "You know its success. You think no doubt I ought to be elated & made happy by it. But you have no knowledge of the many counter checks to this enjoyment, in the misfortunes of my once flourishing family. . . ." He had written of the death of his mother. Now he wrote of how the death of William, "who was every thing to the family" had "encreased my cares and duties; though I feel how apt I am to be negligent of them, and how incompetent I am at best to fulfill them. . . ."

"You wonder why I am not married," he wrote. "I have shewn you why I was not long since—when I had sufficiently recovered from that loss, I became involved in ruin. It was not for a man broken down in the world to drag down any woman to his paltry circumstances, and I was too proud to tolerate the idea of ever mending my circumstances by matrimony. My time has now gone by; and I have growing claims upon my thoughts, and upon my means slender & pre-

carious as they are. I feel as if I had already a family to think
& provide for. . . ."

"My time has now gone by. . . ." It would sound as if
Flora had been correct in saying that he "confessed a hopeless love," a love to which Emily did not respond and which
he dared not press because of the commitments he felt elsewhere.

"You want to know some of the fancies that distress me,"
he wrote finally. "I will mention one as a specimen of many
others. I was one evening going to a Ball at the Countess de
Hohenthals. I had not slept well the night before & after
dressing myself I lay down on the sopha & fell asleep. I
dreamt of my poor Brother whom I had lost about eighteen
months before, & whom I had not seen for years. We walked
& talked together. The dream was most vivid and consistent
& affecting. When I went to the Ball I was engaged to dance,
I think with both Emily & Flora, I tried to dance but could
not; my heart sank at the very sound of the music and I had
to give up the attempt & go home. Do you want some of the
*real* causes. While at Dresden I had repeated _____"

And there, for everyone other than the Fosters, who read
the letter in 1823, the document breaks off.

What had he "repeated" in Dresden? A tendency toward
"cheerfulness and even gaiety" at times when he had "real
cause to grieve"? An attitude of "selfish indulgence" that
"seized him with compunction"? Or a surrender to a love for
a young woman, a young, young woman, which for quite
other reasons than his first love seemed impossible of con-
summation?

One other passage in the letter, shortly before its conclusion, gave a clue to his refusal to speak generally of what had
wounded him. "I have now talked to you on subjects that I
recur to with excessive pain, and on which I am apt to be
silent, for there is little gained by the confiding of grievances.

It only overclouds other minds without brightening ones own. I prefer summoning up the bright pictures of life that I have witnessed and dwelling as much as possible on the agreeable."

And so, having confessed the matter on which he was generally silent, and having had his confessional letter returned to him by Mrs. Foster, he did not depart at once from Dresden after all, as Flora had indicated in his journal that he was about to do.

In his journal he noted on April 17th, "Determine to quit Dresden soon." But later that day he had an Italian lesson with Mrs. Foster, dined with the Fosters, talked with Emily about *Egmont,* and played with Mrs. Foster and her sons after dinner. The next day he was again with the Fosters and again the next. On the 27th there was a court ball, at which he danced with both Emily and Flora and was made much of by the old Queen. On May 1st, he walked in the *grosse garten* from half-past five till seven o'clock. It was a beautiful, sunshiny morning. "Birds singing—partridges bursting on the wing—hares—squirrels—clouds and breeze come up toward seven. . . ." Later that day he was again at the Fosters, and the next day he went out driving with them after dinner in their carriage.

He was a man "hopelessly in love," at least according to Flora, but still constrained to linger in the neighborhood of the beloved, taking what pleasure he could from her nearness and "dwelling as much as possible on the agreeable." Besides, May 4th was her birthday. There was to be a birthday dinner for her and he was writing a poem in her honor. When the poem was completed, he was overcome by shyness and sent the verses to her mother.

"My Dear Mrs. Foster," he wrote. "I will be with you at two to-day, to be ready for dinner at whatever time it may be served. I had declined an invitation that I might dine with you, as I recollected it was Miss Foster's birth-day. I send you a few lines which I have scribbled on the occasion. If you think them in any way worthy of the subject and that they would give her any pleasure, slip them into her scrap-book; if not, slip them into the stove, that convenient altar, and sacrifice them as a burnt offering to appease the Muses. I have no confidence in my rhymes.

God bless you, Yours truly,

Washington Irving."

Perhaps he was right in mistrusting these particular rhymes. They began easily enough:

Twas now the freshness of the year
When fields were green and groves were gay,
When airs were soft and skies were clear,
And all things bloomed in lovely May—

Blest month, when nature in her prime
Bestows her fairest gifts on earth—
This was the time, the genial time,
She destined for her favorite's birth. . . .

But in five more stanzas he seemed unable to raise himself above such commonplace conceits to a phrase that expressed real emotion.

Mrs. Foster did not slip the verses into the stove but presented them to Emily who noted them in her journal. "That good dear nice Mr. Irving sent me delightful verses, the first almost he ever wrote I hope it is not vain to transcribe them I do it more for his sake than for the partial compliments (are a cold word) to me. . . ."

Whatever Irving had confessed to Mrs. Foster, however she, Emily, and Flora had pored over his letter, the girlish entry hardly showed the same uneasiness about him that previous notes about "signore autore" had done. He was that "good dear nice Mr. Irving" again, a family friend.

He had, it would seem, once more retreated from showing

his emotions so intensely that they frightened her. But after her birthday, his plans to leave Dresden hung fire. One day he was talking of leaving for Paris. The next day he had spoken to a young English officer, John Cockburn, who was interested in touring the Risen Gebirge, or Giant Mountains, and visiting various cities in Bohemia, and thought he might accompany him and then return to Paris.

Finally, he was definitely decided on the tour. His last evening in Dresden he spent, as always, with the Fosters. For a while he stood with Emily—Miss Foster—on the terrace, looking out over the moonlit garden. Emily—Miss Foster—talked of how easy it was to believe in heaven on such a night and how near God seemed. This was not the sort of conversation with which Irving felt at ease. He had banished speculations about heaven and hell from his mind when he banished his father's religion, but with Emily standing beside him, so slender, so silvery fair, he managed to make the proper responses.

The next morning, he left Dresden with John Cockburn. "Mama suspects he meant not to return," Emily wrote in her journal that bright May morning, "he said he had thought of it—but that he would he could not help it."

The journey was, by and large, a misbegotten venture, accomplishing nothing that Irving had hoped from it. Distance did not decrease his dependency on the Fosters nor the disturbing feelings he had for Emily. He was not a day's journey away before he began a long letter to Mrs. Foster, describing the sights that he and Cockburn had seen, many of them reminding him of his Dresden friends. The next night and the next he continued the letter. In Friedland he wrote, "I have been to the spot from which I presume Emily took her sketch of the castle. I hope she will excuse my apparent familiarity in using her beautiful name instead of the formal one of Miss Foster. Were I writing to any one but yourself

I should not do it; I would have given any thing at the time to have heard her in her own delightful way talk about Schiller's play and the scenes she preferred."

From Prague, which he already had visited the previous fall, he wrote to Mrs. Foster that Cockburn had fallen ill. They would be detained there until he recovered from what the doctor called scarlet fever. A letter from Mrs. Foster reached him and he replied, "I thank you a thousand times, my dear Mrs. Foster, for your letter of Wednesday; I cannot tell you how interesting it was to me, placing the dear little circle of the Pavilion so completely before my eyes. . . ."

Day after day, the stay in Prague was prolonged by Cockburn's illness. Irving nursed him faithfully, watched the activity of the city from the hotel window, and wrote more letters to Mrs. Foster and prayed for answers from her. When one arrived, he sat down at once to answer it. "It seems to me," he wrote her, "as if I am the least fitted being for this wandering life, into which chance and circumstance have thrown me. I have strong domestic feelings and inclinations, and feel sometimes quite dreary and desolate when they get uppermost." In another, he thanked her "a thousand and a thousand times" for her solicitude about him. "Will you tell Emily and Flora, that their kind wishes are more gratifying to me than I can express?" he added. "Good heavens! what would I give to be with you all this evening at the strawberry supper you speak of. . . ."

In one letter Mrs. Foster asked whether or not he planned to return to Dresden. "I am ashamed to say it," he replied, "I am almost wishing myself back already. I ought to be off like your bird, but I feel I shall not be able to keep clear of the cage."

Was he going back? Or was he going to make the break and travel directly to Paris once Cockburn had recovered? He tormented himself by remembering the evenings with the Fosters, spent in such "varied, animated, intelligent, but unforced and unostentatious conversation, with, now and then, but too rarely, a song, and now and then a recollection from some favorite author or a choice morsel from a scrapbook, given with beaming looks and beaming eyes. . . ." When before had he ever been so happy? Or so unhappy?

"Dresden, Dresden, with what a mixture of pain, pleasure, fondness, and impatience I look back on it!"

Gradually, Cockburn recovered from his fever, but Irving did not. The travelers were ready to move on.

Irving went back to Dresden.

The Fosters were now preparing for their return to England after a three-year stay abroad. There was nothing left for Irving to decide. His devotion to Mrs. Foster was just that—devotion. His feelings for Emily, impossible. He would stay in Dresden until they departed, accompany them as far as Cassel on their way toward embarking for England, and then take his leave of them.

Perversely, he was in tearing spirits as the party set off from Dresden in two carriages, the ladies' laps full of flowers which were parting gifts from Dresden friends. A mounted escort of Dresden gentlemen, including Colonel Livius, accompanied the travelers for several miles and Irving took the lead in shouted banter between the carriage travelers and the outriders. Finally, the escort halted, farewells were said, and the two carriages rolled on toward the Harz Mountains.

Various excitements starred the journey. A tremendous thunderstorm overtook the travelers as they approached the mountains. Wind, dust, rain, hail, thunder, and lightning swept about the carriages. The horses became terrified. Irving leaped from the dickey to help the coachman in his efforts to calm them, but in spite of their efforts, the horses of one carriage bolted and dragged their vehicle down a steep bank into a ravine where it overturned. Fortunately no one was hurt, but everyone was more than thoroughly drenched by the time Irving had rushed half a mile through the storm to the nearest house for help, ridden on a borrowed horse to the nearest village, found some workmen to go to the scene of the accident and pull up the carriage, taken rooms at the inn for the party, and then returned to escort the group on foot to the inn. When everyone had changed into dry clothes, however, the mood became festive. The Fosters and Irving sat by the inn fire and comforted themselves with cold tongue and a bottle of wine.

Resuming their journey, they came to the Harz Mountains, which reminded Irving of the Catskills. In these hills, they suddenly found themselves in a lively resort which was centered upon some therapeutic springs and where the nobility of a small German court were currently in residence. Here the group decided to linger for several days to rest from the fatigues of the journey, and here Irving took off on a ramble into the forest which was very like one he had taken years before into the wilderness along the St. Lawrence River. Years before, he had taken a nap in the forest depths and returned hours later to find everyone in a state of alarm about him. During this particular walk, which took place after dark, he lost his way in the woods and met with some suspicious characters, who may or may not have been brigands. Both Emily and Flora recounted the episode in their journals with some excitement, Flora's account being the most colorfully embellished with hints of glinting knives, furtive followings, and so on.

Arrived finally at Cassel, the capital of Hesse, where Irving had planned to part from the Fosters, he had a change of heart. His mood changed also. His liveliness deserted him, and he could not bear to say good-bye just yet. He decided to accompany Mrs. Foster, Emily, Flora and the two boys all the way to Rotterdam where they were to board their ship for England.

So he clung to his love for a few more days. His love for Emily? His love for Emily as the daughter of Mrs. Foster? His love for the three women and the two little boys as a family, the sort of family which he seemed always seeking? He never seems to have asked the questions of himself.

Flora later wrote her own dramatic story of the last day the Fosters and Irving spent together in Rotterdam:

"Mr. Irving, like a man expected to be his own executioner, had been out to take our berths in the steam vessel. We had taken a dismal walk along the slimy canals of Rotterdam, though something neat and old-fashioned in the Dutchmen's houses for a brief moment took up Mr. Irving's attention. We had dined . . . there followed a sorting of our separate property in sketch books, memorandum ditto, umbrellas, boxes, and all the small paraphernalia that accumulate on such a journey as ours. . . . Irving was in terrible spirits. He gave mama a beautiful little copy of Cowper's poems, and to each of us some favorite book. Our tea and evening were as melancholy as our approaching separation. Very little was said; little good was achieved by moving Irving to the sofa. We sat round, looking silently upon one another. . . ."

Emily noted in her journal that "Mr. Irving is sadly out of spirits. We are going to home and friends; but he, to wander about the wide world alone."

The final parting came the next day. Emily, unsure of just how strong were the emotions that she had roused in this famous author who had been a family intimate so long, knowing only in a confused way that there were emotions, tangled and obscure, to which she could not respond, wrote: "After bathing, we were hurried pele-mele into the steamboat. Mr. Irving accompanied us down the river, quite into the sea, when he was put down into the little open boat to return to the shore. I shall never, however long I may live, forget his last farewell, as he looked up to us, so pale and melancholy. It was a very painful moment to us all. We have not often felt so grieved at parting with a dear friend."

Returned to shore, Irving made his way to Paris and a few days later wrote to Peter. "At Rotterdam the Fosters embarked. I accompanied them down to the Brille and then bade them adieu as if I had been taking leave of my own family; for they had been for nearly eight months past more like relatives than friends to me."

He had taken lodgings at the Hotel de Yorck on the Montmartre, and determined to settle down to the writing he had in the main neglected for the last eight months. But a depression came over him. He was "wretchedly out of spirits," he wrote Peter. "I have, in fact, at times a kind of horror on me, particularly when I wake in the mornings, that incapacitates me for almost anything. . . ." He had his own explanation for this. "I am aware that this is all an affair of the nerves, a kind of reaction in consequence of coming to a state of repose after so long moving about, and produced also by the anxious feeling on resuming literary pursuits. I feel like a sailor who has once more put to sea, and is reluctant to quit the quiet security of the shore. . . ."

With which confused view of himself as both coming to rest and putting to sea, he tried to bury the emotions that had racked him in Dresden ("Ah Dresden, Dresden, with what a mixture of pain, pleasure, fondness and impatience I look back on it!"), and told himself and Peter that "If I can only keep the public in good humor with me, until I have thrown off two or three things more, I shall be able to secure a comfortable little independence, and then bread and cheese is secure, and perhaps a seat in the pit into the bargain."

# 23

# Tales of a Traveller

"In the time of the Rump
As old Admiral Trump,
With his broom swept the chops of the channel;
And his crew of Big Breeches
Those Dutch sons of ———"

HERE IRVING broke off, smiling, and put his hand over his mouth.

Payne laughed, seeing exactly what Irving had in mind for the song. The old captain would start the song over and over during the course of the play, but his niece would always clap her hand over his mouth before he could sing the final word. It would make for a nice comic effect that could build throughout the comedy of *Charles II, or The Merry Monarch*.

Laughing, counting up the scenes into which the song could be interpolated, Payne felt suffused with a sense of the good fortune which had been coming his way at last. In May, his play, *Clari, or The Maid of Milan*, had been produced in London and met with great success. A song in the play for which he had written the words had struck the public fancy with such impact that people everywhere were soon singing "Home, Sweet Home," and he was becoming known as its author. The popularity of the song had not meant any extra money for Payne, but he had made enough from the whole production to pay his most pressing debts. He could now move freely from Paris to London and back. And now Irving had agreed to collaborate with him on some of his current and future projects. Payne's optimism bubbled to new highs. With Irving, famous author of *The Sketch Book,* writing with him, what successes the future could hold!

As for Washington, the decision to try his hand at some writing for the stage was neither sudden nor whimsical. During the Dresden months, when he had been unable to make anything of his German notes, he had filled some of his hours at his desk with dramatic experiments above and beyond the adaptations of little comedies for the amateur theatrical group. Karl Maria von Weber, the resident musician at Dresden's court, and known all over Europe for his opera *Der Freishütz,* had composed an earlier work, *Abu Hassan,* which caught Irving's interest. Through the April days when he fretted over whether or not he should leave Dresden and the insoluble emotional problems there, he had made a translation and adaptation from the German story by Franz Karl Heimer on which von Weber had based his opera. Irving then listened on several occasions as von Weber played his own music for the tale. He had also translated and made an adaptation of another German tale which von Weber had used, *The Wild Huntsman.*

Both the manuscripts were in his luggage when he returned to Paris, and Payne had offered eagerly to present them to producers in London on his next visit. Payne was sure that if Irving would consent to sign the works he would have no trouble selling them, but since this was a venture into a new field, Washington fell back on his old need to be anonymous.

Still, the idea of writing for the theater, which he had loved all his life, had begun to tantalize him. If some form for his German notes continued to elude him, he could help Payne rework the French play by Alexander Duval about Charles II, which Payne thought would go well in London. He could, when that was finished, assist in translating and adapting another Duval play, this one a tragedy based on some aspects of the life of Richelieu.

Working on these projects, so removed from the subjective essay or story forms of his books but in a field with which he had always been familiar, the theater, Irving gradually began to lose the wretchedness of spirit that had assailed him when he arrived in Paris.

Payne, who had been living in the suburbs during the summer, decided to take an apartment in the city for the winter and urged Irving to share it with him. He promised that much of the time he would be in England, and so Irving would have the apartment almost as his own. The suggestion became even more inviting to Washington after he made a short visit to Peter, in Havre, and learned that Peter might spend some of the winter months in Paris with him. When he returned to Paris, Washington found that Payne had already rented the new quarters at 89, rue Richelieu and was eager to have Irving join him so that they could lose no time in polishing the two plays, *Charles II* and *Richelieu*.

The move turned out to be an agreeable one for Washington. "My apartments consist of bed room, sitting room, and dining room, with use of kitchen and appurtenances and a cellar," he wrote to Peter. "Payne has furnished them very handsomely. They have a warm southern exposure, and look into a very spacious and handsome court. . . . I shall have a bed for you whenever you choose to pay Paris a visit."

By December, Payne had left for England to meet with Charles Kemble, the actor, and negotiate with him about the sale of *Charles II* and *Richelieu,* on both of which Irving was still putting some finishing touches. Soon after that, Peter arrived. It was the first time the two had been together for any prolonged period since the publication of the *Sketch Book,* but the easy companionship they had known all their lives was not changed.

Washington could tell Peter his hopes that writing for the stage might offer him new enthusiasm and inspiration and explain why any form for the German material still eluded him. "There are such quantities of these legendary and romantic tales now littering from the press both in England and in Germany that one must take care not to fall into the commonplace of the day. Scott's manner must likewise be widely avoided. In short, I must strike out some way of my own, suiting to my own way of thinking and writing. . . ." Peter was pleased when it seemed, briefly, that Washington had thought of "some way of his own" to use the material and understood his depression when the idea seemed unworkable.

If Washington also confessed to this understanding brother some of the emotions he had known in Dresden, and admitted, at least to a degree, the confusion of his feelings in regard to Emily Foster he left no record that he did so. The Dresden days were over. The door was closed on them.

The family group in Paris was enlarged that winter by the two older Van Wart boys who were attending a boarding school in the city. On school holidays and Sundays they were often with their uncles Washington and Peter. "Read the morning service to them," Washington noted in his journal one Sunday in January, 1824, "and pointed out the beauty and solemnity of the prayers." He did not seem to remember how he had balked at hearing prayers when he was their ages. Or perhaps he felt that since he was reading Church of

252 · THE HEART THAT WOULD NOT HOLD

England prayers, which had none of the old Calvinist feroc-
ity, the situation was somewhat different.

Letters came from his publisher, John Murray, asking
when he could expect another book, and Washington began
to grow frantic. He took out a sketch about a literary dinner
which he had deleted from the *Sketch Book* and pondered
whether he could make a novel from the adventures of its
hero, Buckthorne. Stopping in at Galignani's in the morning
to read the papers and greet the usual group there, or dining
out of an evening, he listened always for some story, some
remark that would spark a train of inspiration.

One of the nephews became ill and Washington moved
him to the apartment on the rue Richelieu in order to nurse
him. He gave the boy his bed, making his own on the sofa
in the sitting room, and stayed up several nights with him,
thinking between times of what he was to write next.

Just when the pattern came to him he did not note in his
journal, but by mid-February he was beginning to write "the
Italian story." Shortly there were references in the journal
to the story of "the Bold Dragoon," and the "Robber tales."
By March he was writing to John Murray that "I have the
materials for two volumes nearly prepared, but there will yet
be a little re-writing and filling up necessary. . . . I think the
the title will be Tales of a Traveller, by Geoffrey Crayon,
Gent."

The plan, as it finally came to him, ignored the German
material altogether. What he was projecting was a book in
several sections, almost, but not quite as miscellaneous as *The
Sketch Book*. One section would comprise the story of Buckthorne and his literary friends, which he had not been able
to write as a novel after all, but only as a series of sketches
about literary life in England. Another section would consist
of ghost and mystery stories, "Strange Stories by a Nervous
Gentleman." The stories in the third section recalled his fasci-

nation with the tales of Italian banditti in the long-ago year when he had lingered in Genoa, and were based on some of the notes he had made then. Finally, to balance the pattern, he added a fourth section of stories with an American setting, more fragments from the papers of Diedrich Knickerbocker, but these generally oriented to tales of greed and its punishment and titled, "The Money Diggers."

According to his letter to Murray, "two volumes were almost prepared" by mid-March. Like all authors, he was exaggerating. He had written an enormous number of pages in the weeks since the idea for the Tales first occurred to him, but everything he had written needed pruning and polishing and more sketches were needed to fill out the various sections. Through the rest of March and April, he continued to write so rapidly that he was vastly encouraged. Surely this easy composition augured well for the material.

The news of Byron's death in Greece came in early May. Irving found it difficult to believe. Through so many years he had read and admired Byron's poetry and had heard anecdotes of Byron's life from Byron's friends who were his friends as well. He had read through the Memoirs that Byron had entrusted to Moore, and it had seemed only a matter of time and circumstance until he should meet the poet in person. But Byron was dead, struck down by a fever. The meeting that Irving had taken for granted would never take place.

He went back to his Tales and then heard from Payne, in London, that *Charles II* was being produced. Suddenly he decided to pack up his manuscript and, following the same impulse that had made him think he could finish *Bracebridge Hall* more easily in England than in Paris, took off for London.

He arrived in London in time to join Payne at the theater for the second presentation of *Charles II*. With Payne was a slender, intense-looking young woman whom Payne introduced as Mrs. Mary Wollstonecraft Shelley, the widow of the poet. Irving could see Payne's anxiety to please the lady and felt some sympathy for him. Mrs. Shelley so obviously took Payne's devotion for granted, while Payne seemed not to notice her condescension and bustled about to make everything comfortable for her. Toward Irving, on the other hand, Mrs. Shelley was extremely gracious, and Washington spoke politely with her, remarking on his admiration of her late husband's poetry (although he had never cared for it as he did for Byron's) and complimenting her on her own talent for novel writing. *Frankenstein* was indeed a fascinating work. No wonder it had known success, he said.

He was much more interested in the proceedings on stage, listening and watching avidly as lines and scenes which he had written were brought to life by the actors. All in all he thought it went very well, though the first act was slow, but later he learned that the critics had attacked the *language*. What language did they mean? The word that was carefully *not* spoken? "His crew of Big Breeches/ Those Dutch sons of _____?" After the performance he talked with Payne about cuts that might improve the first act, and they planned a meeting to do some revising. But the song, Irving was determined, would remain. And so it did, to the pleasure of many viewers, including Charles Lamb, who told Payne that the last line kept him awake at nights.

Meantime, Irving visited with his artist friends, Leslie and Newton, to see and comment on their latest paintings and catch up on the latest gossip in the art world. "I am rejoiced that I got my work ready before coming here," he wrote to Peter, who was staying on in the apartment at the rue Richelieu, "or I should have been full of perplexity and annoyance, as I am kept in a continual whirl. Moore is in town. I was with him a great part of the day before yesterday; yesterday he passed in the country; today we dine together."

He rejoiced, for the work was ready enough so that he could accept Murray's offer of the 1,500 guineas for it, sight unseen. But still it was not quite ready to deliver to Murray. A few more stories were required. It was ready enough so that he felt free to accept Samuel Rogers' invitations to breakfast, and so that he could accept an invitation to a country house in Hampshire where he knew another June idyll like the one the year before in Somerset. He might work for a while on his manuscript in the morning but "at 12 we set out on a fishing party Mr. Compton Mr. Mills on horseback one of the Boys on pony & I drove Mrs. Compton . . . two of the children & the tutor in a low car drawn by black horse . . . thro beautiful forest scenery—glades, heather, groves of birch—saw herds of deer—repast under tree by brook. . . ."

After a week of such pastimes in Hampshire, he joined Moore and Bessie at Bath for a music festival. They heard Catalani sing. They walked along the terraced streets of the fashionable town, observing the visitors who thronged to the resort for its waters, its entertainment, for a chance to find beaux for their daughters and to show off new bonnets. They made mocking comments on the motley crowd, and they gossiped some more about Byron. Moore told Irving of how he had bought back Byron's original memoirs from Murray, and then, at the insistence of Byron's executors, burned them. Moore's next project was to be his own biography of the poet he had known so well. There is no record that they spoke of another writer, who had lived for several years in Bath and whose novel, *Northanger Abbey*, had mocked the town more neatly than they were able to. Somehow, for all his familiarity with many of the best-known writers of his time, Irving never indicated any awareness of the one writer, Jane Austen, whose quiet and amused observations of society might have matched at least to a degree with his own. She was eight years older than he. She had been dead seven years when he visited

Bath. But her vision of the town was destined to remain fresh and funny for generations.

Some concern about the manuscript he owed Murray began to agitate Washington at last, and so he accompanied the Moores from Bath to their cottage in Sloperton where Moore had promised he would have the quiet he needed to finish the book. But even there, social distractions intruded. One evening Moore took Irving to dine with his benefactor, Lord Lansdowne, who owned Sloperton Cottage. Moore was disappointed that Irving, so lively in private conversation, had acquired a habit of sleepy withdrawal when part of a large company. The Fosters had grown to know this habit of Irving's in Dresden when he retreated into some nook at the appearance of other callers. Moore, cheerful and gregarious whatever the size of the gathering, was a little annoyed as he noted in his journal: "Took Irving . . . but he was sleepy and did not open his mouth. . . . Not strong as a lion, but delightful as a domestic animal."

In spite of dinner invitations and other social activities, Irving did manage to do some more work on his Tales, and, as once before, Moore offered him an inspiration for a story. Irving quickly wrote it up as an added entry for his section of "Strange Stories."

But he was growing somewhat uneasy. He had rejoiced that the work was ready when he arrived in London at the first of June. By mid-June it was still in no shape to hand over to Murray. Once again, following an old pattern, he traveled to sister Sally's in Birmingham where good luck always seemed to attend his writings. From the Castle Van Tromp, where he had written his legend of Rip Van Winkle six years before, he was at last able to send off a packet of manuscript to Murray, sufficient to make up the first volume of *Tales of a Traveller*.

Shortly thereafter he returned to London to make sure the

manuscript went to press as soon as possible so that no delay in the English edition would make possible an earlier American publication.

And then, a year after his melancholy parting with the Fosters in Rotterdam, he was on his way to visit them in their own home, called Brickhill, near Bedford in Bedfordshire.

What had it all meant, really—that time of pleasure and pain in Dresden? He had written one letter to Emily in the year since the parting and several to Mrs. Foster, who had invited him for the visit. He had accepted, and now he was going to see them in their natural setting, which was bound to be quite different from the Dresden world in which he had first known them.

The stage put him down before the inn in Bedford where the Fosters' gig was waiting for him. He stepped into the vehicle and was whirled along the village road and finally up the rise to where the Foster home, Brickhill, stood on a sweep of land with a fine view of the countryside around it.

All of the family were waiting at the door to greet him, "in the kindest manner." There was Mrs. Foster, warm and welcoming. There was Emily, still fair and slender and beautiful. There was Flora, clasping her hands in excitement. There were the boys, those "manly little fellows." And there, as there had not been in Dresden, was Mr. John Foster, an upright, civic-minded Englishman, a magistrate of the county, endlessly concerned with better roads, better crops, and general community improvement.

Did Mr. Foster's presence alone make the difference? Mrs. Foster, Emily, and Flora all had a slightly changed manner because of him. If there were any spontaneous suggestions of walks through the gardens or a visit to the stables the decision had first to be referred to Mr. Foster. He might have some other plan. After dinner, the gatherings in the drawing room no longer brought forth the same easy, rambling discourses on personalities, poetry, or theatricals as in the Dresden evenings. Mr. Foster, sitting on his high-backed chair, smiling courteously and making polite conversation, did not so much prohibit such conversation as make it impossible.

Other visitors to Brickhill, most of them of a strongly religious bent, added to the strangeness. Had the Fosters shown such a concern for religion in Dresden? Certainly groups of pious souls had not appeared at all hours in the old rented palace in Dresden, and certainly Irving had never been surprised in the library there by a group suddenly entering and its leader crying, "Let us pray!" When it happened at Brickhill, Irving jumped from his chair and as everyone else dropped to his knees so did he, but with a muffled exclamation of dismay. And certainly in Dresden, and on the adventurous journey from Dresden to Rotterdam, Emily had never talked to him about the state of his soul, asking him gently if he were convinced of his salvation.

He had looked forward to a stay of two weeks or more at Brickhill and told Murray to forward proof sheets of *Tales of a Traveller* to him there. But in spite of jaunts about the countryside, picnics, and other excursions, the days began to be filled with tension for Irving. Everyone seemed to be trying so hard where once all had been spontaneity.

Within a week he was making his excuses for having to get back to London at once. He had suddenly realized that two sections of his book needed more material and he would have to write it and get it to the printer at once.

Hands were pressed, good-byes were said with a great show of feeling, but everyone knew the visit had not been a success. Settled back in the stagecoach, staring out at the landscape, Washington did not try to analyze what had happened. The intoxication he had felt was over, that was all.

What he had written in his letter to Mrs. Foster the year before was only the simple truth, "My time is now gone by." He turned his thoughts to the Tales and which of the fugitive ideas of the past months he might write up as additional sketches.

Writing had once been only a matter of whim, an expression of high spirits, no more meaningful to him than a sudden burst of song. After financial reverses, it had become more important, a means to reinstate himself in the world's opinion. Now it was something even more than that—the one element in his life that gave him meaning and solidity, the thing that did not fail.

In London, he wrote the additional material that was needed for *Tales of a Traveller*, some introductory material for the Buckthorne section, and another "robber tale." He corrected the proofs as they came from the printer, and then on August 13th took a coach for Brighton, to sail from there to France.

August 25th, Murray published *Tales of a Traveller* in two volumes. At almost the same time, Ebenezer had arranged for the manuscripts Irving had forwarded to him to be published in America in four parts, at two-week intervals. Both in England and America, the reputation of Geoffrey Crayon, Gent., was such that the books sold well from the beginning. To Irving, who had rented quarters in Auteuil, outside of Paris, so that he might be free of social engagements for a while as he proceeded with further literary endeavors, the news of this good sale was cheering but only what he had expected. He was sure that the *Tales* were the best things he had ever done.

Irving took a brief excursion with Peter through the Loire Valley in October, spending several days in the half-abandoned castle of the Duke of Duras, tended by the two old servants who were retained on the place. "We rambled over the old apartments, and the grass-grown terraces and avenues of the castle, and among the pines and fig trees laden with their fruits; and in the evening had a blazing fire lighted for us in the library," he wrote Sally. Washington did not know when he had been "lodged so much to my humour."

On their return from the trip, Peter continued to stay with Washington in the apartment at 89 rue Richelieu.

Only then, in November of 1824, did Washington begin to receive news of the bad reviews that *Tales of a Traveller* was getting both in England and America. At first he could hardly believe what he read. Sensitive as he was to criticism, he had actually known very little. From his first ventures into print he had been praised.

Suddenly his luck had turned. Love had failed him. Now the faith that he put in his writing also failed him.

# 24

# Indecent and Obscene

" 'ARE THEY CRUEL to travellers?' said a beautiful young Venetian lady, who had been hanging on the gentleman's arm.

'Cruel, signora!' echoed the estafette, giving a glance at the lady as he put spurs to his horse. 'Corpo di Bacco! They stilleto all the men; and as, to the women'—Crack! Crack! crack! crack! crack!—The last words were drowned in the smacking of the whip, and away galloped the estafette along the road to the Pontine marshes."

Irving had no need to reread the passage. He knew what he had written. But "Obscene?"

"If the truth of the charge be denied, we refer for proof of it to . . . the indecency drowned in the crack! crack! of the postillion's whip at Terracina. . . ."

The reviewer for the *United States Literary Gazette* also cited the story of "The Young Robber," where a "scene the most revolting to humanity is twice unnecessarily forced on the reader's imagination."

Irving had no need to reread that story either. A young

member of a robber gang had kidnapped a maiden with whom he was in love, a deed forbidden by the gang's code, and for good reason. This story was one of the more realistic ones in the section on Italian banditti, a true story that he had heard in Italy, but what had he forced on the reader? He had *indicated* what had happened. "His triumphant look, and the desolate condition of the unfortunate girl, left me no doubt of her fate. . . ." Later, after the gang members had drawn lots for their individual turns, the narrator of the story, in agony and rage, had "beheld the wretched victim, pale, dishevelled, her dress torn and disordered. . . ."

Perhaps, Washington admitted to himself, the story, true though it was, was too harsh and cruel, and he had made a mistake to include it. Yes, he could grant that. But then, how could the *London Magazine* find "The Bold Dragoon," that innocent and merry story, "offensive to the chastity of the Georgian home?"

Besides, that story had been all invention, so how could the critic of the *Edinburgh Magazine* write that "invention seems to be the quality in which he is most deficient."

Plots?—"dull." Descriptions of London life?—"decidedly unfortunate; for the double reason that as a picture of the past they are not original, and, as of the present, they are not true."

"The sterner criticism" that Washington had feared for *Bracebridge Hall* since the novelty of an American writing decent English had faded was now being levelled upon him. "Geoffrey's fame was occasioned by the fact of his being a prodigy for show—such as La Belle Sauvage, or the learned pig; up to the time of Geoffrey, there were no Belles Lettres in America, no native *littérateurs*, and he shot up at once with true American growth."

"Obscene . . ." "Untrue . . ."

And at the same time: "Nothing that can excite controversy, nothing that can occasion dissatisfaction; all, pensive, *gentlemanly*, and subdued; all, trifling and acquiescent as a drawing room conversation . . . a little pathos, a little sentiment . . . a little point and a little antithesis to . . . divert the attention from the lamentable deficiency of solid matter."

The very way the critics contradicted one another in their disparagement should have indicated to Washington that they were now reacting, as he had feared they would before, against a feeling that he had been overpraised in the past. But he had no heart for that sort of logic. He tried to put the words and phrases out of his mind as he had always attempted to banish what was unpleasant and to concentrate on the new projects he had begun before the reviews reached him.

Playwriting he had decided was not for him. He had worked on one or two more plays with Payne in the spring and toyed with the idea of original drama about Shakespeare as a youth. But the two plays on which he had done the most work, *Charles II* and *Richelieu*, and which were finally produced in London, brought in such a small financial return that Irving became convinced the effort he expended in this field was not worth his while. However, he had contracted with Galagnani to edit a series of British classics with his own critical introductions, and had already begun on the first volume, dedicated to the works of Goldsmith. Payne had suggested that he write a life of Cervantes, so he was reading what he could find on that Spanish master and was also doing some research on the life of William the Conqueror.

But a weight of depression hung over him, making it almost impossible to pursue any creative activity. Sitting at his desk, he wrote letters instead. He wrote to Leslie, a long, superficially cheerful letter, commenting on a visit that Leslie had made to Scott at Abbotsford, and discussing Leslie's current paintings at some length, for which he predicted much success. At last he spoke glancingly of himself. "Of my own fate

I sometimes feel a doubt. I am isolated in English literature, without any of the usual aids and influences by which an author's popularity is maintained and promoted. I have no literary coterie to cry me up; no partial reviewer to pat me on the back; the very review of my publisher is hostile to everything American. . . . I have one proud reflection, however, to sustain myself with—that I have never in any way sought to sue the praises nor deprecate the censures of reviewers, but have left my works to rise or fall by their own deserts."

So he tried to stiffen his back against the inner soreness the comments had caused. A New Yorker, Dominick Lynch, whom he had known in the *Salmagundi* days, appeared in Paris. Washington and Peter both were pleased to see him, to dine with him, and to take him to their favorite Paris haunts. After talking with Lynch about the old days in New York, Washington was inspired to repair the long lapse in correspondence with the friend who, more than any other, was the companion of those days, Henry Brevoort.

"I cannot tell you what pleasure I have received from long chats with Lynch about old times and old associates. His animated and descriptive manner has put all New York before me, and made me long to be once more there. I do not know whether it be the force of early impressions and associations, or whether it be really well-founded, but there is a charm about that little spot of earth; that beautiful city and its environs, that has a perfect spell over my imagination. The bay, the rivers and their wild and woody shores, the haunts of my boyhood, both on land and water, absolutely have a witchery over my soul."

He came at last, as he had to, to some comment on his latest book. *Tales of a Traveller* was having "a good run" in England, he wrote, but "has met with some handling from the press. However, as I do not read criticism, good or bad,

I am out of reach of attack. If my writings are worth anything, they will outlive temporary criticism; if not, they are
not worth caring about."

But, of course he did read criticism. And just now, in case
he should fail to see some particular blast, he seemed to have
acquired some unknown ill-wishers who made sure that he
did. Some habitué of Galagnani's reading room whom Washington identified in his journal simply as his "evil genius" was
taking pleasure in reminding him, every time he appeared
there, that the critics were attacking him "like the very devil
in England." Some unknown "friend" in America was for-
warding American newspapers that contained unfavorable
reviews. How could he not at least glance at these arrivals in
the post to see if they were fair or foul?

Writing to Brevoort, he attempted to defend himself by
an analysis of his style. "I fancy much of what I value myself
upon in writing, escapes the observation of the great mass of
my readers, who are intent more upon the story than the way
in which it is told. For my part, I consider a story merely as
a frame on which to stretch my materials. It is the play of
thought, and sentiment, and language; the weaving in of
characters, lightly, yet expressively delineated; the familiar
and faithful exhibition of scenes in common life; and the
half-concealed vein of humor that is often playing through
the whole;—these are among what I aim at, and upon which I
felicitate myself in proportion as I think I succeed. . . ."

For another page and more, he continued to explain "the
line of writing peculiar to myself," until at last he could
present that line as the reason why he had not embarked on a
novel, as Ebenezer often suggested, and as Brevoort himself
had also ventured to advise. "I believe the works that I have
written will be oftener re-read than any novel of the size that
I could have written. It is true that other writers have
crowded into the same branch of literature, and I now begin

to find myself elbowed by men who have followed my footsteps; but at any rate I have had the merit of adopting a line for myself, instead of following others."

He would have found it pleasanter if someone else had been writing these things for him, but facing up to attack for the first time in his life, he did the best he could.

More unhappy news came from America, sadder than adverse criticism. Maria Hoffman had died of a lingering illness in the fall. Washington left no comments on his reaction to this information. He was already suffering nostalgia for "the beautiful city of New York and its environs." Now the woman who had filled him with so many delicate and youthful emotions during his early years there was gone. He did not write about his memories. They too belonged to an enchantment that was past, the door in the mountain closed against them.

He had a letter from Ebenezer's oldest son, Pierre Paris, who had been a newborn infant when Washington returned to America from Europe in 1806. Pierre Paris was now a youth of eighteen, going to college, and trying his hand at writing. He sent a copy of a little periodical, *The Fly*, to his uncle in Paris, to let him read his contribution.

Washington replied in a dismally cautionary vein. He admitted that Pierre's articles "gave proof of a very promising talent," but added, "I am sorry, however, to find you venturing into print at so early an age, as I consider it extremely disadvantageous." With no mention of the fact that he himself had known admiration at nineteen for his Jonathan Oldstyle letters, he played heavy uncle for page after page. "I hope your literary vein has been but a transient one. . . .I hope none of those whose interests and happiness are dear to me will be induced to follow in my footsteps, and wander into the seductive but treacherous paths of literature. There is no life more precarious in its profits and fallacious in its enjoyments than that of an author. I speak from an experience which may be considered a favorable and prosperous one. . . ."

What else could he say? He knew that Henry Brevoort, who had admired and appreciated literature along with him, but who had kept his main energies for business, was now among the wealthiest men in New York. He knew that the brother next oldest to him, John Treat, was also a wealthy man, having pursued the legal career that Washington himself had found impossible. Casting his mind back to the country that he had left nearly ten years before, it seemed that everyone, except his financially unlucky brother, Ebenezer, was living in a sort of golden abundance, and certainly without fear of cruel attacks for "lack of creativeness," or "obscenity," or "triflingness."

"There is a large family connection of you growing up," he reminded his nephew. "I wish to urge the cultivation of a common union of interest and affection among you. The good of one should be considered the good of the whole. You should stand by each other in word and deed; 'in evil report and in good report'; discarding every petty spirit of jealousy; prompting each other's happiness, and building up each others' prosperity."

The family was a unit that had always been important to him: his own, where he had been the youngest, pampered and cherished by all save his father; the Hoffman family; the Brevoort family; the family of his sister, Sally Van Wart; the Foster family in Dresden; and now, in Paris, the Storrow family. Without such families how would he have endured?

He took his downcast spirits to the Storrows day after day. Mrs. Storrow scoffed at the criticisms he received through the mail or from his "evil genius." She entreated him to remember that in spite of such mean-spirited attacks, his book was selling, as indeed it was, and that she thought it perfect, which she did. The children clambered about him, as always, teasing for stories. At the Storrows' he spoke one day of a desire to learn Spanish. Learning German had been a distraction back in 1817 when P. and E. Irving Company was sliding toward bankruptcy. Now Minny and Susie Storrow declared that they wished to learn Spanish too. Clasping them like talismans to enforce his resolution, he engaged a tutor to teach them all the language.

The year of 1824 dragged to its close. "Dec. 29th.—A restless, sleepless night, full of uncomfortable thoughts—woke before four—studied Spanish after breakfast—took lessons from eleven to twelve—went to Galignani's—read a very favorable critique on French translation of Tales of a Traveller—two French translations have appeared—called at Mr. West's—Mrs. Patterson sitting for her picture.—Lynch there—stayed till half past three—walked in Palais Royal—returned home—dined with Peter—studied Spanish in the evening—a triste day, though laughed a good deal both at West's and at dinner—a merry head may sometimes go with a heavy heart. . . . 31st.—Retire to bed at eleven—this has been a dismal day of depression, and closes a year, part of which has been full of sanguine hope, of social enjoyment, peace of mind, and health of body; and the latter part saddened by disappointments and distrust of the world and of myself; by sleepless nights and joyless days. May the coming year prove more thoroughly propitious!"

The new year of 1825, however, started off very like the last half of the old year. He studied Spanish to such purpose that he was soon reading the works of Lope de Vega and Calderón, transcribing various scenes into his notebooks, and reading Spanish history in its own language. A Spanish tale caught his fancy and he thought of adapting it. He began to write in a rather haphazard fashion a series of essays on American manners and customs. Having been so long absent from his own country, he felt he saw more clearly the differences between the culture in which he had grown up and the one in which he had lived for ten years. Still his journal entries continued the monotonous theme. "Awoke with low spirits—read in Calderón—a misty chilly day."

In March, Peter, once again half-crippled with rheumatism, departed for a protracted visit with Sally in Birmingham. Left by himself, Washington continued to read Spanish, to fret with the American essays, and to dine out and go to the theater. Payne was still in England but Washington heard from him frequently about his various theatrical hopes, on some of which Washington advised him from time to time. He was reminded of Payne even more frequently by calls from various of Payne's creditors who were constantly appearing at the apartment on the rue Richelieu.

"I wish," Irving wrote to Payne, not for the first time, "that you would send money to pay off these petty scores, as they continually threaten to seize the furniture; and make my residence in the apartment very uncomfortable. I never have been placed in such a situation before—I am tenacious in money matters. I pay down for everything, and cannot bear to have an account outstanding against me; much less to be dunned for one. I am sensitive in this respect. Since I have lived in this apartment, however, I have been so beset and persecuted with a degree of impertinence, that I actually begin to feel as if I were grossly in debt & bilking my creditors."

John Howard Payne, devoted to Irving but incompetent to deal with money whether he was flush or impoverished, sent dribs of money from time to time to pay on his accounts, but Irving's harassment by Payne's creditors went on.

Spring came and then summer, and Irving's life continued in the same uninspired pattern. Alexander Everett, newly appointed United States Ambassador to Spain, appeared in the city, and meeting him, Irving mentioned his desire to visit

Spain now that he had some knowledge of its language and history. Everett suggested that such travel might be made easier for him if he were given some vague attachment to the embassy, but no action was taken on the suggestion.

Payne appeared in Paris in August, excited by a contract to write a number of plays for a London producer, but with a curious agitation in his manner. Washington thought that was explained when Payne admitted that in spite of pleasing prospects he was currently out of funds and needed to borrow a few napoleons. Soon, however, it developed that something more was disturbing him. Payne began to speak somewhat hesitantly about Mrs. Shelley. He had been honored by her friendship and made deeply happy that he could serve her from time to time by obtaining theater tickets for her. None of this was especially astonishing to Irving. He had seen for himself, a year before, how devoted Payne was to Mary Wollstonecraft Shelley, and how lightly the young woman accepted Payne's homage.

But now, in a stumbling way, Payne was talking about how natural it was that Mrs. Shelley's admiration should not be for him but someone else. Irving raised quizzical eyebrows. Finally Payne declared he would give Irving a packet of the lady's letters which would make everything clear. Thrusting the packet into Irving's hands, he departed for his own room.

Later, in his bedroom that warm August night, Washington untied the string on the packet and read, first of all, a note from Payne.

"My dear Irving, I have reflected a long time before I determined to show you this correspondence, because from its nature it might appear indelicate to expose the letters—especially to you—as you are more involved in it than you even appear to be. It was some time before I discovered that I was only sought as a source of an introduction to you—and I think you will, on reading the papers, feel that I might have mistaken the nature of my acquaintance with the writer, without any gratuitous vanity—But at the same time you will admit that she is a woman of the highest & most amiable qualities & one whose wish for friendship it would be doing yourself injustice not to meet—Of course, it must be a perfect secret between ourselves that I have shown the letters—They are at present not known to any one—You must not look upon the affair in a ridiculous light, as, if you should I shall never forgive myself for having exposed so fine a mind to so injurious a construction . . ."

A little startled, a little mystified—but not so mystified as he might have been, Washington recalled the evening in the London theater with Mrs. Shelley and Payne. He remembered something he had tried not to notice at the time—a certain languishing look in Mrs. Shelley's eyes when she turned them on himself.

Payne's letter continued, doggedly honest, making clear how often Mary Shelley had turned the conversations she had with him to the subject of Irving, and of why, realizing his own love for her was hopeless, he was giving Irving the proof of her undisguised interest in him.

"I do not ask you," he wrote, "to fall in love—but I should even feel a little proud of myself if you thought the lady worthy of that distinction."

A good deal bemused, Irving turned to the letters that Mary Shelley had written to Payne. Soon he saw that he was indeed "involved" in the correspondence. Mrs. Shelley frequently referred to his writings. In one letter, she begged Payne to let her see at least one of the letters that Irving had written to him—any letter—to prove to herself how much Irving's influence had meant to him. Payne had obliged with a letter and Mrs. Shelley had studied it carefully and then returned it to Payne with a comment on how much the friendship of someone like Irving would mean to her. But "it cannot be—though every thing I hear & know renders it more desirable—How can Irvine—surrounded by fashion, rank & splendid friendships pilot his pleasure bark from the gay press into this sober, sad, enshadowed nook?"

Alone in his room, picking up the letters and reading them one by one in the flickering lamplight, Washington must have paused to conjure up the pale face of the author of *Franken-stein*. Shelley's widow. Daughter of William Godwin, that brilliant old man who had so praised his *Sketch Book*. An intimate of Byron's. A talented writer of Gothic romance herself.

Somehow, though, there must have been something very unromantic to Washington about the way Mary Shelley revealed herself to Payne in these letters, something distastefully egocentric and heedless of the feelings of others. How could a woman of sensibility make light jokes about the possibility of marrying Irving to a man whom she knew was in love with her?

When Irving had read the last letter, he folded it and stacked up all the letters into the same kind of packet that Payne had given him, then set them on his desk to return to Payne tomorrow. He noted in his journal: "Read Mrs. Shelley's letters," and added no comment, but undressed, blew out the light, and went to bed.

Love, after all, was not come by in this fashion. Not through someone fantasizing romance in her loneliness, inventing ridiculous pictures of the beloved. "How can Irvine," she had written, carelessly misspelling his name, "surrounded by fashion, rank & splendid friendships pilot his pleasure bark from the gay press—?" It is possible that a wry smile twisted Washington's lips in the darkness as he recalled that sentence and contemplated the fashion and rank and splendid friendships that surrounded his "pleasure bark." No, love was something else. Love was someone very young, very shy and kind, with a mind that "unfolded itself leaf by leaf—."

An invitation for him and Peter to go to Bordeaux to observe the grape harvest and the making of the wine came in
the next week or so. Peter, returned from Birmingham after
a stopover at Havre, where the steamboat project was still
causing concern, expressed himself agreeable to accepting the
Bordeaux invitation. Both he and Washington had a number
of American and English acquaintances in that city, and a
new friend, M. Guestier, who had a château outside the city
and was the owner of many vineyards, was the one who
had proffered the invitation.

They left Paris in mid-September and the journey southward across France in the fine early fall weather bolstered
their spirits. At Bordeaux they were welcomed by their
friends and carried off at once by M. Guestier to his château
in the Médoc country. They were late for the winemaking,
but Washington visited the caves where the wines were
stored and investigated every aspect of the winemaking pro-
cess until he had made himself an amateur expert on *les vins du
la pays.*

Later, he and Peter returned to Bordeaux and took lodgings. Washington began to work on his American essays
again. Day after day, his journal noted, "Mind tranquil—slept
well." A brief flare of worry that arose at the news of the
failure of an English banker with whom he, Peter, and Henry
Van Wart had had dealings was extinguished when further
mails brought the news that the failure had not affected the
finances of Henry or any of the Irvings.

Christmas came and he and Peter lingered in Bordeaux.
"For some time past, indeed ever since I have resumed my
pen, my mind has been tranquil. I sleep better and feel
pleasanter," he noted in his journal. On the last day of 1825,
he was again insisting on his tranquility. "Write letters—walk
out—fine cool weather—all the world buying *bonbons*—dined
at home—afterward walked out with Mr. Johnston—evening
at Mrs. Johnston's—play chess—in the night, military music in

the street. . . . So closes the year—tranquil in mind, though doubtful of fortune and full of uncertainties—a year very little of which I would willingly live over again though some parts have been tolerably pleasant. . . ."

There was no hint here, as there had been ten years before when he suddenly left America, that he had reached some sort of dead end in his life and was determined to strike out for something new, something that once again might make "quite another being" of him.

# Part Three

By the Alhambran
Fountain

# 25

# An Entirely New Line

"I THINK I TOLD you that I would write you a letter from the Alhambra," he wrote to the young woman back in Madrid. "It is now near the hour of sunset of a warm day, the sun is still shining upon the towers which overlook this court, and a beautiful, mellow light is spread about its colonades and marble halls. The fountain is immediately before me, ever memorable from the tragic fate of the gallant Abencerrages. I have just diluted my ink from its waters. . . ."

It was March of 1828. He had been in Spain for more than two years. The time seemed almost a blur to him now, a blur of days spent at a desk from dawn until nightfall, reading old Spanish documents and volumes, checking and rechecking notes, making notes and outlines, and then, writing, writing, writing. He had seen very little of Spain during his first year there, except for his evening walks in the wild gardens of Madrid's Retiro at sunset, and, now and then, a bullfight. Washington tried to gloss over the attraction that bullfights had for him. Objectively, he felt that he should disapprove the cruelty to bulls, horses, and men, but there was a fascination in these ancient spectacles that drew him back, week after week. Still, the pattern of the days, weeks, and months had been exercise of the brain and the pen.

"Good heavens!" he continued the letter he was writing by the Alhambran fountain, "after passing two years amidst the sunburnt wastes of Castile, to be let loose to rove at large over this fragrant and lovely land!"

The "two years amidst the sunburnt wastes of Castille" had begun suddenly and unexpectedly. At the beginning of the year 1826, Irving had written to Alexander Everett in Madrid to remind him, somewhat diffidently, of his hope to have a journey to Spain facilitated by some connection with the American embassy there. Everett had replied promptly, giving Irving a nominal attachment to the legation. Everett also mentioned the imminent publication of a new and definitive work by the Spanish historian, Don Martin Fernandez de Navarette, on the life and voyages of Christopher Columbus. How fitting, Everett had written, if America's most admired man of letters, Washington Irving, were to undertake the translation of this work into English for the benefit of his countrymen in the New World discovered by Columbus. Nor need this be altogether a labor of love, Everett had continued. He imagined that Irving might make as much as a thousand or fifteen hundred pounds from the endeavor.

The months Washington had spent studying and reading Spanish with no particular goal in view seemed oddly fateful. He destroyed the American essays he had been writing as though he had never taken them seriously, convinced Peter to make the Spanish journey with him, and within days they were on their way. They had a rapid trip over the mountains and then across the Castilian plain, in a diligence drawn by galloping mules with bells on their harnesses, and Washington was caught by a picturesqueness that seemed to exceed that of Italy. He dashed off a note to Leslie, in London, expressing the wish that he and Newton were with them. Every Spaniard was "a subject for the pencil," and they could "lay up ample materials" for their Spanish pictures.

Arrived in Madrid, however, the sightseer's mood had quickly vanished. He called on Everett, who greeted him warmly and was eager to have him started at once on his translation of the Navarette work. Seeing Irving first of all as a literary man, Everett took him to meet Obadiah Rich, an American who had long been a resident of Spain and was currently American consul in Madrid. More importantly, Rich was a dedicated book and manuscript collector, and his library, gathered through years of effort, contained what was perhaps the finest treasury of Hispano-American literature in Spain. The amiable, consecrated Mr. Rich soon was not only offering Irving free run of his library but suggesting that he and Peter take up their lodging in one wing of his house. The charge? But why should there be a charge, Mr. Rich asked. Well, very well, five dollars a week.

Washington and Peter had settled into the empty wing of Mr. Rich's vast, rambling house. It was situated not far from the center of the city but somehow, once inside its walls and in the rooms which all faced inward on a courtyard garden, the Irvings felt isolated in quiet, broken now and then by the sound of convent bells. Everett brought Washington the Navarette volumes and he settled down to study them. Almost at once Washington saw that the Navarette work was simply a compilation of all the discoverable documents having to do with Columbus' life and voyages—a huge, comprehensive, and masterly compilation, but still just that—a reference for scholars, not a readable history for ordinary laymen. A new idea began to present itself, an idea that would entail much more effort than a mere translation of the work and yet might be much more satisfying ultimately. For days, even for several weeks, he pondered the choice. He

felt that he knew his own talents, his ability to sketch colorful backgrounds, to suggest character and to let "the play of
thought, and sentiment and language," be stretched across
the framework of a story. At last he came to the conclusion
that shaped the next two years for him. He would put his
talents to work in adapting the material Navarette had collected to fashion a comprehensive history of America's discoverer that would be appealing to the average educated reader,
the same reader who had already enjoyed Irving's earlier writings.

Irving had no conception then of the work that would be
involved. A translation would have been simplicity itself by
comparison. His plan demanded not only the translation and
study of the documents Navarette had collected but a search
for connective material as well. He pored through the books
and documents in Obadiah Rich's library. He sought permission to examine documents in official libraries and museums,
permission not easy for a foreigner to obtain. In Spain, he
was not known as an author as he was in France and Germany, and even with the sponsorship of Everett he could not
always gain admission where he wanted it. But he went
where he could and meantime he had Obadiah Rich's library
as a resource. So he read, he checked, he outlined, he began
writing, he found discrepancies, he rechecked, he rewrote,
and then read, checked, and rewrote again.

"Columbus all day . . ." "All day Columb . . ." "Columb
. . ." were the entries in his journal night after night through
most of 1826 and part of 1827.

Social life as he had known it in Paris and London almost
ceased to exist. At Everett's suggestion, he and Peter called
upon the heads of the various legations in Madrid, but the
invitations to dinners, soirées, and balls which followed he
steadfastly refused. Every two weeks or so they had dinner
with Mr. Everett and his family. Sometimes they took tea

with the Rich family. A young American visitor in the city, the twenty-three-year-old Alexander Slidell Mackenzie, was too lively and interesting a new acquaintance to be ignored. A captain in the United States Navy, Mackenzie (who had been born Slidell but taken an uncle's last name) was spending a wandering year in Spain, taking the sort of eager, voluminous notes on everything he saw that Washington had made years before on his first European tour, although Mackenzie's were a bit more candid. Amused and entertained by the young man, Washington spent a good many hours with him before he departed in April. Aside from such diversions, his pattern was to be up at dawn, then into the library where he worked until dusk signaled the hour for a turn in the garden or a stroll through the Retiro. Except when now and then he went to a bullfight.

Pierre Munro Irving, William's fourth son, arrived unexpectedly in Madrid during the summer. Washington and Peter learned of their nephew's presence in the city with some chagrin. Had the lines of communication with home broken down so far that neither Ebenezer nor John Treat Irving, the only surviving brothers, knew that Washington and Peter were in Madrid when they sent Pierre off on his grand tour of Europe? Hiding their bewilderment, Washington and Peter hurried to greet the young man and escort him about the city, taking sightseeing walks and rides that they themselves had neglected. Pierre, at twenty-four, was an agreeable and intelligent young man, fond of both of his uncles and full of admiration for the one who was a famous author. Washington, in turn, developed a fondness for Pierre whom he had last seen eleven years before, and suggested that when Pierre's travels through Europe had finally taken him to London he might be able to render some services in the publication of the Columbus manuscript.

Such a suggestion was actually premature and without any

definite basis. Washington had queried Murray about his interest in a life of Columbus when he began the project, but Murray had refused any commitment until he saw a completed manuscript. Talking with Pierre as they walked in the Prado or visited galleries, Washington himself had no idea when the manuscript would be finished. Unaware of this, Pierre promised happily to do what he could when he arrived in London and then took off for the north.

Washington's journal again began to carry the monotonous entries, "Columbus all day . . . all day Columb." He had written a lengthy comic history once, first in a rush of high spirits and then in a flight from grief, but it had not taken him very long, all told. Writing a serious history, he was discovering, took a great deal more time and effort.

The time lengthened further when he was enticed into a digression from the main project. The presence of the Moors in Spain had interested him when he was a boy, reading whatever books of adventure or geography came his way. Somehow he had become acquainted with the story of Boabdil, last king of the Moors. Now, reviewing the reigns and activities of Ferdinand and Isabella, who played such important roles in Columbus' life, he was again running into Boabdil and the Moors as the Spanish monarchs ignored Columbus in their overriding desire to expel the Moors from their last stronghold in Spain, Granada. Washington became so entranced with the events of this conquest, and with the character and behavior of Boabdil, that the idea for another book leaped into his mind. He laid aside the Columbus manuscript to outline it and title it *The Conquest of Granada*.

He had thought to have his book on Columbus finished by the end of 1826. Writing and thinking about a pendant manuscript as well, Irving saw 1826 end and the winter months of 1827 succeed each other with neither manuscript anywhere near completion. Washington, and Peter too, began to feel that these particular labors had been going on forever. From time to time, Washington tried to reassure himself that he was progressing. He wrote to Thomas Storrow in Paris, "I reflected that this was a trial of skill in an entirely new line in which I had to satisfy both the public and myself. I determined therefore that it should be a fair one, that I would enter minutely into every research & investigation & in short execute every thing to the best of my abilities. The task has been laborious and I have much work still before me. . . ."

In the spring of 1827, Henry Wadsworth Longfellow, making a tour of Europe before assuming a professor's post at Harvard, called upon Irving with a letter of introduction from the American historian, George Ticknor, who had recently returned to America from several years abroad. Washington was gracious. He arranged for Longfellow to meet all the people he knew in Madrid. He himself was available in the evenings. But the daytime hours were devoted to work. Years later, Longfellow wrote his recollections of Irving that spring and summer in Madrid. He remembered a handsome man, "all mirth and good humor in society," but he also remembered the hours Irving spent at his desk.

"One summer morning, passing his house at the early hour of six, I saw his study window already wide open. On my mentioning it to him afterwards, he said, 'Yes, I am always at my work as early as six.' Since then I have often remembered that sunny morning and that open window,—so suggestive of his sunny temperament and his open heart, and equally so of his patient and persistent toil."

Longfellow was bemused by the outward mildness of Irving's manner. Washington would not impose on others the anxieties that secretly beset him, the growing desperation about his financial situation, the need to have this interminable book finished, and the worry always present as to whether Murray would like it or not. He regretted now that he had ever undertaken such a mountainous labor and Rich's library, once a delight, now seemed a prison cell.

Finally, in July of 1827, a year and a half after coming to Spain, he ground his way to the end of the narrative and sought, with generally poor luck, for copyists to begin writing out the manuscript for him, so that he could send copies to America as well as England. The book was not really finished. Dozens of loose ends needed tying up, many portions needed rewriting, and he still had to locate many old prints and maps that he wanted to use as illustrations. Still, by the end of the month, it was complete enough so that he could bundle up half of it and send it off by envoy's pouch to the American consul in London, Colonel Thomas Aspinwall, who had agreed to act as his agent. Along with the manuscript, Washington sent an anxious letter hoping that the Colonel could not only sell it to Murray but achieve a good price for it. The next month he sent the remainder of the bulky work.

Then he began waiting for word from London.

The friends whom he had made, almost in spite of himself, during his months of labor, filled a larger part of his life. From his first days in Madrid, he had found a welcome at the home of M. D'Oubril, the Russian Ambassador to Spain. Madame D'Oubril was a friendly, attractive woman. There were three young children, and a delightful young lady who was Madame D'Oubril's niece, Mlle. Antoinette Bolvillier. The irresistible pattern had formed once more, a family circle that included a sympathetic older woman, a pretty and intelligent young woman, and a cluster of small children to add their innocence and liveliness to the group. In the weeks of waiting for word from Aspinwall in London, the D'Oubril house became another of his homes away from home where he could find affection and encouragement. Here also he found good conversation with a young Russian prince,

Dmitry Ivanovitch Dolgorouki, who was attached to the legation as a secretary.

Not until the end of October did Irving finally hear from Aspinwall that Murray had accepted the manuscript of Columbus on the best terms Irving had yet received—three thousand guineas, payable three hundred pounds down and the balance in three-month installments over a period of two years. Aspinwall sent no hint that Murray had shown a good deal of hesitation about accepting the book. He wrote only of the cheerful conclusion of the business, and Irving was almost delirious with relief.

That fall he found it possible to take some excursions into the countryside away from Madrid with Peter and other friends, and to visit the Escorial, Toledo, and Aranjuez. Returned to Madrid, Rich's library no longer seemed a "nagging shrew" and he could settle down there to begin serious work on *The Conquest of Granada*.

In February of 1828, as Murray was publishing *The Life and Voyages of Columbus* in England (though Irving had no hint of that), Washington was at last planning the sort of excursion he had longed for, a journey that would take him into the Spain about which he had been reading and writing so long—the plains of La Mancha, Cadiz, Seville, and at midpoint, the highpoint, Granada itself, the last home of the Moors.

When it came to the issue, Peter, who had grown more and more unhappy with the climate of Spain, decided to return to Paris; so Washington took off on the journey with two congenial members of Madrid's diplomatic society.

In a diligence, with hired outriders to guard them against the ever-present threat of bandits on Spain's wilder trails, the party set forth, into cold rain, biting winds, and bleak vistas. But the way led southward, and after three days traveling they reached the warmer airs of Andalusia. They lingered a while in Cordova, making trips on horseback into the mountains behind the city. For Washington, however, Granada was the goal and at last he was on his way to it. One day, as the diligence turned around a promontory of the mountains, there it was: "Granada, with its towers, its Alhambra, and its snowy mountains burst upon our sight."

The travelers spent the night in a *posada* in Granada, but with the morning Washington hurried to ride up the winding trails of that curious hill in the center of the valley which was crowned with the ruins of the Moorish palace, the Alhambra. No restoration work had been attempted yet on the huge old structure. Irving came upon it in 1828 just as the years had left it, many of its walls crumbled, its courtyards and patios overgrown with roses, other flowers, trees, vines, and weeds. In the nooks and crannies of some of its courts, beggars, gypsies, and criminals made their makeshift homes and sometimes hung their laundry on ropes stretched from one delicate column to another.

The beauty that remained filled Washington with wonder. The decay and ruin that blurred it and the encrustations of everyday life springing up in cracks and corners, heedless of finding shelter where kings once had lived in luxury, echoed the one teaching of his father that he had accepted as truth. All—all passes. Man is as grass.

All day he explored the halls, rooms, and terraces and then sat down at last in the courtyard by the great fountain to write to Mlle. Bolvillier. He wrote of how his admiration was awakened by "the elegant habits and delicate taste of the Moorish monarchs." He loved the intricately ornamented walls, the aromatic groves, the enlivening sound of the fountains, the balconies and galleries open to the mountain breeze and overlooking the loveliest scenery of the valley of the Darro. It seemed to him "an earthly paradise," a paradise that had the added charm of being imbued with the past and its mysteries like a haunting perfume.

One small mystery had been particularly on his mind as he roamed the palace. In the course of his study of old chronicles he had read somewhere that Boabdil, on leaving the castle to surrender its keys to Ferdinand and Isabella, had begged that the door by which he departed be walled up so no one might ever walk through it again. Was there really such a walled door? All morning, as Washington had walked through echoing chambers and along crumbling walls, he had looked for some sign of a walled-up portal. At last he asked an old man who lived in a shack in one of the outer courts if he had ever heard of such a door. The old man consulted with several other inhabitants of the palace even older than himself, and one of these pointed out to Irving a gateway that had been walled up for the duration of everyone's memory, a gateway which the ancient creature remembered to have heard his parents say was the gate by which the Moorish king departed.

The seal of satisfaction was set on the day for Irving when he looked on the very outlines of the gate by which the unfortunate Boabdil was expelled from paradise. The gate in the wall, filled with stone—like the cleft in the Catskills, forever hidden behind a waterfall, like the cavern in the German mountains, within which Emperor Charles and his army lived through their enchanted eternity—was a basic image on which his fancy seized.

In the courtyard where he sat writing his letter to the sound of the plashing fountain, shadows were lengthening. "The old halls begin to darken around me," he wrote to Mlle. Antoinette, "and the bat is flitting about the court in place of the birds which were lately chirping here. I have performed my promise and have written to you from the halls of the Alhambra. . . . The present letter I will finish by lamp light at the posada. I will gather you a flower, however, from the Court of the Lions, and enclose it in the letter to atone for the want of flowers in my style. And so farewell at present to the Alhambra and all its tragical and poetical associations."

"Farewell at present . . ." But already the idea for another book was teasing at his mind. Surely, he thought, he could gather enough material to write a book about this "ancient pile." He could describe it as it was now, with its strange, ragged inhabitants, and then describe it as it had been. He could recount some of the legends connected with it. Meantime, there was *The Conquest of Granada* in his luggage, still half-finished, awaiting the descriptions he could add after viewing some of the sites of the story firsthand. Meantime, also, he had piles of notes on other voyagers contemporary with Columbus which he had not been able to make use of in *The Life* but which he was sure would make another book.

Sitting by the fountain as darkness fell, a wave of homesickness came over him. It had been so long since he had seen his friends in America, so long since he had gazed on the city of his boyhood. His mind was full of projects that would keep him in Spain for at least a few months to come, but he resolved that as soon as *The Conquest of Granada* was finished and his notes were in order for the other ideas, he would fulfill what he now thought of as his dearest wish. He would go home.

# 26

# The Alhambra

IN AMERICA, John Quincy Adams, last of the Presidents in the gentleman-statesman, New England or Virginia tradition, was campaigning for re-election against his chief rival of the preceding election of 1824, the people's hero, Andrew Jackson. Much had changed in the mood of the country since Washington Irving had left it in 1815, thirteen years before. Growth in itself had done much to change the mood. Cities were larger and more populous. Settlements were pressing out and out toward the west and north, overrunning the country that Irving had known as frontier land, leaving that country domesticated. The land around Lake Otswego in central New York that James Fenimore Cooper had known as wilderness when a boy had become a region of towns and farms, thanks to his father's activities in developing it. The wild land along the St. Lawrence River, to which Washington had journeyed with the Hoffmans and Ogdens in 1803, was settled country also, boasting, among other villages, a town called Ogdensburg.

All this spreading out and taking up of land had led, one way or another, to a spreading out of democracy as well.

Property qualifications for the right to vote had been abolished in most of the Northern States. A host of craftsmen, dockers, loggers, riverboat men, and laborers who had never been able to vote before were enfranchised. As a result the patriotism that the Lads of Kilkenny had mocked in 1806 was as nothing to the boasting of thousands of newly prideful Americans. Thumbs in gallusses, they bragged of being citizens of "the greatest Republic of all time." They were "cute" and "smart" and spat tobacco juice into the spittoons which were the newest commodity of civilization, or onto the floors, or the carpets or whatever, and they tolerated no criticism from anybody, native or foreign. For this large and vocal group, there was pride in everything American—pride in the country's leveled forests, its harnessed streams, its new steamboats, its new canals, and in the fortunes men were making as they chopped down the trees, dammed streams for factories, and built and operated the steamboats.

There was just as fierce a pride in American cultural activities, however vaguely some might understand or enjoy them. There was pride in the paintings of Washington Allston, who had won some acclaim abroad, and in the paintings of his pupil, Samuel F. B. Morse (though not enough to win him the commission to paint the panels in the Capitol building, which disappointment turned him to inventing things). Charles Wilson Peale's paintings were admired, as were those of his artist sons, namesakes of artists every one, from Rembrandt on through Rubens and Titian.

People felt pride in the continuing literary activity of James Kirke Paulding, Washington's old collaborator, and joy in the novels of James Fenimore Cooper, for Cooper's thorny prose style could not hide his blazing talent as a storyteller and he wrote, moreover, of American scenes, American frontier types, and of Indians, both good and bad. The poems of William Cullen Bryant and of Fitz Greene Halleck were further proof that Americans had no need to import any such fripperies from abroad.

As for Washington Irving, pride in him had become a sort of national touchstone, like "the pursuit of happiness," for those who had not read him as well as those who had. Washington really had not needed to cringe as he had done under the bad reviews of *Tales of a Traveller* when they were forwarded to him in Paris. His name, his fame had already been established in America, and thousands bought and read that book simply because his name (or Geoffrey Crayon's) was on it, not even aware that the *Literary Gazette* had been offended by its indecencies. Thousands were now buying *The Life and Voyages of Columbus*, the publication of which Ebenezer had arranged immediately after it was published in England by Murray. The book was indeed the first readable and comprehensive life of the great discoverer of America, and it seemed fateful that Washington Irving should have written it.

Irving had always been first. The first writer to make New Yorkers laugh at themselves with *Salmagundi* and the first writer to throw a veil of sentiment and legend over the city, its river, and its highlands. Knickerbocker, by this time, had become a synonym for any New Yorker, and Knickerbocker Fire Companies or insurance companies had already begun to spring up. Rip Van Winkle was a figure known to the illiterate as well as the literate. Added to this was the fame Irving had won abroad. He had been the *first* American writer to be so lionized. Edgy questioning about why he did not return continued, but the very concern Americans felt about that gave some measure of his importance to readers and nonreaders alike. Had he not won such fame, no one would have cared.

But of course he did not really know the nature of his reputation in America. Of the reviews he had received there, he remembered the bad ones. The letters he received from Ebenezer, John Treat, and Brevoort gave him no measure of the general feeling. He had no sense of a country waiting for his return.

As it was, he continued to think of himself as homesick and to do nothing about returning. "It would seem you shape your course by pleasant companions," William had written to him once when he was dallying through Italy. He had a much greater commitment to his writing now, but pleasant companions still shaped some of his hours.

From Granada, he traveled on to Seville, where he planned to do some research. There he was soon joined by a young artist, David Wilkie, whom he had first met in London through Leslie and Newton. Wilkie was a brisk and out-spoken Scotsman, and embarked on a tour of the continent; he could not go through Spain without stopping for a while with Irving. For two weeks Washington put writing aside while he and Wilkie toured the galleries and cathedrals of Seville. They admired some of the accepted masterpieces, held their own opinions about others, and discovered to their satisfaction, unrecognized gems that dated before the days of Murillo. At times Wilkie corrected some of Washington's enthusiasms, rebuking some of his admirations as "too costumy—too costumy." He also worked at a portrait of Washington, which was to be forwarded to America and Henry Brevoort.

Then Wilkie departed and Washington lingered in the lodgings he had taken in a boardinghouse and set to work again on *The Conquest of Granada*. He had borrowed something from the format of *Knickerbocker's History* for this new chronicle, and was having a mythical narrator tell the story. By purporting that an old and somewhat ironic priest, Fra Antonia Agapida, was the author, Washington was enabled to recount the substance of the history of the conquest as he had learned it, while enlivening it from time to time with Fra Agapida's digressions into legend or admiring or deprecatory comment. He was pleased with the freedom this gave him, so much greater than that he had known in writing *Columbus*. Even so the work proceeded slowly, for he was now also revising *Columbus*, that book having done so well in England that Murray was planning a second edition. Washington had picked up enough new information to want to make additions and corrections.

Drudging away in Seville, he missed the Madrid friends who had given a homelike atmosphere to his months there. He wrote a number of letters to Antoinette Bolviller and to the children of the D'Oubril household. To Prince Dolgorouki he wrote, "I regret extremely that there is no likelihood of your visiting Seville while I am here. The chances of my return to Madrid are very slight, and yet I cannot endure the idea that I am to leave Spain without seeing anything more of your household."

As summer advanced the weather grew uncomfortably warm. Washington had become acquainted with a young lodger at his boardinghouse, a consumptive Englishman named John Hall. Suffering from the heat in the city, he and Hall decided to find quarters outside the city where the air might be cooler. Soon thereafter, they moved to a small cottage some eight miles from Seville, the Casa de Cera.

The house was set in the midst of a vast and sunburnt plain, the "Tablada," but was itself surrounded by walls within which were gardens and orange and citron trees. Here, while the ailing Hall passed his days in a desultory study of Arabic, Irving plugged away at *Granada*, interrupting the silent hours now and then to ride into Seville on horseback to consult books in the library there. In the evening, Hall would take a little exercise by riding the horse out onto the plain and Washington would walk along beside him.

His brow was often damp as he worked. His hand, holding his quill, stuck to the paper as he wrote. But in the almost perfect solitude, he progressed so well that he was moved to one of his rare moods of hortatory advice.

"Fix," he wrote his young Russian friend, Dolgorouki, "your attention on noble objects and noble purposes, and sacrifice all temporary and trivial things to their attainment. . . . Above all, mark *one line* in which to excel, and bend all your thoughts and exertions to rise to eminence or rather to advance towards perfection in that *line*."

Fixed on one line himself, hewing away to one purpose as he had done only intermittently in the past, he followed up his revisions on *Columbus* with thoroughness. The port of Palos, from which Columbus had set sail on his great voyage, was only twenty miles distant from the Casa de Cera. Traveling in a calesa, Irving journeyed to Palos and poked about the town for several days, taking notes for an enlarged description of the port.

When he returned to the cottage on the "Tablada," he found the heat so intense that he decided that he and Hall should make another move. Within a few weeks, they had crossed the Bay and were settled in a two-story house, called Caracol, on the outskirts of Puerto de Santa Maria, a few miles from Cadiz.

From this house in Puerto de Santa Maria, Washington was able to send off a good portion of *Granada* to Colonel Aspinwall, asking him to offer it to Murray. As always, he sent a duplicate of the material to Ebenezer in New York. Along with this, he also sent corrected manuscript for the second edition of *The Life and Voyages of Columbus* both to England and America. Then he went back to work on the last portion of *The Conquest of Granada* and began to write as well about the personalities and voyages of some of Columbus' contemporaries.

"I am haunted," he wrote to Peter in September, "by an incessant and increasing desire to visit America, and if I once get in motion it is a chance if I come to anchor again until I find myself in New York. I will endeavor, therefore, to provide against the possibility of such restlessness." This he proceeded to do by taking notes on the life of Mahomet for still another possible book.

Puerto de Santa Maria offered more opportunities for friendship than had the lonely Casa de Cera, chiefly with a certain Johann Nikolaus Böhl von Faber and his family. Von Faber was a German scholar and bibliophile, married to a Spanish wife at whose insistence he had settled in Spain. He was manager of the William Duff Gordon wine company in Puerto de Santa Maria, but his chief interests remained literary, and he had made himself especially learned in old Spanish poetry and drama. A quick sympathy sprang up between Irving and von Faber, both of them so fascinated by the history and literature of a country not their own. Irving found encouragement in von Faber's conversation and books alike, and they spoke with some bewilderment about the lack of interest that Spaniards themselves seemed to have in their past. "They turn their backs upon their old writers and then are piqued when they find strangers appreciate them more than they do themselves," Irving wrote later. "They are like some husbands who neglect their wives but are ready to draw their swords the moment they detect a stranger ogling them." Undeterred, both Irving and von Faber continued their love affair with Spain.

Irving maintained his pattern of work, research, reading, note-taking and writing. In November, the heat having abated somewhat, Irving left Hall at the house in Puerto de Santa Maria and traveled to Seville to spend a few weeks of research in the Archives of the Indies, a collection which he had finally won permission to visit.

Von Faber's daughter, Cecilia, who was married to the Marquis of Arco Hermoso, lived in Seville. She was a young woman as much interested in literature as her father and the center of a literary group in the city. Washington was soon on friendly terms with the Marchioness, who enjoyed telling him tales and anecdotes about the Spanish peasantry she had known in her childhood. He also talked with her about poetry and soon was encouraging her in her attempts at novel writing. Some years later this Seville friend would become an admired Spanish writer under the pseudonym of Fernan Caballero, and Irving would recall the pleasure he had felt in reading some of her first sketches, "thrown off," as he wrote at the time, "with great freedom and spirit."

News from Puerto de Santa Maria that John Hall was dead came as a shock. Irving had left him, he thought, in improving health. But Hall had taken a horseback ride, the horse had bolted, and Hall had been thrown. The fall brought on a fatal hemorrhage. Von Faber had taken charge and arranged for the funeral and burial of the young man. To Irving remained the task of writing to Hall's sister in England to tell her the news.

Remembering their evening walks together, Irving recalled several talks they had had about immortality and whether or not spirits of the dead could return to communicate with the living. Hall had half wanted to believe they could, but wondered if such visits would be welcome to the living. Abruptly, he had turned to Irving and asked whether he would be willing to receive a visit from him after death. "Why, Hall," Irving had replied, "you are such a good fellow, and we have lived so amicably together, I don't know why I should fear to welcome your apparition, if you are able to come." But Hall had been unwilling to leave it at a joke, and Irving had promised that if Hall should die before him, he would make a real effort to invite a visit from his spirit.

The idea of ghosts and spirits had always tantalized Irving. He had written about them in many of his sketches, but generally only to laugh them away at the end. He was in a graver mood when he rode out to Casa de Cera, a few weeks after Hall's death, to keep his promise of inviting Hall's spirit. Standing in the twilight near the vine-hung cottage they had shared, looking out over the darkening and ocherous "Tablada," he may have had some trepidations lest the spirits he had teased so often should prove to be real. Whatever his emotions, Hall's spirit did not appear. In the darkness, Irving mounted his horse and rode back to Seville.

As the year 1828 came to a close, still another writing task came along to keep him "fagging" at his desk. He heard from Peter that an American publisher was planning to make an abridged one-volume edition of *Columbus*. Businesslike as he had become, he saw no reason why someone else should profit by such a venture and hurried to abridge the *Columbus* volumes himself and to get the condensed version on its way overseas to be published under Ebenezer's auspices. Cheering him on through this effort was the news from England that Murray had accepted *The Conquest of Granada*. The terms were not as favorable as those for *Columbus* had been, but the subject did not seem to Murray to have the same wide interest.

On the last day of the year Irving put down his pen for a while and called on his friend, the Marchioness, who had a new collection of Spanish tales to tell him. Back in his lodgings, he made notes on some of these and then took out his journal.

"Thus ends the year—tranquilly.—It has been one of great literary application, and generally speaking, one of the most tranquil in spirit of my whole life. The literary success of the History of Columbus has been greater than I anticipated, and gives me hopes that I have executed something which may have greater duration than I anticipate for my works of mere imagination. . . . The only future event from which I promise myself any extraordinary gratification is the return to my native country, which, I trust will now soon take place."

But the days and weeks went by and he remained in Seville.

Honor came to him unexpectedly in January, 1829. Unknown as a writer when he arrived in Spain two years before, he had made no attempts to promote any of his past works which had won fame for him in America, England, France, and Germany. He had devoted himself to his researches and writing on Spanish themes, getting acquainted as he did so, with a number of Spanish historians, antiquarians, and librarians. He had corresponded also, quite naturally, with Navarette, whose documentary history of Columbus had both inspired and provided the indispensable framework for his own book. This debt he had acknowledged at some length in the introduction to his *Life of Columbus*. But once Irving's books on Spain were completed, he sent them off to England and to America and went on to the next project, with no thought of having them considered for translation and publication in Spain.

He was surprised to learn, in early January, that, in recognition of his services to the study and dissemination of Spanish history, he had been elected a corresponding member of the *Real Academia de la Historia*, one of Spain's most learned and prestigious societies. He was the second American to be so honored. George Ticknor, the American scholar and professor who had resided for a while in Spain before Irving's arrival, was the previous recipient of the honor.

Touched and flattered, he hurried to compose a letter of acceptance in Spanish and soon received a gracious letter in return from the secretary of the society.

Through the winter he continued to gather the material and to write on the books that were to be his backlog, he hoped, when he took off for America. Then, in April, Prince

Dolgorouki wrote that he was leaving for Seville and hoped to take a holiday trip with Washington through southern Spain with Granada and the Alhambra as their goal.

The prospect of seeing Dolgorouki again and of making another visit to the Alhambra was delightful. The young Russian arrived in Seville, and for several days the two men walked about the city, lingering in the cathedral and visiting Irving's favorite paintings. Then, on the first of May, they set off by horseback for Granada where Irving planned to indulge himself "with a luxurious life among the groves and fountains of the Alhambra." He was going to be there in May and June, after all, the region's most splendid season, when everything would be in bloom.

Their journey was just full of enough difficulties, mildly alarming adventures and fatigues, to be interesting without being exhausting. Arrived in Granada in the middle of May, they took lodgings and then went to call on General O'Lawler, the Governor of the city. Washington spoke of his interest in the ruined palace on the hill and his hope of spending many hours there during his stay in Granada. O'Lawler listened sympathetically, then remarked that the royal apartment in the palace was furnished and maintained for him as Governor but that he never used it. Would the two gentlemen who were so interested in the Alhambra care to make their headquarters in that unused apartment while they were in Granada?

Not just visitors to the Alhambra, but residents of the palace! Irving and Dolgorouki looked at each other and smiled with pleasure.

The haunting desire to return to America, the nagging homesickness for the scenes and friends of his youth which Irving had been feeling for a year and more, were suddenly put aside. With a chance to step into a fairy tale was he to refuse?

To be pleased with everything, and if not pleased, amused,

had been his credo years before. He was older, forty-six this spring. He had become more serious, hard-working, even ambitious, no longer a youth swinging on whims. But he would not have been the person he was if he could have resisted this invitation to live for a while—all summer if he wished, O'Lawler said—where Boabdil had lived. The sealed door was reopening, the cleft in the mountains was uncovered again, Hendrick Hudson's crew was playing at ninepins—and Boabdil's perfumed seraglio was to be his.

# 27

# Another World

"On waking, he found himself on the green knoll whence he had first seen the old man of the glen. He rubbed his eyes— it was a bright sunny morning."

So Rip had wakened after a dream of twenty years. So, in a way, Irving wakened, though the dream had not lasted so long—only two months and a little more. For a week, Dolgorouki had shared the royal apartment in the Alhambra with him, then Dolgorouki had ridden down the hill and off across the vega to continue his travels. For a few days more Irving had played host to Ebenezer's second son, Lieutenant Edgar Irving of the United States Navy, who, when his ship put in at Gibraltar, had found his way to Granada to visit his uncle Washington. Then the solitude had enclosed him. The quiet, which was not really quiet but the murmuring obligato of plashing water, birds singing, and bees humming, had risen up around him and he had floated, suspended, through the sunny days and moonlit nights.

An old woman connected with the place, who was known as Tia, and her niece, Dolores, had cooked and cleaned for him. A bumptious lad, Mateo Ximenes, had appointed himself Irving's valet, guide, and companion and busied himself seeking out or inventing stories to fit the various suites, portals, paintings or towers of the vast and rambling palace. After a week or so in the governor's apartment, Irving found a more secluded suite of rooms and moved into it, over the objections of Tia and Dolores who were sure the rooms were haunted, or if not that, a likely goal for robbers who might steal in at night and slit his throat. There, in the heart of the cavernous edifice, he found the retreat which he had always sought. One window looked out on the gardens of the Lindaraxa with the fountains playing among the flowers. Another window looked down upon the valley of the River Darro and faced a mountainside covered with gardens and groves. Rising to this beauty each morning, Irving splashed water on his face from the fountain and Tia and Dolores brought his breakfast to the courtyard. After that, he spent a few hours at the desk, writing or making notes on his surroundings, the fancies they aroused in him, and the legends he was hearing concerning them. Later he wandered idly around the palace, sometimes with a book or manuscript in his hand. Sometimes he walked out, with Mateo as his guide, down the storied hill. Now and then, but not often, he descended all the way to Granada, to the home of the Duke of Gor, with whom he had become friendly. The duke was "between thirty and forty years of age," he wrote to Peter, "extremely prepossessing in his appearance, frank, friendly, and simple in his manners; one of the best informed and most public spirited men in the place." Besides all this, the duke had an excellent and curious library which he put at Irving's disposal.

The days passed and the weeks passed. "I am so in love with this apartment that I can hardly force myself from it to take my promenades," he wrote Dolgorouki. "I sit by my window until late at night, enjoying the moonlight and listening to the sound of the fountains and the singing of the night-ingales; and I have walked up and down the Chateaubriand gallery until midnight."

"In one of the great patios or courts," he wrote to Peter, "there is a noble tank of water, one hundred and twenty feet long and between twenty and thirty feet wide. The sun is upon it all day, so that at night it is a delightfully tempered bath, in which I have room to swim at large."

The pouch of letters that broke the spell came in mid-July, 1829. A letter from Washington, D.C., informed him that the new President of the United States, Andrew Jackson, was pleased to appoint Mr. Washington Irving Secretary of the United States Legation in London.

A clutch of other letters, from Ebenezer, from John Treat, and Henry Brevoort and James Paulding, among others, confirmed the appointment and urged Washington not to hesitate in accepting it even though he might feel that the post of secretary was not as important as he deserved. One or two other letters brought the news that in the course of the new President's sweeping changes, he had not seen fit to reappoint Alexander Everett as Ambassador to Spain.

Dazed by the unexpected summons from the outside world, Washington focussed for a while on the latter news and grieved that Everett had "fallen beneath the edge of the old general's sword." But at last he had to face the matter of his own decision. Should he accept the appointment or refuse it, as he had once refused the Navy appointment obtained for him by William? He thought of the pile of manuscript—legends, stories, and descriptions of the Alhambra—which he had been planning to finish before he left his retreat. Did he have enough material in hand to work up a whole volume while in England? Again he read the letters from Ebenezer, John, and Brevoort. He smiled to read in Brevoort's letter that it had been a one-time companion of the Lads of Kilkenny, a cheerful naval officer named Jack Nicholson, now advanced in rank and with some prestige in Washington, D.C., who had proposed his name to Jackson's Secretary of State, Martin Van Buren.

"That I should have that fat, jolly little tar, Jack N., for a patron," he wrote to Peter. "I confess there is something so extremely humourous in this caprice of fortune that I cannot help feeling in good humour about it. Little Jack has had a kind of dogged determined kindness for me now for about twenty-five years, ever since he took a liking to me on our getting tipsy together in Virginia at the time of Burr's trial."

He smiled, he frowned, and he wished he had a letter from Peter as well as from all the others, giving his recommendation. At last, however, the weight of the affectionate pleading in the letters from New York became too much to resist. He looked out at the roses in the gardens of the Lindaraxa outside his window. He stared at the fountain flashing its drops in the sunlight and mentally began to say good-bye.

"My only horror is the bustle and turmoil of the world," he confessed in his letter to Peter, "how shall I stand it after the delicious quiet and repose of the Alhambra?"

The weather had become sultry everywhere but in the water-cooled and stone-shaded palace. It was an impossible time of year to travel away from Granada on horseback as he had come. Fortunately, a young Englishman stopping in the city was about to start for home. Irving and the Englishman agreed to travel together and to make the journey in a sort of covered cart called a tartana and drawn by mule. Mattresses were placed inside the cart, on which the travelers could recline during the hottest part of the day's journeying. Irving packed his clothes, his manuscripts and notebooks into his trunk. On July 29, 1829, he and his traveling companion, Ralph Sneyd, clambered into their "rumble-tumble" conveyance and started on their way.

Centuries before, Boabdil had stopped for one last backward glance at the palace he was surrendering on a rock which became known as The Last Sigh of the Moor. Irving was not quite so romantic as to take his last look at the Alhambra from the same rock, but when he looked back from the cart as the wagon jolted down the mountain road, he did feel "like a sailor who has just left a tranquil port to launch upon a stormy and treacherous sea."

Once again a portal was closed and sealed, a cleft in the mountains buried beyond discovery under a dashing waterfall.

The journey through Spain and then across France brought him by slow stages back into the "bustle and turmoil of the world." In Paris, he lingered for a brief visit with Peter, and then made his way to London and his new position.

London, filled with crowds and carriages, offered him a sort of homecoming of its own. He had many friends in that city now. He made his way first to the American Legation to meet Louis McLane, the new American Ambassador to the Court of St. James's and his superior in his new post. He found lodgings for himself across the street from the Legation which was then at 9, Chados Street, Cavendish Square. After that, he could greet the friends he had not seen for three or four years. He could lunch or dine with Leslie and Newton and Wilkie and go to their studios to examine their latest works. He could meet "Anacreon" Moore, busy these days with his *Life of Byron*, and accompany him on some of his social rounds. Samuel Rogers summoned him to breakfast. John Howard Payne was in the city, still optimistic, with still more plays in hand which he hoped Irving would have time to read. He saw his theatrical friends, Charles Kemble and his wife, Marie Therese, concerned about the financial fate of the family white elephant, the Covent Garden Theater, and placing their hopes on the debut of their daughter, Fanny, who was to play Juliet in a new production of *Romeo and Juliet*. Irving was at the theater on the all-important night to see the dark-haired, dark-eyed nineteen-year-old Fanny leap into stardom with her youthfully sensitive portrayal of the role. He was at the Kemble home later, to smile sympathetically as Fanny laughed and cried over the jeweled watch her father gave her as a token of her success.

But through a good part of every day he was at the Legation getting acquainted with his new duties and briefing himself on the United States government's instructions to its English embassy. He did not expect his duties to be demanding, but he was taking them seriously all the same, which meant bringing himself up to date on political events in America to which he had paid little attention in recent years. Never especially partisan in politics, he had been vaguely sympathetic since youth to the Federalist party and could hardly have been called a "Jackson man" before his appointment by that newly elected President. But, just as years before in Washington, D.C., when he had found good men in both political parties, he was ready to believe that Jackson, hero of New Orleans, was a courageous and honorable man who would endeavor to serve his country well. From McLane, he learned that one of the chief aims of the American Embassy in England was to settle finally the long dispute over open American trading with British ports in the West Indies. Advised on that, and lesser aims and problems as well, he was soon at work writing the letters and inquiries that were required.

That he filled the post of secretary very successfully should not have been the surprise it was to some people at home. Thinking of him as a wanderer, even an idler, who stayed away from his own country so mysteriously, they forgot that his long years abroad, and all the day-to-day talk he had heard in Paris, in Dresden, and in Madrid, had made him familiar as few other Americans could be with the princes and pretenders, the national feuds and ambitions that kept life stirring in western Europe. Irving fitted into the embassy routine easily, picking up more and more responsibility as time went on.

He had hoped that his work in the Legation would allow him time to finish the books he had been writing while at the Alhambra. Before long he found this impossible. Diplomatic chores took up most of his daytime hours, nor was it sensible to give up his evening social life to devote that time to writing. His popularity in England was an asset to the American Legation. In spite of everything, however, he did manage to piece together a book on *The Voyages of the Companions of Columbus*, which he offered to Murray. And Murray, after a curious sort of reluctance, accepted it. But then, Irving reflected, Murray had always been an erratic, evasive publisher, slow to communicate until he had made his final decision.

From time to time Irving was engaged also in aiding fellow writers or fellow Americans. Moore, near to completing his *Life and Letters of Byron*, was eager to have the book published in America. Irving wrote a long, enthusiastic letter to Ebenezer, asking him to offer the book to an American publisher. After some deliberation, the Harper Brothers accepted it and a contract for fifteen hundred dollars was signed. The money itself was slow to arrive, and Irving had a note from Moore who was at Sloperton Cottage.

"I don't like to bother a great diplomat such as you are about matters of the shop—particularly as you won't come and be bothered here where I could have my wicked will of you—but time flies, and the golden moment (or rather the silver one) for the arrival of my dollars from America ought to be here. Do, like a good fellow, poke them up a little about it, as, if the cash doesn't come, I must—go."

Before he left London, Irving also spent some time in finding an English publisher for the American poet William

Cullen Bryant. He first suggested Bryant's poems to Murray, but once again that publisher proved unsympathetic. Finally, Irving found another publisher who accepted the Bryant work on the condition that Irving write an introduction to the book. A difficulty arose as the book was being prepared for the press. In one couplet Bryant had written:

> And the British soldier trembles
> When Marion's name is heard.

Appalled by this slur against British valor, the publisher summoned Irving and said he could not print such a line. If it stood, he would have to give up publication of the book. In this small literary crisis, Irving knew that to write to Bryant for an alteration and then get an answer from overseas would take so long that the book would be shelved. He felt that to make the change himself was to take an unwarranted liberty with another writer's work. In the end, however, he decided that the value to Bryant of having the book published in England was worth the intrusion and he changed the line to, "When the foeman's name is heard." Later, he learned that Bryant was incensed by the change, but still later, a personal friendship between the two men would ease the poet's ruffled feelings.

John James Audubon, in London with his huge and brilliantly precise paintings of American birds, was looking for an inspired engraver and also seeking subscribers for a published volume of his work. Irving gave him assistance also, writing letters of introduction and encouraging him in every other way he could.

The year 1829 came to an end with no entry about "tranquility" in Irving's journal. He had given up the daily journal entries after arriving in England. In some ways, he had too much to report—too many dinners, teas, balls, great names —too many diplomatic details, some trivial, some more vital. In other ways, he had too little. Days went by when he had no time to look at his unfinished manuscript of *The Alhambra* or the still unpolished *Life of Mahomet*. Committed now to the idea of himself as a writer before anything else, this troubled him.

It was somewhat cheering, therefore, to hear on his forty-seventh birthday, April 3, 1830, that the Royal Society of Literature had voted him one of their fifty guinea gold medals for literary achievement. "What makes this the more gratifying," he wrote to Peter, who was currently visiting Sally in Birmingham, "is that the other medal is voted to Hallam, author of the Middle Ages."

A month later, he learned that the University of Oxford had voted to confer on him an honorary degree. He was expected at Oxford on June 23, "the day fixed for the ceremony at which it is usual to confer honorary degrees." A Doctorate of Literature, for Washington Irving, the unwilling student, who had been happy to leave school at sixteen!

The actual ceremony, as it turned out, was postponed, owing to the illness and expected death of King George IV, but the savor of the honor was not displeasing. Perhaps it helped encourage him in readying two more manuscripts for Murray's scrutiny, the long-delayed *Life of Mahomet* and his collection of tales and essays about the Alhambra.

Murray's rejection of both manuscripts, after one of his customary delays, came as a shock. Since the magical success of *The Sketch Book*, Washington had taken it for granted that Murray would never again turn down anything from his pen. Disconcerted, he put the two manuscripts back among his papers. A year and more would pass before he would make any effort to have *The Alhambra* published in England, and *Mahomet* would wait for years.

The months passed, filled with public events and ever more time-consuming labors at the Embassy. George IV died and the succession of his nephew, William IV, kept London agog for weeks with parades, reviews, grand dinners, and dress balls. Louis McLane, Washington's superior, began to have recurring bouts with ill health, which meant that Washington had to take charge in his place. He had developed a real sense of the various issues involved in the relations between England and the United States and of the delicate maneuverings that were required to achieve one seemingly simple goal. He felt, as a result, a true sense of accomplishment when, in November of 1830, he finally forwarded to America the order "passed yesterday, reopening the West India ports to our Shipping. Thus the long Struggle is crowned with success."

For the first time he began to study the economy of England as opposed to the cheerful customs of old English squires. After all, with McLane sick in bed, it was he who had to write the letters to Van Buren, in Washington, D.C., explaining the conditions and pressures that were forcing the country to consider a Reform Bill. An increasing awareness of the misery and despair of England's poor made him sympathetic with political changes that surely would have to come. He was not inspired to any literary works exposing the sufferings of those caught in the toils of the current system. He was not and never would be the sort of missionary writer that Charles Dickens would become within a few years. For him, it was enough to respond personally to life's cruelties and injustices. In his writing for publication he preferred to please, or amuse.

International events and intrigues also concerned him during these months. He listened, he asked questions, he read. And he wrote his letters to Jackson and Van Buren with a liveliness and perception that few other diplomatic secretaries could match.

In June, 1831, the postponed honor at Oxford was conferred. Irving moved through the ranks of undergraduates gathered at the ceremonial exercises, a somewhat stouter figure than he had been, but still a handsome man, his winging eyebrows quizzically raised, the secret smile lurking at one corner of his mouth.

The undergraduates shouted their affection and their familiarity with his writings. "Diedrich!" they cried, "Knickerbocker!" "Crayon," "Rip Van Winkle!" He ducked his head in embarrassment but managed to respond with a few grateful words to the compliments of the citation.

Also in June, 1831, the tumultuous political events surrounding Andrew Jackson and his cabinet in the United States began to have their consequences in Irving's life in London. Jackson's showdown with his Vice President, John Calhoun, over the Union-splitting doctrine of nullification, the foolish, exhausting social crisis in the capital as to whether or not Peggy Eaton would be received by capital wives, the coiling gossip that Jackson was Van Buren's tool, had finally led Van Buren to resign as Secretary of State. Van Buren's resignation was a signal for Secretary of War Eaton to resign also, and with those departures, Jackson was able to dismiss the rest of his Cabinet officers, who were Calhoun men, and make new appointments all around. With this total shake-up, Louis McLane was summoned back to America to become the new Secretary of the Navy and Martin Van Buren was banished from Jackson's side to be the new Ambassador to the Court of St. James's.

Louis McLane departed from London for America late in June, leaving Irving the acting head of the American Embassy until Van Buren should arrive. Once again, as so often before, Irving began to think of returning to America. Unlike the times before, however, his plans now assumed a certain reality. Perhaps the official changing of the staff at the Embassy imposed a pattern that made a definite decision easier to make. Irving had been appointed to serve under McLane.

He decided he would await the coming of Van Buren and then, with no more flights to Paris or anywhere else, board a ship to return to the country of his birth.

The daily routine of the Legation went on through the summer. Van Buren did not arrive in London until mid-September, and Irving was waiting to meet him. He wrote to McLane that he was favorably impressed by this controversial political figure. "His manners are most amiable and ingratiating, and I have no doubt he will become a favorite at this court."

The years, the months, the days in Europe were winding themselves up. In September, Sir Walter Scott was in London on his way to a vacation in Italy. Irving was invited to dine with him, his daughter, Anne, and her husband, Lockhart. The change in Scott, "the golden-hearted man," since the last time Irving had seen him, was shocking. Once—had it really been fourteen years ago?—Scott had carried conversation, laughter, and song through a day and evening like a tireless and merry athlete. Now he greeted Irving from a hunched seat and looked up at him in a moment's bewilderment before he recognized him. "Ah, my dear fellow. Time has dealt lightly with you since last we met."

The dinner that followed was an experience that brought tears to Irving's eyes. Scott sat lost in a sort of misty melancholy, rousing now and then to start a story, then losing its thread, until the rest of the company picked up some other topic to divert attention from his confusion. "Ah," Scott sighed again, taking Irving's arm, "the times are changed, my good fellow, since we went over Eildon hills together. It is all nonsense to tell a man that his mind is not affected, when his body is in this state."

Irving visited Birmingham to see sister Sally, Hal, and the young Van Warts (no longer children but growing to maturity). He spent a few days with a new friend at a country estate, Barlborough Hall, that seemed a projection of Irving's imagined Bracebridge Hall. He gratified a long-standing desire to spend some time at the estate which had once been Byron's ancestral seat, Newstead Abbey. Returned to London, he agreed to accompany Martin Van Buren and Van Buren's young son on a sightseeing journey through the towns of Oxford, Stratford-on-Avon, and other famous locales that were now so familiar to him. With such delays, Irving spun out his time in Europe as though for all his dreams of home he was almost afraid to return.

An epidemic of cholera was frightening the country and talk of the "raging" sickness filled much London conversation. Irving seemed indifferent to the threat. Continued political agitation over the Reform Bill was keeping most businessmen in a state of uncertainty. But with his plan to return to America quite definite, Irving decided he did not want to leave England without arranging for the publication of one manuscript that seemed the fruit of his happiest days abroad, the stories and legends which he had collected under the title of *The Alhambra*. He found a publisher more perceptive of its merits than Murray had been and signed the contract for its publication in England, making sure to send a copy of the manuscript to Ebenezer so that he could have it published in America at the same time.

The date of his departure for home was drawing nearer when he sat at breakfast in a room of the Embassy one morning in February and was brought an astonishing item of news. The United States Senate had refused to confirm Jackson's appointment of Van Buren as Ambassador to England. Pondering this information over his neglected meal, he looked up to see Van Buren in his dressing gown, clutching the letter that had brought him the same tidings. In some agitation, the politician who had been called "the little magician," sat down beside Irving. Did this mean that he was dead politically, Van Buren wondered.

Irving had been detached from practical politics most of his life, exposed to their diplomatic workings only for the last three years. But he shook his head and spoke as though a weight of experience prompted his words. "No," he said. "I think you will have cause to be grateful for this rejection. It may ultimately elevate you to the Presidency."

Van Buren listened to Irving's confident prophecy that this rejection would make him a martyr in America. Returned to that country, he could count on running with Jackson in the next election, and four years after that he could make the easy step from Vice President to President. Meantime, Irving counselled him to stay in London until a replacement arrived and to honor his invitations to the various levees and state dinners being held in honor of the Queen's birthday. Van Buren, a year younger than his amateur advisor, nodded with an air of bemusement.

In March, Irving said good-bye to his friends—Leslie and Newton and Wilkie, Moore and Rogers and Payne. He made last-minute visits to the theater and to say farewell to the Kembles. Finally he wrote Peter: "I shall endeavor to arrange my affairs so as to cross from Southampton to Havre about the 1st of April, and to sail from thence by the first packet that departs."

On April 3, 1832, his forty-ninth birthday, he was in Havre with Peter. A week later he was on his way to New York, where he arrived after a passage of forty days and an absence of seventeen years.

# Part Four

An American Theme

# 28

# A Tour of the Prairies

"The very village was altered; it was larger and more populous. There were rows of houses which he had never seen before, and those which had been his familiar haunts had disappeared. Strange names were over the doors—strange faces at the windows—everything was strange. His mind now misgave him; he began to doubt whether both he and the world around him were not bewitched. Surely this was his native village, which he had left but the day before. . . ."

The return to New York, even more than the departure from the Alhambra, seemed to have been previsioned in the story of Rip Van Winkle—so concerned with the mystery of time, condensing itself, stretching itself out, befuddling the poor rovers who move through it, losing track of it as they sleep or dream. Still, Washington's mind did not really misgive him as Rip's had, when he saw from the rail of the ship the great forest of masts that now surrounded the tip of Manhattan Island. He felt a vague sense of unreality but no shock to see how the city was crowded with new buildings and accented by new steeples for two or three miles farther north than it had been when he last saw it. New York was still the same brick and wood city laced up and down and across with the greenery of trees.

He found it curious, but not shocking, to recognize Ebenezer on the wharf, wholly different with his pate of white hair, and yet, once the eye had adjusted itself, not different at all, still Ebenezer, Captain Greatheart, old Brom. The changes that time made, or the changes in people and their creations as they moved through time, had been his concern for a long while. He had gazed on European ruins and he had sat in the flower-haunted silence of the Alhambra and had slipped himself into time past. Now it was merely a question of slipping himself into time present or time future—another geographical trick—so that he could marvel at the new buildings, the new streetlamps and storefronts, as they rattled along the newly paved streets toward Ebenezer's house on Pine Street, but never feel his mind was leaving him.

"The very character of the people seemed changed. There was a busy, bustling, disputatious tone about it. . . ." he had written years before, of Rip's return to his village. So he looked without undue surprise on the increased bustle of New York as he rode through it, nor was he struck dumb by changes in clothing, in hairdoes, in signs and in street cries.

One surprise there was. Rip had returned to find the inhabitants of the town that had once been his staring at him with curiosity and hostility. "Does nobody know poor Rip Van Winkle?" he had cried.

Everybody knew Washington Irving, it seemed. He might have changed in his rovings through time, just as Ebenezer had. He might be stouter, less volatile, less mocking. But everybody knew Washington Irving's name. Everybody knew that Washington Irving had brought honor to American letters not only in his own country but across all England and western Europe. Though he had been absent a long time, almost inexcusably long, still he had returned. Everybody was eager to show his delight in the importance that Irving had conferred somehow on each and every American by his success.

"Wilt thou not smile, oh, Musselman of invincible gravity, to learn that they honor their great men by eating, and that the only trophy erected to their exploits, is a public dinner!" Mustapha Rub-a-dub Keli Khan had commented on the curious American habit years and years before, in *Salmagundi*.

"No sooner does a citizen signalize himself in a conspicuous manner in the service of his country, than all the gormandizers assemble and discharge the national debt of gratitude —by giving him a dinner."

Now there was to be a dinner for Washington Irving—a great public feast tendered in his honor by three hundred of the leading citizens of New York—its literary, social, and political arbiters, gathering to "offer up whole hetacombs of geese and calves, and oceans of wine, in honor of the illustrious living."

He was astonished, he was humbled, he was "topsy-turvy" with his emotions. Once, fourteen years before, he had been "cast down," eager only to regain "the good opinion of the world." He had regained that good opinion in a stroke with *The Sketch Book* and had not lost it with *Bracebridge Hall*. Then had come word of his countrymen's displeasure that he stayed so long in Europe. There had been the bad reviews of *Tales of a Traveller*. There had been a few querulous comments on his serious historical works, *The Life and Voyages of Columbus* and *The Conquest of Granada*. Murray had rejected *The Alhambra*. True, Irving had later sold it elsewhere and it was soon to come out in America, but these rejections had been magnified by him. In spite of such honors as his election to the Spanish Historical Society and the medal and degree that he had been awarded in England, he had no idea that he was coming home to fame. The querulous comments had been forgotten, it seemed, and the sharp criticisms. He was *famous*.

He was, above all else, terrified, because he would be the center of all eyes at the dinner and would have to make a speech. He was, as his friend Moore had said, "no lion in public."

The chief salon of the City Hall was the scene of the banquet. Three long lines of tables seated three hundred diners. Washington was pale and distraught as the hearty good will of the dinner clanged and chimed around him. Down the three rows of tables people ate and drank in a Lucullan apotheosis of banqueting. And the time would come when he would have to rise and speak.

In the end, he did better than he had feared. Grasping a table knife for support, he affirmed his abiding love of "his own, his native land."

"I am asked how long I mean to remain here," he said. "They know but little of my heart or my feelings who can ask me this question. I answer, as long as I live."

The hall rang with bravos. In the custom of the day, handkerchiefs were waved and cheer after cheer was sounded until Irving, abandoning the rest of whatever else he might have thought of saying, ending by quavering forth a toast. "Our City—May God continue to prosper it."

So he was accepted after his long absence, his long dream, and now he had to show his gratitude for such an outpouring of affection.

He excused himself from facing the problem directly for a time. A returned member of a government embassy, he had to go to Washington, D.C., to report to President Jackson on his years in London. There was talk, while he was in the capital, of some new diplomatic or governmental post for him. He refused, with gratitude, to consider any thing like that. He had come home and his first wish was to grow reacquainted with his native land.

In the capital and in Baltimore also, hosts of friends were eager to greet him and entertain him. Word came that the citizens of Philadelphia wanted to tender him another public banquet. He replied in a panic saying that he was grateful for the sentiment, but had to decline being the object of such public distinction any more.

The threat of a banquet averted, he traveled to Philadelphia. Breakfasting in the Mansion House, he saw his old actor friend of the Park Theater days, Thomas Cooper. They had a "dish of chat" and then Washington joined Cooper on the steamboat to travel up the river to Bristol where Cooper now lived. There he met again, after so many years, Cooper's wife, Mary Fairlie, the "Sophy Sparkle" of *Salmagundi*. "She was pale, and thinner than I had expected to find her, yet still retaining much of her former self," he wrote to Peter. He said nothing as to what had happened to the extravagant laughter they had shared when they were young.

Philadelphia also meant someone else, a dark-haired, dark-eyed figure, also from long ago. Rebecca Gratz too was older and slimmer but with a quiet air of dedication about her that seemed to insulate her from the sort of endless roving that agitated Washington. Having helped to raise her younger brothers, she was involved in raising nieces and nephews and much concerned as well with the Orphans' Home in Philadelphia and a variety of Jewish philanthropies.

A good-looking, middle-aged man and a handsome, middle-aged woman, they talked with ease and affection of the friends they had known—Maria Hoffman, Mary Fairlie, Henry Brevoort, James Paulding, and Thomas Sully, Rebecca's brothers and sisters and their various destinies. The talk came around to Washington's years abroad, and they spoke of his friendship with Scott and of the heroine named Rebecca in *Ivanhoe*. Did Washington admit that he had spoken to Scott of her and her doomed romance? Neither she nor Washington ever said. But of course they finally spoke of

Washington's writings. Rebecca told him how much she had enjoyed his books and asked what he planned to write next. She hoped that he might return to an American theme. Yes, he nodded. This was what he wanted to do, what he was determined to do.

If only, Rebecca said, he could do something in the line of *Salmagundi* again. Themes for satire had certainly existed twenty-five years ago when "Old Sal" had flourished, but perhaps he had not been home long enough to see how many more there were now, crying out for the mocking observations of someone like Launcelot Langstaff.

Washington admitted that he had already noticed some of the excesses that marked American life these days, the braggadocio, the spoiling in the name of profit, the shrillness and the coarseness. In letters to friends abroad, he had commented on some of these. But he was not the youth that he had been when he stood on the veranda of Cockloft Hall and mocked the follies of the Establishment. Then he had laughed as he mocked, but he no longer felt the same sort of laughter. He had tried, while in Bordeaux, to write some searching essays about the nature of his country and countrymen, but he had destroyed those efforts. They were not his style. Besides, he was an established man himself now, to a degree. His writings had brought pride to his countrymen. Could he turn and criticize the country from which he had been absent so long? He was no self-assured landowner and son of a landowner, like James Fenimore Cooper, who seemed to feel an autocratic obligation to point out the faults and excesses of his fellow-men and was now astounding both Europe and America with his *Notions of Americans Picked Up By a Travelling Bachelor*.

No more *Salmagundi*, Rebecca said quietly.

He shook his head.

Still, a quest for some sort of American theme engaged

him. Surely, somewhere in the vastness of his native land he could find an inspiration.

After returning to New York, he took off again with James Paulding and two acquaintances from his transatlantic voyage, Charles Joseph Latrobe, and a young Swiss, Count de Pourtales, for a journey up the Hudson. Steamboat travel was not new to Washington, but American vessels had improved in his absence and he now felt "wafted from place to place . . . as if by magic." He gazed again at the hills and valleys he had so longed to see when in Europe and found them as beautiful as ever, but offering him no theme for a book. Another excursion later in the summer took him into New Hampshire and Vermont and then again down the Hudson River Valley. This time he stopped off to visit one of William's sons, Oscar, who had bought a house in the Sleepy Hollow region, and here he had the first notion of buying a little land for himself. Not far from Oscar's land was a property on which stood an old Dutch cottage which had once belonged to the Van Tassel family. Irving's fancy was caught by that, for Van Tassel was the family name he had given his chief characters in "The Legend of Sleepy Hollow." Besides, the land itself was attractive, sloping through woodlands down to the river. He wrote to his sister Catherine about his sudden impulse to buy the place. "I am willing to pay a little unreasonably for it, and should like to have it in time to make any alterations that may be advisable, as early as possible in the spring."

For some reason, however, he made no purchase that fall. Instead, still seeking his American theme, he left on a trip into western New York and Ohio. There, meeting one of the government's Indian Commissioners, just about to embark on an expedition beyond the Mississippi, he decided to accept the Commissioner's invitation to join the party and so visit country that was totally new to him.

What hardships there were on the journey he met readily

and cheerfully. Traveling on horseback through forest and prairies, camping in tents at night, hunting deer, buffalo, and wild turkey could not unduly alarm someone who had braved the trails over the Spanish mountains and down the defiles of the Alps. He resumed his journal, making notes on each day's adventures. Perhaps he had stumbled onto his American theme at last.

Journeying by steamboat on the Ohio River from Cincinnati to the Mississippi and then up that river to St. Louis, he marveled at the "grand scenery of the two mighty rivers." "The magnificence of the Western forests" was quite beyond his anticipations, "such gigantic trees, rising like stupendous columns—and then the abundance of flowers and flower shrubs. . . ."

From St. Louis, the route lay inland by horseback. The party halted at Fort Jefferson, where Irving saw and talked with the famous chief Black Hawk and some fellow chiefs who had been taken captive in the recent Indian wars. Then the group rode onward to Independence and from there still farther west to Fort Gibson and the Little Red River and the Pawnee country beyond it.

"We led a complete hunter's life," he wrote Kitty later, "subsisting upon the produce of the chase, camping by streams or pools, and sleeping on skins and blankets in the open air, but we were all in high health. . . . We got out of flour, salt, sugar, &c., and had to eat our meat without bread or seasoning—." It had been most invigorating. To Peter, he reported that he "had brought off . . . the tongue of a buffalo, of my own shooting, as a trophy of my hunting, and am determined to rest my renown as a hunter upon that exploit, and never to descend to meaner game."

Circling back toward the east, the party arrived at Montgomery's Point, where the Arkansas River met the Mississippi, and here Irving left the group to board a steamboat bound down river to New Orleans. Audubon, whom he had last seen in London, was on board the boat, busy all day with his drawings and paintings of birds. There was a man with no lack for a theme, Irving thought, and wondered if he really did have material for a book in his notes on the journey into Indian country.

For several days he lingered in New Orleans, enjoying the motley character of that cosmopolitan city. Then he set off in a mail stage to travel through Alabama, Georgia, and South and North Carolina toward Washington, D.C. In South Carolina, he stopped in Columbia to seek out an acquaintance from the days in London when he had been awaiting bankruptcy, William Preston, now a member of the South Carolina Legislature. "I passed a day most cordially with him," Washington wrote Peter. "I dined with him at Governor Hamilton's, the nullifying Governor, whom I had known when a young man at New York, and who is a perfect gentleman, but a Hotspur in politics. It is really lamentable to see such a fine set of gallant fellows as these leading nullifiers are, so madly in the wrong."

Irving had always been able to keep politics separate from friendship, but this did not mean he had no convictions of his own. "Come again soon," the Governor said as Irving left. "Oh yes," Irving replied. "I'll come with the first troops."

The tension that was building as to whether or not South Carolina would test her nullifying doctrine brought Washington to a halt when he came to the capital, determined to stay on till he learned if troops would indeed be required to settle the issue. Jackson had been re-elected President, with Van Buren as his Vice-President. Meeting Van Buren again, Irving could feel satisfaction about his prediction that Van Buren's rejection as Ambassador to England was only starting him on his road to the Presidency, and he spent interesting hours with him, discussing the present difficulties of the country. Van Buren reported on Jackson's hopes and Irving commented on the varying sentiments he had heard about the subject in the course of travels in the west and south. The great drama, however, was in the Congress, where nullifiers and Union men were locked in verbal combat day after day.

Irving had planned to be home for Christmas, home now being Ebenezer's house on Bridge Street in New York, filled with nieces and nephews. Ebenezer's wife, Elizabeth, had died several years before, but sister Catherine and her daughter, Sarah, were often there to make it a real family gathering-place. But the activities in the Capitol were too engrossing to Washington for him to leave. Christmas came and went and he sayed on, attending sessions of Congress almost daily. He heard "almost every speech, good and bad, and did not lose a word of any of the best." In the evenings, he found a friendly family circle at the home of Louis McLane.

On and on he stayed, through Jackson's decision to send the troops to South Carolina, through the debates to reduce the tariffs that had so offended the southern state, until finally the crisis had come to an end with the Union intact and Congress adjourned.

After that, he took to the road again, and this time, with Martin Van Buren as a companion, once again toured the Hudson River Valley country, home ground for Van Buren as well as Irving, since Van Buren had been born and raised in Kinderhook.

Had he come back to the United States merely to be the same sort of wanderer that he had been in Europe? To linger here and there wherever he found a spectacle to view, or to travel on when he found good company for the journey? What had become of that steadying impulse to write, day after day, that had given the years in Spain a character of their own?

By fall, Ebenezer was asking openly why Washington was not ready with some new work for the press. In unhappy financial straits himself, Ebenezer worried because Washington had been infected by the speculative fever that was epidemic in America during these years and was making investments in wilderness land and stocks. The abridgment of *Columbus* had been accepted as a school text. *The Alhambra*, published at last, was selling well. Imbued with some of the same soft, discursive magic as *The Sketch Book, The Alhambra* was destined to have a continuing popularity through the years when *Tales of a Traveller* and *Bracebridge Hall* would have slipped from view. But Ebenezer, not gifted with any second sight as to which of his brother's writings might endure, fretted about Washington's investments in America which seemed no more promising to him than had the French steamboat project. A famous man Washington might be, but wealthy, or even financially secure, he was not.

Washington responded that he was worried also and was getting to work at once. Reading and rereading his notes on his western tour he saw no way to make them into anything more than a record of his journey. He decided to write just that, a story of *A Tour of the Prairies*. His skill at sketching colorful scenes and picturesque events had not deserted him. When the book was completed he sent a copy of the manuscript to England. Murray, so harsh in his rejection of *The Alhambra*, did not hesitate to give Irving a contract for this work. Published in both America and England, *A Tour of the Prairies* pleased readers in both countries. The pictures it gave of America's newly opened west were bright, timely, and sharply observed. But Washington knew that interesting and informative as the *Tour* might be, this was not the American theme which he sought, the theme that would engage his imagination as his vision of the Hudson highlands or old New Amsterdam once had done.

In the fall of 1834, Irving finally purchased the ten acres of Van Tassel property just south of his nephew Oscar's holding in the Sleepy Hollow area. He explored the ancient stone cottage on the land with his nephew and several nieces, inventing a history for it as he poked about in its two small, dusty rooms. After the Van Tassels had departed the cottage had been the homestead of a certain Wolfert Acker, he told his companions. Wolfert was a quiet, harmless Dutchman, something like Rip Van Winkle and married, like Rip, to a shrew, and here he had sought peace and quiet. Look! Irving said, was there not a half-obliterated motto over the door that read *Lust in Rust? Lust in Rust*— Dutch for *Pleasure in Rest*. But of course poor old Wolfert's wife had given him little *rust*, and through the passage of years the neighbors had corrupted the word to Roost.

Wolfert's Roost, would be the name of the cottage, Irving announced. He thought of it as a summer retreat for Ebenezer, approaching sixty years of age now, and his nieces and nephews, a sort of cabin where he also might stop for a few days in the summer to relax in the countryside he had always loved. Even so, once it became his, he began to think about changes and improvements he wanted to make in the structure. He began to envision embellishments that would change it from a primitive, Puritan rectangle into a real Dutch house with stepped gables surmounted by weathercocks. Yes, he had to have weathercocks. They were a sort of symbol to him. How often had he referred to his own "weathercock mind"? How often, years before, had he watched the weathervanes in Liverpool as the family business slid into bankruptcy and the wind still blew "due east, due east"? The wind blew fairer now, but still—weathercocks.

He made rough sketches of the changes he wanted to have made at Wolfert's Roost. An English artist with an interest in architecture, George Harvey, lived near the river just south of Irving's property, and Irving consulted with him about working plans for his ideas. He invented further legends about old Wolfert. But still he was fretting and pondering. What was his American theme?

# 29

# Sunnyside

John Jacob Astor—and his ambitious attempt to build a city on the far side of the continent, a city that would be the center of the fur trade in the far Northwest? Surely this was not the theme he sought.

Washington looked at the strong, square old face of his host, the planes thrown into sharp contrast in the lamplight, and sighed. This was not the first time Mr. Astor had broached the project. Whenever Irving dined with him and Fitz Greene Halleck at Astor's new country house near the Hell Gate on the East River, the subject came up some time during the evening.

Once again Mr. Astor was telling him that he had boxes and trunks full of documents that told the story. He had journals, maps, letters, reports, everything Irving would need to trace the history of Astoria, from the moment Astor had envisioned it through its hopeful commencement on to its capture by the British during the War of 1812, and the subsequent failure of Astor's dreams of establishing a line of trading posts from the Mississippi to the Pacific with Astoria as an American outpost in the far west. Actually, Mr. Astor still had hopes that Congress might one day agree to put the recovered town under the protection of the American flag and so establish American territory in the far west. To some degree the book he wanted Irving to write would be special pleading. But it was a grand story beyond any such consideration, full of the adventures of men making their way by land and by sea to a coast which seemed almost as remote as China to most Americans. It was a story of exploration, of natural perils, of encounters with a variety of Indian tribes, of the most basic sort of pioneering—a grand story. And Mr. Astor had the letters, the journals, the diaries to document it all.

Irving nodded. He could see that the story might indeed work up into a colorful, dramatic book and that the time was probably ripe for a true tale of high adventure in crossing the continent to establish a fur trading post on the Pacific coast. But he wondered if he could undertake to write a book for John Jacob Astor and sign it with his own name. Might not his readers feel that he had been bought by Astor to advertise his commercial enterprise? Washington was sure in his own mind that Astor was not asking for any distortions of history that would build him into a hero. He did not think that there was any element of self-aggrandizement in his wish to have the story told nor any desire to have himself depicted as noble when he had been otherwise.

Washington had known Astor all his life and had heard no rumors that he had made his fortune by piratical or despicable means. An immigrant from Germany by way of England, Astor had arrived in New York the very year of Irving's birth, full of the sort of ambition that Irving had never had. He had worked first as a street peddler for a baker. Later he had set himself up in a little shop. Washington had walked past it many times as a boy, its small dusty window a curious mixture of musical instruments and furs. Later still,

Astor had taken to the wilderness himself, bearing a pack of goods to trade for furs with the Indians. Finally, after he had built a trading route and established the foundations of a monopoly in supplying furs to New York and its environs, he had hired Henry Brevoort, a young relative of his wife's, to travel as one of his representatives to Montreal and the various fur-trading stations in Canada and along the Great Lakes. So Irving had also known of Astor during those years, hearing anecdotes about him from Brevoort. Now, visiting him in his new pillared and elegant mansion, Washington was sure that Astor was eager simply that the record of a daring, exciting, and ultimately unsuccessful venture be presented. It was a chapter of American history as Astor saw it, and he wanted Washington Irving, historian of Columbus, to write it.

Washington's doubts about the propriety of doing so began to waver. In their place came thoughts of the immense amount of work that would be required to sort through those masses of documents that Mr. Astor was promising, the hours that would be needed just to arrange them chronologically, and the further hours to extract the pertinent material. He was already at work preparing a new book, a collection of some of the Spanish sketches that he had in his trunk, to which he wanted to add some new material as well. He had in mind another *Sketch Book* really, a miscellany, which he was planning to call just that—*Crayon's Miscellany*.

Mr. Astor suggested that someone might be hired to do the preliminary sorting out and arranging of the material. He would be glad to pay for the services of anyone Irving suggested. With this, Washington was reminded of his nephew, Pierre Munro, who had recently gone out to Jacksonville, Illinois, on some business venture but was not really settled on a career. Perhaps, for a fee, Pierre would be willing to undertake the preliminary work of examining the records and preparing a rough outline of the Astoria chronicle. He mentioned the possibility to Mr. Astor who leaped at the idea and urged him to write his nephew at once.

"Mr. Astor is a strong-minded man," Washington noted in his letter to Pierre, "and one from whose conversation much curious information is to be derived. He feels the want of occupation and amusement, and thinks he may find something of both in the progress of this work. You would find him very kindly disposed, for he was an early friend of your father, for whose memory he entertains great regard; and he has always been on terms of intimacy with your uncle Peter and myself, besides knowing more or less of others of our family. Halleck, the poet, resides a great deal with him at present, having a handsome salary for conducting his affairs."

Pierre considered the proposition his uncle had made, found it attractive, and was soon in New York, settled in Mr. Astor's house, and busy at work in the library.

That project out of his hands for a while, Washington returned to polishing various manuscripts for the *Crayon Miscellany* and to writing the accounts of his visits to two English homes that had filled him with special emotion—Scott's home and Byron's.

A surge of nostalgia came over him as he wrote of the visit to Abbotsford that had meant so much to him. Scott, had died the year Irving returned to America. Washington looked back across the years to 1817, when his carriage stopped above the country house that Abbotsford had been and Scott came limping up the drive in the morning sunlight to greet him. Remembering the joy of that visit, when he had actually "known he was happy," he wrote on and on, recreating the conversation, the songs, and the family evenings of the five days he had spent in Scott's company.

Then he wrote of Newstead Abbey, Byron's ancestral seat, which he had visited some years after Byron had sold it and a year or so after Byron's death. Byron, his next hero after Scott, he had never met, but to Irving the Gothic halls and galleries of the old Abbey had seemed a sort of frame or projection of the poet's passionate and mocking personality, and his sketch of Newstead Abbey did not lack a sense of the poet's presence.

It was probably only an accident of circumstance that as he wrote about those homes of the men he admired he was arranging for work to start on the rebuilding and embellishing of his own little "roost" near Tarrytown. By spring of 1835, George Harvey had prepared some architectural drawings for the projected renovation. Washington pored over them with him, making suggestions and offering further ideas. Should there not be an entryway, which could hold a small bedroom on the second floor, and could not this tiny ell have a stepped gable? Harvey had already provided for stepped gables at either side of the house and for the wing at the rear, but Washington could not have enough of them. Somehow they spelled the charm of old and vanished New Amsterdam to him.

"The cost will not be much," he wrote to Peter. "I do not intend to set up any establishment there, but to put some simple furniture in it, and keep it as a nest, to which I can resort when in the mood. In fact, it is more with a view of furnishing the worthy little Bramin [his latest name for Ebenezer] a retreat for himself and his girls, where they can go to ruralize during the pleasant season of the year."

So he wrote in the spring. By the fall of 1835, after a summer that he spent at Astor's Hell Gate mansion, working on the Astoria manuscript from the material collected by Pierre, he had begun to discover how a modest plan for remodelling can grow less modest from day to day.

"Like all meddlings with stone and mortar," he wrote Peter in November, 1835, "the plan has extended as I built, until it has ended in a complete, though moderate-sized family residence. It is solidly built of stone, so that it will last for generations; and I think, when finished, it will be both picturesque and convenient."

A great fire swept New York in early December, causing not only vast property damage but many personal losses from investments in insurance companies. Writing about it to Peter, Washington reported that Brevoort had lost about fifty thousand dollars, while "Brother John estimates his loss at forty-one thousand dollars—that is to say, he has insurance stock to that amount. Some of the companies in which he holds, however, will not be bankrupt. His son Gabriel thinks his father will not really lose much above half that amount; but Brother John is rather tenacious on that point, and we allow him to have the full merit of his misfortune. As his fortune is estimated at some three or four hundred thousand dollars at least, his case is not considered desperate. . . . I lost three thousand dollars."

In the same letter, he wrote of his joy that Peter was finally contemplating a return to the United States in the spring. "My cottage is not yet finished, but I shall drive at it as soon as the opening of the spring will permit; and I trust, by the time of your arrival, to have a delightful little nest for you on the banks of the Hudson. It will be fitted to defy both hot weather and cold."

Through the winter he put the finishing touches on the manuscript of *Astoria*, and sent it to the press. Then, in the spring, to the delight of the entire family, Peter arrived, pale, frail, but somehow intact, after an absence from America of twenty-seven years. He settled in at the "Hive," with Washington and Ebenezer and his family, to spend the next few months slowly getting reacquainted with the city of his youth and marveling at the changes in it.

The cottage was still not complete. To Pierre, who had taken off for Toledo, Ohio, after completing his work on *Astoria*, Washington wrote that it was "slowly approaching to a finish. . . . For such a small edifice it has a prodigious swallow, and reminds me of those little fairy changelings called Killcrops, which eat and eat, and are never the fatter."

A few weeks more and it would be finished, he had thought in June. A few weeks more he thought in July. In midsummer news came that another investment he had made in speculative lands was not about to pay off so quickly as had been promised, so he slowed his purchases of furniture for the Roost.

Finally, in October of 1836, he, Peter, and sister Catherine's daughter, Sarah, who had somehow endeared herself to Washington above all his other nieces in the years since his return, took a boat from New York to Tarrytown, disembarked there and hired a carriage to drive them to the little house and to take up residence there at last.

The dirt road curved through the woods where the trees were a brilliant transparency of yellow, gold, and red. Fallen leaves muffled the sound of the horse's hooves and the carriage wheels. Birds, in their swift and erratic fall skirmishings, darted through the air. Through the spangle of color to one side, they could see the river shining silver in the sun.

The road curved again and suddenly there was the house before them. What was it? A miniature Gothic castle, all steeples and battlements on the smallest possible scale? Or the absolute synthesis of an old Dutch house run mad with stepped gables wherever a gable could be? Or some sort of mixture of the two, stirred up in Diedrich Knickerbocker's most whimsical style?

The three in the carriage looked and did not bother with descriptions or definitions. The Roost was finished, and it was perfect. Three weathercocks posed on various gables, moving gently from side to side in the October air. There was supposed to have been a fourth but the bad financial news had checked Washington in its purchase until a future date. No one missed the fourth at this moment. Nothing seemed wanting. All was as it should be.

Washington helped Sarah Paris from the carriage and then Peter. They walked across the leaf-strewn lawn to the front door. Washington stood back for them to enter and then followed, pointing out the charms of the interior arrangement. Peter and Sarah had both seen it before its completion, but that did not discourage the new householder. Here, on the right of the entrance, was his study. See! how well arranged it was for his desk and his books. There, on the left, was the dining room. Look at the views of the Hudson from the long windows. Beyond the dining room was the parlor, and look, here too, what a vista of the river! Across the hall, the kitchen—see how spacious! And the pantry. And upstairs, come, everyone must see again—all the bedrooms, some tucked under the eaves, with slanting ceilings, so to sleep in them would be something like sleeping in a tent, but all would have fresh breezes blowing in from the Hudson in the summer, and look! there were snug iron stoves in each room so that they would be warm in winter.

So Washington took possession of his house at last. He had thought it would be a retreat to retire to from time to time. "I do not intend to set up an establishment there," he had said. But once settled in, the thought of actually living any place else did not seem to occur to him again. He would leave the Roost for shorter and longer periods, but he would always come back to it. A few years later, when the house had become home, not only to him and to Peter, but to Ebenezer and his daughters, when it had become beyond a doubt a "family place," Washington would change its name from the Roost to something he felt more fitting for such a homestead—Sunnyside. But settling in at the Roost that day in 1835 really marked a change in his life almost as profound as his departure for Europe in 1815, when he had hoped to become "quite another being."

He was fifty-three in 1835, and for most of his adult life he had wandered from place to place finding most of his comfort in "homes away from home." "Strange tenant of a thousand homes," he had somehow never envisioned himself in his own place. Now he had bought his own land and imagined his own house and built it and would keep changing it and improving and enlarging it through the years as though he could never weary of such efforts.

A home of his own, on the banks of the river which he had helped to make legendary—a home to which his friends could make their way through the years to come, instead of his always making his way to their homes—a home of his own to which many of the best-known or aspiring writers, artists, and editors of the time, along with hosts of admiring readers, would travel as if on a pilgrimage—this he had achieved at last.

It was not, perhaps, the American theme that he had thought he was seeking when he returned to his own country but it was, in its way, an American theme that would give a new steadiness to his emotions for the rest of his life. He had found a place where his heart could hold.

# 30

# I Have Been Astounded

IN THE END he found the literary theme he wanted, one for which he seemed to have been destined ever since he took pen in hand—a biography of the man for whom he had been named, America's greatest hero, George Washington. Actually, he had been thinking of writing such a biography for years. He had talked of the possibility of doing so with both Moore and Payne during the years in Paris. The idea had drifted through his mind after his return to America in 1832 and he began to plan it in 1840. But it was not until after he returned to America again in 1846, after four years as American Ambassador to Spain, that he really set to work on it.

Ambassador to Spain? He professed himself astonished when the news of his appointment reached him; but it was, in fact, one of the more logical appointments of the Whig administration in 1842, when Vice President Tyler took over as President after the death of William Henry Harrison. Irving was, by that time, if not the best-known American writer (Cooper and Bryant were making their names as novelist and poet), certainly the best-loved. Whatever he wrote, the reputation he had won as Diedrich Knickerbocker and Geoffrey Crayon did not desert him, and he had kept on writing. In the course of completing *Astoria*, he had met with a lively soldier-adventurer, Captain Bonneville, who was trying to put his own journal of western experiences into publishable form. Washington had bargained with him and taken over the material to shape into a work of his own. *Astoria, Captain Bonneville, U.S.A. A Tour of the Prairies* which was later included in the *Crayon Miscellany*—the list was not unimpressive for a ten-year span, and even though some of the books were reportorial and some were filled out with manuscripts written years before in Spain, they all pleased his audience. His "singularly sweet" style endeared him to thousands who read about obscure Moorish heroes when the subject in other hands would have bored them.

For a while, he had thought the theme which would be a logical sequence to his *Life and Voyages of Columbus* would be a history of the conquest of Mexico. He began to do some research on that subject in 1835, soon after settling down at the Roost. His notes piled up. His interest began to catch. And then, in 1838, life fell apart for some time. The real blow was not when John Treat Irving died in March of that year. John, obsessed by his legal career and piling up a fortune, had never been close to his brothers, nor had he assumed the same responsibility as Washington for Ebenezer and his children, Catherine and her daughter, and bachelor, Peter, when their lives fell on difficult ways.

Peter's death, in June of 1838, was something else. Peter had been a semi-invalid for years, his health the operative factor in his life. But no one had expected his sudden illness to end as it did. Washington was unprepared and stricken. Three months later he was still trying to adjust to the blow, writing to sister Sally, "Every day, every hour I feel how completely Peter and myself were intertwined together in the whole course of our existence. Indeed, the very circumstances of our both having never been married, bound us more closely together. . . . I was not conscious of how much this was the case while he was living, but, now that he is gone, I feel how all-important he was to me. A dreary feeling of loneliness comes on me at times, that I reason against in vain . . . for though surrounded by affectionate relatives, I feel that none can be what he was to me."

Surrounded by relatives he was. Ebenezer's five daughters were now residents of the cottage. Catherine and her daughter, Sarah, were there most of the time. Ebenezer often came up from New York. Other visitors, friends, or admirers kept the small cottage overflowing. But none could take the place of Peter to Washington, Peter who had begun with him the long-ago jape of *Knickerbocker's History*, who had shared the dismal days in Liverpool, who had trekked across half of Europe with him, and who had finally come to enjoy the domestic pleasures of Sunnyside.

Trying, in the fall, to restore himself by "resuming his pen," and engaging his mind in some intellectual task, he set himself again to the subject of the conquest of Mexico. He had gone into the city to do some research in the "City Library," later known as the New York Society Library, when he met with Joseph Cogswell, editor of the *New York Review*, a friend of Mr. Astor's, and a friend as well of the young historian, William H. Prescott. Prescott, half-blind, but dogged in his application and determination, had recently published a *History of the Reign of Ferdinand and Isabella*, which had met with much acclaim. The subject being what it was, Washington had read it with interest and admired it. Now he wondered what Prescott was contemplating next.

"Is he engaged on an American subject?" he asked Cogswell.

"He is," Cogswell replied.

"Is it—the conquest of Mexico?" Irving asked in a rush, not knowing why he should feel sure somehow of the answer.

"It is," said Cogswell.

There was a pause. Then Irving spoke almost reflexively. Whether it was a reflex of admiration and pity for the young man who had labored under such handicaps to produce a beautifully researched and written history of Ferdinand and Isabella, or whether he felt some doubts about his own interest in handling such a tremendous theme as he knew the conquest of Mexico to be, no one would ever know.

"Well then," Irving said, "I *am* engaged upon that subject, but tell Mr. Prescott I abandon it to him, and I am happy to have this opportunity of testifying my high esteem for his talents, and my sense of the very courteous manner in which he has spoken of myself and my writing in his Ferdinand and Isabella, though they interfered with a part of the subject of his history." Or so his nephew, Pierre Munro Irving, later reported the conversation as it had been related to him by his uncle.

After that, Washington retired to Sunnyside and expressed his exasperation, confusion, and possible relief by working in his garden and "planting cabbages most furiously."

Three weeks later, he broke the vow he had made years before never to be connected with a magazine and agreed to make monthly contributions to a new periodical which had borrowed from his writings for its name—the *Knickerbocker Magazine.* He was writing not only because it had become a habit but because he had to. Month after month, he ground out or tossed off some sketch or essay or story for the *Knickerbocker.* He had a family dependent on him at Sunnyside—Ebenezer's daughters, Catherine's Sarah; they were his "womankind."

A wife, just one example of womankind, had eluded him, and with that he had lost forever the need to adjust to and somehow accept the differentness of someone of the other sex living with him in the closest and most exacerbating of relationships. He had instead, "womankind"—a generic group, dear girls, young and sweet and eager to please him. Their gossiping, their tears, their worries about what to wear, their general natterings were carried on at a distance from him, in their rooms, in the kitchen, in the laundry. He saw them smiling and loving and merry.

A good uncle, he admired each niece for her special characteristics and noticed the several contributions each made to the pleasantness of life at Sunnyside and took none of them for granted. If he loved Sarah Paris, Catherine's daughter, the best, he tried not to show it. She was the oldest of the nieces, twenty-seven in 1840, and in some ways the most scatterbrained. But she had the instinctive gift of understanding and sympathy that Irving had sought in women all his life and found—in Maria Hoffman, in Rebecca Gratz, briefly, so briefly in Matilda Hoffman, and later, in another country, in Emily Foster.

Sooner or later, such a lovable member of his "womankind" was bound to attract a suitor. Irving felt mixed emotions when young Thomas Storrow, Jr., son of his old friend in Paris, visited the United States on business for his father and became the favored one. Undeniably, there was a sense of family continuity in this joining of his family with one that had so long offered him one of his homes away from home. He was reassured by the fact that he had known Thomas since he was a boy and had observed the forming of his character. It was hard to think of the cottage without Sarah and to realize she would not even be living nearby but making her new home in Paris. But that last consideration had its compensations. Sarah in Paris would give him whatever excuse he needed to make periodic returns to a city he had always enjoyed.

The wedding was held at Sunnyside at the end of March, 1841, before spring had flung any pale green veil over the countryside, but when the clear black and white vistas of tree shapes, river, and hills all around seemed to accent the warmth, color, and cheer inside the cottage. Then Sarah and her new husband were gone.

He was concerned with the welfare of his many nephews as well as that of his nieces, though his assistance to them was directed chiefly toward trying to find them posts or positions in government or elsewhere. Working to this end, he did not hesitate to call upon any of the famous, important, or powerful friends he had made through the years. From the beginning of his friendship with Martin Van Buren, he was in correspondence with him, writing in an assured fashion curiously at odds with his usual diffidence. After Van Buren's election to the Presidency, Irving wrote him a congratulatory letter which quickly turned to sermonizing and moralizing. "You have now arrived at the most distinguished post in the world, at the head of the *great republic*: it depends upon yourself to make it the most honorable. There is but one true rule for your conduct: act according to the sound dictates of your head and the kind feelings of your heart, without thinking how your temporary popularity is to be affected by it, and *without caring about a re-election.*" Neither did he hesitate in the years that followed to write various letters to President Van Buren, urging him to use his influence in behalf of some nephew or other, or of his brother Ebenezer, or some old friend, like James Paulding.

Biographers through the years have winced at some of those letters, seemingly so out of character for the shy, unassuming Irving. A few of Irving's contemporaries, chiefly his one rival as America's most popular literary man, James Fenimore Cooper, seized on the way Irving made use of powerful friends to accuse him of expediency, sycophancy, and trimming his sails to suit political winds. That Irving should have been at times as aggressive as anyone else in trying to win security for his family, that he should have acquired some sense of personal importance, even superiority, appeared an outrage to these critics, themselves quite accustomed to using whatever means they had to achieve similar goals. Perhaps it was his candor in asking for help for his nephews that repelled them. Nor were they mollified when Irving turned down Van Buren's invitation to become his Secretary of the Navy. His refusal simply showed he was waiting for something better, they insisted. They could not see him as a man beyond the flow of his sweet and singularly pleasing prose, a man who had taken on responsibility for his brothers' and sisters' families in lieu of having the responsibility for a family of his own. A vein of practicality in a man who had reinstated himself in the world's eyes by the use of his pen was unthinkable.

Responsible for the family at Sunnyside, and the nephews who were here, there, and everywhere, Irving kept turning out his sketches, sometimes little more than squibs, for the *Knickerbocker Magazine*. Yielding to personal whim, he embarked on a short biographical venture, a sketch of the life of a young poetess, Margaret Miller Davidson, who had attracted much public sympathy before her death of consumption at the age of seventeen. Irving's picture of her life and that of her ailing but sensitive mother and equally ailing and gifted younger sister, also doomed by consumption, was the most sentimental writing he had ever done. Public taste, growing ever more softened and attuned to hectic flushes, rapturous trances, inspired utterances, and doomed declines was pleased and gratified by the book. But Irving had had no thought of profiting by a cynical exploitation of current fancies. He assigned all profits from the book to the dead poetess' mother. Besides, the subject, a young girl of seventeen dying of consumption, was one that struck at his deepest memories—Matilinda-dinda-dinda—dying before his eyes so many years before. The control and discipline that he was used to exercising over his writing vanished as he indulged himself in a public flood of tears for Margaret Davidson.

Not all was indulgence, or the monthly pieces for *Knickerbocker* either. For now he was at last settling down to the theme that he knew was his, the life of the hero who had patted his head and blessed him more than fifty years before.

The letter from Charles Dickens came as he was outlining the first volume. Irving and the English novelist, who was riding the crest of his popularity, had corresponded previously, each expressing his admiration of the other's accomplishments. Now Dickens wrote that he and his wife were going to visit America and had booked passage on a steam packet to cross the Atlantic at the start of the coming year, 1842.

"I look forward to shaking hands with you with an interest I cannot (and I would not if I could) describe," Dickens wrote. "You *can* imagine, I dare say, something of the feelings with which I look forward to being in America. I can hardly believe I am coming.'

Irving also looked forward to meeting the Englishman of such prodigious talent, and all America, when it heard the news of his impending visit, prepared to lash itself up to a public banqueting to outdo anything Mustapha Rub-a-dub had ever witnessed. Meantime, Irving continued with the preliminary work on the life of Washington. He went into the city to consult various books in the Society Library. While there he went to the theater and the new Italian Opera, and attended a dinner of the Saint Nicholas Society, a club of New Yorkers of Dutch ancestry which he (with Diedrich Knickerbocker as his Dutch godfather) had helped to found. Then he returned to the "dear little, bright little cottage," and his "womankind" there, for Christmas holidays and the New Year.

He was in the city again in February when the news of his appointment as Ambassador to Spain came to him. Daniel Webster, long an admirer of his writings, had proposed him for that diplomatic post first to President Harrison, and then to his successor, President Tyler. William Preston, companion of the London years and currently a Senator from South Carolina, added his second to the proposal, and there were a host of other friends in Washington, D.C., to concur.

"I have been astounded, this morning," Washington wrote to Ebenezer who was at Sunnyside, "by the intelligence of my having been nominated to the Senate as Minister to Spain. . . . Nothing was ever more unexpected. It was perfectly unsolicited. . . . I have determined to accept. . . . It will be a severe trial to absent myself for a time from dear little Sunnyside, but I shall return to it better enabled to carry it on comfortably."

Like the tails of two comets crossing, Dickens' arrival in New York coincided with Irving's preparations to leave for Spain. Crowds had surrounded the English author and his wife from the moment of their arrival in Boston, and the more boisterous elements of American life had disported themselves around the celebrated couple twenty-four hours a day. Washington, involved in the details of arranging for a long absence from the country, and swept up in a series of farewell dinners and receptions of his own, was in New York when Dickens and his party arrived there. The city, the nation, seemed to be standing on tiptoe, peering, as America's great literary man went to pay his respects to England's great literary man at the Carlton House. Dickens was at dinner in the suite that had been taken for him. Irving's card was carried in to him. Almost at once, Dickens erupted into the reception room, napkin still in hand, and rushed toward Irving with open arms.

"Irving! I am delighted to see you." After this greeting, Dickens dragged him into the suite, hospitably urging a drink on him. "What will you have to drink? A mint julep or a gin-cocktail?"

The next night the old Park Theater was transformed with bunting, medallions, statues, the arms of all the states, painted scenes from Dickens' books, and a portrait of Dickens to brood over the entire décor, for the great Boz Ball. Three nights later came the inevitable dinner, the great Dickens Dinner, and Washington had been invited to preside.

"I shall break down, I know I shall break down," he prophesied as he looked forward to the event. And when it came to the moment, he did indeed manage only a few sentences before some cries from the audience, "Admirable! Excellent!" threw him off balance. He could only croak the conclusion of his speech, "Charles Dickens, the literary guest of the nation." After which he fell back in his chair to murmur in an almost satisfied tone, "There, I told you I should break down, and I've done it."

Dickens, a born showman, was never for a moment in danger of breaking down as he addressed the gathering. In the course of his remarks he spoke lavishly of his admiration for Irving. "Why, gentlemen, I don't go upstairs to bed two nights out of seven—as a very reputable witness near at hand can testify—[his wife and some other ladies had been permitted to sit on a balcony overlooking the all-male event]—I say I do not go to bed two nights out of seven without taking Washington Irving under my arm. . . ."

In the next few days, Irving and Dickens saw each other frequently, and before Dickens left New York he made the trip by boat up to Tarrytown to visit Sunnyside. The two men thought it would be their last meeting, but a week or so later, when Irving had traveled to Washington, D.C., for his instructions as ambassador, Dickens was in the capital also, and they had another afternoon together, drinking julep through straws from one immense bowl.

Finally, all was ready for Irving's departure. He had chosen two young men as aides, Alexander Hamilton, grandson of the famous statesman, and Carson Brevoort, son of his long-time friend, Henry Brevoort. Their youthful excitement about the forthcoming venture added savor to the last-minute briefings. On April 10, 1842, a few days after his fifty-ninth birthday, Irving and his aides were embarking for Europe. Irving planned to go to London first, to visit his friends there, then to Paris for a visit with Sarah Paris Storrow, and from Paris would travel to his new post in Madrid.

He was a good Ambassador. He came upon the Spanish scene when the country was in a political turmoil, quite different from the state he had known in the years when he had been there before. Ferdinand VII had died, leaving only daughters to succeed him and a fine quarrel brewing between those who believed that his oldest daughter, Isabella, should be queen as he had wished, and those who favored his younger brother, Don Carlos. Ferdinand's widow, Maria Christina, the Queen Regent, was in and out of exile while Irving served as American Minister. The government was in and out of the hands of the military leader, Espartero. There were battles, which sometimes invaded Madrid itself, between monarchists and so-called liberals. Irving, familiar with the language, the country, and its history, threaded his way through the various intrigues, difficulties, and alarms with aplomb, writing long letters to Webster to keep the government in Washington, D.C., apprised of the constantly changing situation.

It was inevitable that he should have romanticized the young Queen Isabella, who was just twelve years old when he arrived, and overlooked her plainness to see her as a fairy-tale princess caught in the toils of her elders' maneuverings. It was predictable, also, that he should have rounded up a group from the diplomatic community to rush to the palace to protect her and her younger sister one night when an attack on the capital seemed to threaten the children.

Romancing aside, he accomplished a good deal for the United States during his years in Spain, perhaps more than any other diplomat could have done. He now was known in Spain for his writings, which had been translated there, and admired and honored as an author who knew and loved the country. However, his hopes that he could continue to work on his life of Washington while in Madrid were dashed by the diplomatic activities required of him. For the first two years, his chief efforts were directed toward easing trade tensions between the United States and Spain and winning Spanish recognition of the independence of Texas. Later, the island of Cuba, so close to the American mainland, became a focal object of concern as England and France both seemed to eye the island covetously. This problem too he dealt with satisfactorily and gracefully.

Now and then while in Madrid he was tormented by a return of the old illness that manifested itself in a swelling of his ankles. But every summer he was able to travel to Paris and spend a month or two with Sarah Storrow, her husband, and their new baby, and those visits generally caused an improvement in his condition.

At the end of 1844, he had news of the results of the election in the United States. James K. Polk was the new President. As always, when a new administration took over, there was the promise of change in all appointments. Irving waited through the spring and summer of 1845 for news from Washington, D.C. In September, he was, as usual, with Sarah in Paris. There he met with Louis McLane and was caught up in McLane's agitation over the "Oregon question" which promised to bring on a new conflict between the United States and England. Yielding to McLane's pleas, Irving traveled to London to do what he could to combat English fury at the American campaign cry of "54-40 or fight." His presence in London, his conversations with various important political figures, and his writings on the subject were of some help in easing tensions, until finally the whole problem was settled by the fixing of the Northwestern borders of the United States at the 49th parallel.

By now Irving was weary of being neither approved nor dismissed by the new President and sent in his resignation as Minister to Spain. Communications being what they were and transatlantic travel what it was, it would be seven months before a new Minister would arrive and he could return home. The time seemed long to him. He still loved Spain—the gaunt and haunting beauty of its landscapes, the mingled dignity and wildness of its people, but he had known and loved it best fourteen years before when he had traveled its mountains as an unknown wanderer and lived for enchanted weeks in the courts of the Alhambra. During this stay in Spain he did not even visit that fabled palace.

He was able at last to return to America in September of 1846. There were no public dinners this time. He made a brief visit to Washington, D.C., to report on his final months in Spain and then he was traveling to Sunnyside.

Perhaps only someone who had for so many years been a "strange tenant of a thousand homes" could have felt such a sense of homecoming as he when he saw again the great curves of the Hudson, the comforting hills on its banks, and then, the "cocked hat" of a cottage that was his own. The nieces, his "womankind," were in a frenzy of welcoming. Days went by in visiting old friends and acquaintances and riding past familiar scenes. Days and weeks went by in an extravagant planning of improvements and additions to Sunnyside.

At last, however, with the visits to New York accomplished, the plans drawn for a tower that would add guest rooms to Sunnyside and living quarters for a servant, Irving turned again to work on the book that was to be his great effort on an American theme—his life of Washington.

# 31

# All Sails Set

"Will it ever be finished?"

The question became a combined groan and joke between Washington and Pierre Munro Irving in the years that followed. The task was immense. True, Jared Sparks had published his biography of George Washington in 1837, and this provided an outline of events; but Irving was determined to consult personally every document pertaining to the great man's life that he could find and to visit personally every place he had been. He traveled to Mount Vernon again and again, to learn whatever he could there, and to speak to anyone still alive who might have memories or anecdotes of Washington. He traveled to the capital to consult records there and he visited battlefields all over New York, New Jersey, and Pennsylvania.

Meantime, even as he worked on Washington's life, he took time out to write other volumes, or to collect earlier writings into new books. In 1848, he wrote an amiable *Life of Goldsmith*, with whom he had so often been compared, and the book had a pleasant success. That same year, a young New York publisher, George P. Putnam, offered to publish a collected edition of Irving's works. Irving wanted to revise and correct his earlier efforts for this new edition, and this took weeks and months of time. The next year, his study of *Mahomet and His Successors*, a souvenir from the Spanish years, was published, and the year after that he collected some of the sketches and essays that he had written for the *Knickerbocker Magazine* for publication under the title *Wolfert's Roost*. While most of the pieces were fugitive, one memorable phrase from it, "the almighty dollar," soon entered the common speech.

The notes and the chapters on Washington's life piled up on his desk.

"Will it ever be finished?"

The nieces made his home life easy and comfortable. Pierre Munro Irving had taken over as his agent and business manager. The details of life no longer needed to worry him although too many visitors sometimes did. Sunnyside had become a sort of obligatory shrine for Americans who admired his work and for literary visitors from abroad. Thackeray visited the house and commented rather loftily later on "a funny little in-and-out cottage . . . little bits of small parlours . . . a little study . . . old dogs trotting about the premises . . . flocks of ducks sailing on the pond. . . ."

Autograph seekers came unbidden to the door. One who had insisted on seeing Irving and getting his signature on a day when he was not feeling well received the autograph finally and said briskly, "And now I will pay you. It is a principle of mine always to pay for something like this."

"It is a principle of mine not to accept payment," said Irving coldly and returned to his study.

He received floods of letters as well; hundreds of people wrote him, great and unknown alike, and he tried to answer every letter, though the endless correspondence became like a cobweb, softly and irritatingly delaying him.

Once he had been a youth who mocked at ambition and thought life should be lived by whim. He had not given up whims entirely. There were junkets, excursions, parties, trips to Saratoga Springs, trips to Baltimore to visit a friend of recent years, John Pendleton Kennedy, a man who managed to combine literary activity with politics and other gentlemanly pursuits. He was charmed, as always, by pretty young women and by children. But all the while the life of Washington weighed on him.

Irving was seventy-two years old when the first volume was published in 1855. He had carried the story only as far as Washington's career before the Revolution and had ended with his arrival at Boston after being appointed Commander-in-Chief of the Continental Army. There was a quick interest in the book in America and Murray picked it up for publication in England, but the prospect of how much more of the story remained to be told loomed ahead for Irving like a long road.

His health was good and he liked to ride horseback for relaxation. Then once, twice, and again, he was thrown from his horse, Gentleman Dick, when he went out for his afternoon's ride. His nieces pled with him to sell the animal and do no more riding. He was agreeable to selling that horse but was not willing to give up riding altogether. "I am now looking out for a quiet, sober, old-gentlemanlike horse," he wrote to Sarah Storrow in Paris, "if such a thing is to be met with in this very young country, where everything is so prone to *go ahead*."

Letters praising him for the first volume of *The Life of Washington* were welcome bonuses in the pile of correspondence. George Bancroft, already emerging as America's first distinguished historian, wrote to express his pleasure in "the happy magic that makes scenes, events, and personal anecdotes present themselves to you at their bidding . . . and take color and warmth from your own nature."

Through the rest of 1855, Irving worked at the second volume. "I live only in the Revolution. I have no other existence now . . . can think of nothing else." Through the summer, he lived that existence so completely that by the fall of the year, the second volume of *The Life of Washington*, which took the story through the New Jersey campaign of 1777, was going to press. By the first of the New Year, when the house was still hung with its Christmas greens, he was receiving comments on the new book. William Prescott, to whom he had relinquished the *Conquest of Mexico* some years before, and with whom he had been in correspondence ever since, wrote to say, "You have done with Washington just as I thought you would, and, instead of a cold, marble statue of a demigod, you have made him a being of flesh and blood, like ourselves—one with whom we can have sympathy."

By then Irving was at work on the third volume, sitting in his study while the snow piled up around the windows and ice floes clogged the Hudson, and picking up one pile of notes after another, writing, rewriting, shuffling and reshuffling. A timely gift from his publisher, G. P. Putnam, arrived on George Washington's Birthday—a big new table for his study. It had more conveniences than Irving was used to. "I must get everything in a mess," he said, "and then I can go on comfortably."

April 3, 1856, he was seventy-three. "I must say," he wrote to Sarah Storrow, "I am sometimes surprised at my own capacity for labor at my advanced time of life—when I used to think a man must be good for nothing." Surprised but unflagging, he saw the third volume of *The Life of Washington* through the press, and it was published in July, 1856.

One letter among the hundreds woke echoes from the past just then.

"My dear Mr. Irving: I think I ought to begin by telling

you who is writing to you—Emily Foster, now Emily Fuller. . . ."

The long-closed door on a pleasant, painful winter in Dresden opened briefly. Emily, he read, was writing to him because her oldest son, Henry, was coming to the United States, and she hoped that he could meet her friend of long ago, and perhaps, since he desired to settle in the States, Irving could give him some advice as to situation and so on.

Irving replied at once, expressing his "surprise and delight." "A thousand recollections broke at once upon my mind, of Emily Foster as I had known her in Dresden, young, and fair, and bright, and beautiful; and I could hardly realize that so many years had elapsed since then, or form an idea of her as Mrs. Emily Fuller, with four boys and one little girl. . . ." He told her something about his life in his "little rural retreat . . . in a beautiful part of the country . . ." with a "house full of nieces, who almost make me as happy as if I were a married man." He mentioned a small drawing which Emily had made that long-ago winter in the Dresden gallery and told her that it hung over the piano in the drawing room at Sunnyside. "I treasure it as a precious memorial of those pleasant days." And, of course, he told her he would be happy to meet her son and do what he could to aid him. Then the door closed again. He was seventy-three. He had, as he sometimes mentioned, passed the biblical threescore and ten, "beyond which all was special grace and indulgence." And there was still so much of the life of Washington to complete.

On his seventy-fourth birthday, April 3, 1857, the fourth volume was going to press and still the story was not finished.

"Will it *ever* be finished?" he groaned to Pierre, with one of his old lopsided smiles, as they labored over the proof-sheets together.

His humor had not left him. An aspiring young author had visited him and then written up the interview for publication.

"I can only say," Irving wrote the young man, "that I wish
... I had known our conversation was likely to be recorded;
I should then have tasked myself to say some wise or witty
things, to be given as specimens of my *off-hand table-talk*.
One should always know when they are sitting for a portrait,
that they may endeavor to look handsomer than themselves,
and attitudinize."

He could even find some humor in his desperate effort to
get on with the fifth and final volume of Washington's life.
"Whimsical as it may seem," he wrote to a friend who congratulated him on the fourth volume, "I was haunted occasionally by one of my own early pleasantries. My mock admonition to Diedrich Knickerbocker not to idle in his historic wayfaring, rose in judgment against me: 'Is not Time,
relentless Time, shaking, with palsied hand, his almost exhausted hourglass before thee? Hasten, then, to pursue thy
weary task'—."

The year 1857 was not a happy one in America. A financial
panic was sweeping the country, and the long struggle between the North and the South, over tariffs, over state's
rights, above all, over the South's "peculiar institution" of
slavery was building to a climax. Irving, impulsive investor
that he had always been, could not hold himself aloof from
the financial reverses of the year. Difficulties in the publishing
world required that his contract with Putnam's be modified
and adjusted. But from the national financial crisis he emerged
with "only a moderate loss" in his investments.

From the other impending crisis, he tried to shield himself.
He could not believe that the country was going to divide.
That slavery was an evil he had always believed, and he had
tried to bring out George Washington's sentiments against
the system in his biography, to the irritation of some Southern readers. But he was not an abolitionist, like William
Cullen Bryant, John Greenleaf Whittier, or that recently risen

star, Harriet Beecher Stowe. He had seen, in his American wanderings, Negroes whose lot he pitied; he had seen other black people, strong, laughing, singing, following some exotic life-vision of their own, and he had written of them, now and then, as he wrote of the early Dutch settlers in New York. In *Knickerbocker's History*, when he had reviewed various theories about the creation of mankind, he had not neglected an African theory, in which he anticipated a phrase that would become popular generations later. "The negro philosophers of Congo affirm that the world was made by the hands of angels, excepting their own country, which the Supreme Being constructed himself, that it might be supremely excellent. And he took great pains with the inhabitants, and made them very black, and beautiful. . . ."

But his was never a missionary nature, attempting to change the world and mold the future. His fancies had always played over the past, and what he brought to life was from the past and not the future.

An asthmatic condition began to trouble him in 1858 as he worried over the fifth and final volume of Washington's biography. "I work more slowly than heretofore," he wrote to Sarah Storrow. "For two or three years past I have been troubled by an obstinate catarrh, but this winter it has been quite harassing, at times quite stupefying me. Recently I have put myself under medical treatment, and begin to feel the benefit of it."

*Would the book never be finished?*

Through the summer of 1858, he "fagged away" at it, taking only short vacations. In the fall, he went to the city for a few days of relaxation and theatergoing, a pleasure still. He traveled by the railway which had been installed along the river a few years previously, occasioning much protest and horror from him at first. When all his efforts to prevent

the laying of tracks across his property failed, he had accepted
the intrusion with what grace he could, and endeavored to
shield the view of the trains with shrubbery and trees, though
there was no way to escape their racket. By now, he sometimes
found the "cars" almost an attraction, bringing guests so near
to his door and taking him so easily and quickly to the city.

"How are you?" Pierre asked when he called on his uncle
at the hotel in New York.

"Had a streak of old age. Pity, when we have grown old
we can not turn around and grow young again, and die of
cutting our teeth," Irving replied.

Pierre and his wife, Helen, accompanied Irving back to
Sunnyside. Irving lay on the couch in the study while Pierre
read over the most recently completed chapters of the fifth
volume, exclaiming now and then in approval. But soon it
became clear that Irving was not merely weary but ill. The
nieces were summoned. Irving was put to bed. The next day
Pierre rode the cars into town for a doctor whom he brought
back with him.

"An intermittent fever" was the doctor's diagnosis. Irving
himself felt that the strain of trying to finish *The Life of
Washington* was injuring his brain. This was what he feared
most.

"I do not fear death," he said, "but I would like to go
down with all sails set."

The fever waned and he struggled up and back to work.
By the beginning of 1859, with Pierre's help in editing, locat-
ing missing pages, and checking for notes that had vanished,
he was able to send to press the last chapters of the fifth
volume of *The Life*. On his seventy-sixth birthday he celebrated the fact that all of the manuscript, including the
preface, had gone to the printer.

It was finished. He had done it. No sails slackened, he had
written in the eighth decade of his life a five-volume biog-

raphy of the nation's hero. Later biographies would super-
sede it. Its length and the unvarying smoothness of its style
would become less and less pleasing to following generations,
and it would gradually become one of Irving's forgotten
works, taking its place with the *Columbus* volumes as worthy
but dull pioneering efforts. For some years after its completion, however, it held first place as the most popular and
readable history of Washington's life.

The great effort over, the "dismal horrors" began for
Irving, the nights when he could not sleep, and:

> Not poppy, nor mandragora
> Nor all the drowsy syrups of the world,
> Shall ever medicine thee to that sweet sleep
> Which thou ow'dst yesterday. . . .

He quoted the lines to his family with an apologetic smile.

At Irving's request, Pierre and his wife moved up to Sunnyside permanently, and Pierre slept regularly in the tiny room
next to Irving's bedroom so that he could wake whenever he
heard his uncle moving about in a sudden spasm of nameless
fear. Where had these anxieties come from? Did they echo
the long-ago "dismal horrors" that he had known after
Matilda's death? He never tried to explain them.

Summer came and Sunnyside was a bower of green with
silver flashings from the river and occasional hoots from the
trains that passed along the riverbank. The family life at
Sunnyside revolved around its troubled, ailing master. Some
days Irving felt revived and merry and was full of reminiscences of his long life. There were evenings of card-play-
ing. "I do not like to be guilty of pretension," Washington
said, "but I must say I'm the very worst player that ever was."
Later in the evening one of the nieces or Pierre would read
to him, hoping that would help him get to sleep. But they
learned to avoid Alexander Mackenzie's *A Year in Spain* or

almost any book that had to do with that country, for such writings excited him too much.

Pierre Munro's journal became a chronicle of his uncle's health. "Mr. Irving wretchedly nervous. . . ." "One of his 'perverse wretched nights' as he calls them. . . ." "A nervous night. . . ." "Great oppression and shortness of breath during the day."

Still Irving laughed when he had struggled through the horrors of the night to another day. He enjoyed the views from the veranda, and the sunsets over the river. He talked of the actors he had known in the past. He talked of fellow writers. He spoke of James Fenimore Cooper, the one literary countryman who had long borne a grudge against him. "The easily pleased Washington Irving," Cooper had sneered once and Irving had been hurt. But he spoke now of Cooper's genius in creating Leatherstocking.

"No one will care to meddle with that class of character after Cooper. Strange—in life, they judge a writer by his last production; after death, by what he has done best."

October came, and then November and the leaves were gone, baring the vista to the river so that on the evening of November 28th the sunset colors flooded the dining room at Sunnyside. Over and over, Irving called on his "womankind" and on Pierre to admire the beauty of the sight.

Later that evening, he grew more depressed. One of his nieces went up to his bedroom with him to lay out his medicines. He sighed at the thought of another sleepless night and then as if weary of his own self-pity, said "When will this end? When will it be finished?"

Then he caught at his side, clutched the bed post and fell to the floor.

It was finished.

"If my character and conduct are worth inquiring into,"

he had once written to Henry Brevoort, who had died several years before, "they will ultimately be understood and appreciated according to their merits; nor can anything I could say or do in contradiction place them an iota above or below their real standard. . . . With the world, therefore, let the matters take their course."

With the world, matters took their course. In an unusual tribute to a private citizen, the flags in New York City were lowered to half-mast after the news of his death was received. A parade of carriages bearing dignitaries and neighbors attended the funeral as he was buried in Sleepy Hollow Cemetery, next to the other members of his family, whose remains he had caused to be brought there for reinterment. People were pleased that it was a beautiful Indian summer day—"one of his own days," they said. Later, there were many ceremonial gatherings in his honor with all the literary great pontificating. "This country delights in such displays," Mustapha Rub-a-dub Keli Khan had once written to his friend in Tripoli.

And with the world, matters went on taking their course. A war came, at which he might have quailed. Then there was a peace of sorts. But he was still not forgotten. His "character and conduct" were first overpraised, and then underpraised. He was damned for not being as great a writer as many who followed him, Ralph Waldo Emerson, Edgar Allan Poe, and Herman Melville. He was dismissed as a shallow thinker who had never grappled with the great problems of existence. He was anthologized—even his sternest critics could not wholly ignore some of his best sketches—but they called him a "comfortable, genial idler." It did not matter. It was finished.

# Bibliography

PRIMARY SOURCES

Hellman, George S.: *Letters of Washington Irving to Henry Brevoort*, N. Y., G. P. Putnam's, 1915
————, *Letters of Henry Brevoort to Washington Irving*, N. Y., G. P. Putnam's, 1916
Irving, Pierre Munro: *The Life and Letters of Washington Irving*, N. Y., G. P. Putnam's, 1863.
Pochman, Henry: Genl. Editor, the ongoing publication of the *Complete Works of Washington Irving*, Vol. 1, *Journals and Notebooks*, 1803–1806, Nathalia Wright, editor, Vol. 3, *Journals and Notebooks*, 1819–1827, Walter A. Reichart, editor, Madison, University of Wisconsin Press, 1969
Williams, Stanley T.: *The Life of Washington Irving*, N. Y., Oxford University Press, 1935

OTHER JOURNALS AND NOTEBOOKS:

McDermott, John Francis, ed.: *The Western Journals of Washington Irving*, University of Oklahoma Press, 1944
Myers, Andrew B.: ed.: *Washington Irving's Madrid Journal 1827–28 and Related Letters*, Bulletin of the N. Y. Public Library, 1958

Penney, Clara Louisa, ed.: *Journal of Washington Irving, 1828–29*, N. Y., The Hispanic Society of America, 1926
Trent, William P. and Hellman, George S., eds.: *The Journals of Washington Irving* (From July 1815 to July 1841)
Trent, William P., ed.: *Notes and Journal of Travel in Europe 1804–05*, N. Y. Grolier Club, 1921

OTHER BIOGRAPHIES; SPECIALIZED STUDIES

Bowers, Claude G.: *The Strange Adventures of Washington Irving*, Boston, Houghton, Mifflin Co., 1940.
Brooks, Van Wyck: *The World of Washington Irving*, N. Y., E. P. Dutton, 1944
Hedges, William L.: *Washington Irving, an American Study*, Baltimore, The Johns Hopkins Press, 1965
Hellman, George S.: *Washington Irving, Esquire*, N. Y., Knopf, 1925
McClary, Ben Harris, ed.: *Washington Irving and the House of Murray*, The University of Tennessee Press, Knoxville, 1969
Wagenknecht, Edward: *Washington Irving, Moderation Displayed*, N. Y., Oxford University Press, 1962
Warner, Charles Dudley: "Washington Irving," in *American Men of Letters*, Boston and N. Y., Houghton, Mifflin Co., 1881

There are as well a number of small collections of letters to specific friends or acquaintances, and numerous scholarly articles on various aspects of Irving's inspirations or sources.

NEWSPAPERS AND PERIODICALS

The files of the *N. Y. Morning Chronicle*, 1802–1806, the files of the *N. Y. Post*, and other New York newspapers of the period. The annual issues of David Longworth's *City Directory*. The files of the *Analectic Magazine*, 18—. The files of *Knickerbocker Magazine*, 18—.

SECONDARY SOURCES

Armstrong, Margaret: *Fanny Kemble, a Passionate Victorian*, Macmillan Company, N. Y., 1938

Beghard, Elizabeth L.: *The Life and Ventures of the Original John Jacob Astor*, Bryan Printing Co., Hudson, N. Y., 1915

Flagg, Jared B.: *Life and Letters of Washington Allston*, N. Y., Charles Scribner's Sons, 1892

Johnson, Edgar: *Charles Dickens, His Tragedy and Triumph*, Simon and Schuster, N. Y., 1952

————: *Sir Walter Scott, The Great Unknown*, N. Y., Macmillan Company, 1969

Jones, Frederick L.: edit. *The Letters of Mary W. Shelley*, University of Oklahoma Press, 1944

Lockhart, John Gibson: *Narrative of the Life of Sir Walter Scott*, Edinburgh, R. Cadell, 1848

Moore, Thomas: edit. *Letters and Journals of George Gordon, Lord Byron*, N. Y., Harper's, 1830

Osterweis, Rollin G.: *Rebecca Gratz, a Study in Charm*, G. P. Putnam's Sons, N. Y., 1935

Overmyer, Grace: *America's First Hamlet, John Howard Payne*, Washington Square, New York, University Press, 1957

Paulding, William I.: compiler, *The Literary Life of James K. Paulding*, N. Y., Charles Scribner and Co., 1867

Philipson, Rabbi David: *Letters of Rebecca Gratz*, Philadelphia, Jewish Publication Society, 1929

Russell, Lord John: edit. *Memoirs, Journal and Correspondence of Thomas Moore*, London, Longmans, Brown, Green & Longmans, 1853–56

CHRONOLOGICAL LISTING OF IRVING'S WORKS

1802—*Letters of Jonathan Oldstyle, Gent.*
1807—*Salmagundi*
1809—*Knickerbocker's History of New York*

1819—*The Sketch Book*
1822—*Bracebridge Hall*
1824—*Tales of a Traveller*
1828—*The Life and Voyages of Christopher Columbus*
1829—*The Conquest of Granada*
1832—*The Alhambra*
1831—*The Voyages of the Companions of Columbus*
1832—*A Tour of the Prairies*
1835—*The Crayon Miscellany*
1836—*Astoria*
1837—*The Adventures of Captain Bonneville, U. S. A.*
1841—*Biography and Poetical Remains of the Late Margaret Miller Davidson*
1849—*Life of Oliver Goldsmith*
1850—*Mahomet and His Successors*
1854—*Wolfert's Roost*
1855-59—*The Life of George Washington*

Four of the dramas which Irving adapted or collaborated on with John Howard Payne were also published: *Abu Hassan, Charles II, Richelieu* and *The Wild Huntsman.*

# Index